Juz Tabārak

Part 29 of the Qur'ān

Husain A. Nuri

ISBN 13: 978-1-936569-11-3

First edition: 2012
Second edition: 2017
Reprint: 2019

Cover Design: Mansur Ahmad

Taqwa Prints
A division of Weekend Learning Publishers
5584 Boulder Crest St.
Columbus, OH 43235
www.taqwaprints.com

Printed in China

Preface

This book is intended to help students learn, memorize and understand Part 29 of the Qur'ān, conventionally known as Juz Tabarak. Students who have finished Juz 'Amma may advance to this book with the twin objectives of memorizing the sūrah and understanding its message.

Students who have advanced to this part of the Qur'ān are expected to have learned how to read the Arabic text. For this reason, I have not provided an English transliteration of the āyāt as this would be redundant for students' needs. However, I have used large Arabic fonts in order to make the book easier to read. Additionally, I have provided color-coded āyāt to facilitate recitation with proper tajweed. I have explained the color-codes on the next page. These codes are increasingly used by a large number of *mushaf* of the Qur'ān.

Unlike in *Juz 'Amma*, in *Juz Tabarak*, I have provided many detailed explanations. In many cases, I have provided additional literary notes in order to bring out the linguistic marvels of the Qur'ān. I hope students with advanced learning skills will benefit from these notes. If some parts of the book seem too difficult to comprehend, I advise students to seek proper guidance from a qualified teacher. I have based the explanations on works by Syed Qutb, Ibn Kathir, Yusuf Ali, Zohurul Hoque and Nouman Ali Khan. In case further elaboration is needed, an authoritative commentary should be consulted.

I have adopted Zohurul Hoque's translation of the Qur'ān, as it follows the Arabic text literally. I have taken the liberty to modify some of his translation for easier reading. Translation of the Qur'ān is, indeed, a huge challenge and is truly considered impossible. Words of the Qur'ān carry different shades of meaning. When translated into a different language, it may reflect only one meaning, and sometimes it may deviate from the meaning intended in the Qur'ān. With this limitation in mind, my effort is to provide a simple, single and as-close-as-possible meaning of the words.

The "Words to Know" section is intended to help non-Arabic-speaking students learn a few words arising from the same root word. For the "Word-by-Word meaning" section, I have frequently consulted the works of Zohurul Hoque and a translation by Aftab Alam Khan. I have also extensively used *Dictionary of the Holy Qur'ān* by Abdul Mannān Omar, and *A Dictionary and Glossary of the Koran* by John Penrice. I also acknowledge adopting the translations of Abdullah Yusuf Ali and M.A.S. Abdel Haleem. May Allāh (swt) bless all of them, Amin.

During the typesetting of the book, I obtained extensive help from several individuals. I express my sincere thanks to Lenni Nazir for color coding the āyāt and typesetting parts of the book. Noor Alshafie helped me format the āyāt in the word-by-word meaning section. I am indebted to Brenda Rusch for editing and proofreading the manuscript. She has not only eliminated grammatical, punctuation, and spelling errors, but she has also improved the content flow, transitions, and overall organization of the book.

I am thankful to Allāh (swt) for giving me the ability to compile this book. I pray to Allāh (swt) to accept my effort in communicating the message of Islam. Any mistakes or errors in the book are my responsibiity. I appreciate receiving meaningful comments and suggestions to improve this book.

رَبَّنَا تَقَبَّلْ مِنَّا إِنَّكَ أَنتَ ٱلسَّمِيعُ ٱلْعَلِيمُ ۝

"Our Rabb! Accept from us, you indeed are the all-Hearing, all-Knowing." (2:127)

April 25, 2012   Husain A. Nuri

Color Coded Tajweed Rules

■ **Ikhfa:** Blue Arabic font is used to indicate a slight nasal sound. If any one of the following letters ج ث ت ك ق ف ظ ط ض ص ش س ز ذ د appear after a نْ or ◌ٌ, ◌ٍ, ◌ً, it will be pronounced with a light nasal sound.

For example, see āyah 67:3. ط after ◌ً in سَمَـٰوَٰتٍ طِبَاقًا, ت after نْ in مِن تَفَـٰوُتٍ.

■ **Ghunna:** Orange Arabic font is used to indicate *ghunna,* or a nasal sound. When م or ن have a shadda on it, the letter is pronounced with a strong nasal sound.

For example, see āyah 67:4. م has a shadda on it in ثُمَّ, and ن has a shadda on it in إِنَّ in 67:12.

■ **Ikhfa Meem Sakin:** Pink Arabic font is used to indicate *ikhfa meem sakin.* When the letter ب appears after a م, it will be pronounced with a slight nasal sound.

For example, see āyah 67:12 where م and ب combination are shown رَبَّهُم بِٱلْغَيْبِ.

■ **Idghām:** Dark green font is used to indicate *idghām.* If any of these letters و م ن ى appear after a نْ or ◌ً, ◌ٍ, ◌ٌ, the letters become assimilated and will be read with a *ghunna.*

For example, see āyah 67:4. و after ◌ً as in خَاسِئًا وَهُوَ, or ى after نْ as in أَفَمَن يَمْشِى in 67:22.

■ **Qalqalah:** Red Arabic font is used to indicate *qalqalah.* The five letters of qalqalah are ج د ط ق ب. When any of these letters in a word has a sukun on it, or if deciding to pause on any of these letters that appear at the end of a sentence, it will appear to have an echoing or jerking sound.

For example, see āyah 67:2, 5, 22 وَجْهِهِ, وَلَقَدْ, لِيَبْلُوَكُمْ.

■ **Qalb:** Purple Arabic font is used to indicate *qalb.* If after نْ or ◌ً, ◌ٍ, ◌ٌ the letter ب appears, then the nūn sakin or tanween will be incorporated into the letter م and it will be pronounced with a *ghunna.*

For example, see āyah 67:11 وَعَادٌ بِٱلْقَارِ 69:4, عُتُلٍّ بَعْدَ 68:13, بِذَنْبِهِمْ.

■ **Idhgām Meem Sakin:** Light green font is used to indicate *idhgām meem sakin.* If after مْ there appears another مّ, the two meems will become incorporated and will be pronounced with a *ghunna.*

For example, see āyah 67:12 أَمِنتُم مَّن 67:17, لَهُم مَّغْفِرَةٌ.

Table of Contents

Sūrah 1 | Al-Fātihah

Revealed in Makkah

The Opening

Introduction:

Sūrah Al-Fātihah is not part of Juz Tabarak, but it is included in this book as this sūrah is the most frequently recited. We must recite this sūrah in every rakah of a salāh. This is the first sūrah in the Qur'ān and it is a prayer to Allāh. By reciting this sūrah, we establish our relationship with Allāh. He is the Lord of the whole universe. He provides us with everything we need and rewards our good efforts. We are His servants, and we pray only to Him for any help. Allāh shows us the Right Path—the path that is favored—and not the misleading path.

بِسۡمِ ٱللَّهِ ٱلرَّحۡمَٰنِ ٱلرَّحِيمِ ۝

1. In the name of Allāh, the most Kind, the most Rewarding.

ٱلۡحَمۡدُ لِلَّهِ رَبِّ ٱلۡعَٰلَمِينَ ۝

2. The Praise belong to Allāh, the Lord of all the worlds

ٱلرَّحۡمَٰنِ ٱلرَّحِيمِ ۝

3. Most Kind, most Rewarding

مَٰلِكِ يَوۡمِ ٱلدِّينِ ۝

4. Master of the Day of Judgment

إِيَّاكَ نَعۡبُدُ وَإِيَّاكَ نَسۡتَعِينُ ۝

5. You alone we do worship, and to You alone we seek help.

ٱهۡدِنَا ٱلصِّرَٰطَ ٱلۡمُسۡتَقِيمَ ۝

6. Guide us on the Right Path,

صِرَٰطَ ٱلَّذِينَ أَنۡعَمۡتَ عَلَيۡهِمۡ غَيۡرِ ٱلۡمَغۡضُوبِ عَلَيۡهِمۡ وَلَا ٱلضَّآلِّينَ ۝

7. the path of those on whom You have granted favors, not of those on whom wrath is brought down, nor of those who are lost.

Explanation:

1. The meaning of the title "al-Fātihah" is "the opening." The word is derived from the root word *fataha*, which means "to break open."

   The first āyah of Sūrah al-Fātihah is the beginning of the Qur'ān. This āyah is recited before beginning any good work. This āyah includes two of the most beautiful names of Allāh (swt)—*ar-Rahmān* and *ar-Rahīm*. Ar-Rahmān means "the most Merciful." This name tells us that Allāh (swt) is full of mercy and kindness toward everything. The name ar-Rahmān shows that we receive mercy from Allāh (swt) even if we do not ask for it. Ar-Rahīm means "extremely loving and merciful." This name is very similar to Ar-Rahmān. This name shows the quality of Allāh's (swt) mercy that we receive as a result of our good work and the mercy that we will receive in the Hereafter based on our good deeds.

2. All praise belongs to Allāh (swt). He is the Rabb, or Lord of all the worlds. Rabb is the one who not only creates us, but also feeds us, takes care of us, perfects us, preserves us, maintains us, and controls us. He does many other things for us so that we can survive in this world. He is not only our Rabb, but He is also the Rabb of the entire universe. Whatever He does to us, He also does to the Universe.

   The first four āyāt of the sūrah are part of an invocation, or a formal prayer. These four āyāt are stated without reference to the worshipper. In other words, these āyāt are not stated from a specific viewpoint. It does not matter whether the praise is made by a man, a worshipper, an angel or nature—the praise belongs to Allāh (swt).

3. We again remember Allāh (swt) by using His two beautiful names—ar-Rahmān and ar-Rahīm. The meaning of these names is explained above.

4. Allāh (swt) is the Master of the Day of Judgment. He is the Master because on that Day, He will give us our due based on how we behaved in this life.

5. Now that man recognizes that there is a Day of Judgment, he must prepare for the Day by surrendering to Allāh (swt). In this āyah, we confirm that He is the only One we worship. As we say this, we are making sure that we do not worship any idols, stones, people, the sun, the moon, animals, or anything else. We do not worship anything or anybody other than Allāh (swt), so we depend on Him for all help. Then, in the āyah, we respectfully mention that Allāh (swt) is the only one from whom we seek help. Notice that the object "you" (*iyyāka*) is repeated twice—first before the verb (*na'budu*, meaning "we worship") and again before another verb (*nasta'īn*, meaning "we ask for help"). The placement of *iyyāka* is significant because it places emphasis on the word "you," and, thus, excludes everything else from being a deity.

   The first four āyāt are stated in the third person. But this āyah is stated in the second person. The worshipper now speaks. He not only worships Allāh, but he also seeks His help. The shift from third person to second person, a beautiful Qur'ānic style, begins a two-way process where man worships Allāh (swt) , and, in return, he expects help from Him. Allāh (swt) is not only the recipient, but He is also a giver.

6. We ask Allāh (swt) to guide us on the Straight Path. This straight path is the Right Path. This is the path of Islam. The path does not have any twists or surprises. It is the perfect path for our survival. This path will lead us to the best result in the Hereafter. The guidance requested is spiritual guidance, but the request is made in the image of a straight path (*sirātal mustaqīm*). It appears that man is standing at a crossroads and is not sure which path will be ultimately beneficial.

The petition for guidance recognizes that Allāh (swt) knows which path will lead to a blessed destination and which path will lead to destruction.

7. The path that we want to follow is the path of the past messengers and other good people. Allāh (swt) blessed these people who walked on this path. Even if it is argued that we do not know whether the path was tested earlier, we submit to Allāh (swt) to guide us on the path that He has blessed. Thus, even in the petition, we are humble enough to leave the decision to Allāh. We want to be blessed like them, therefore, we pray to Allāh (swt) to help us walk on the path. Any other path is a wrong path. Those who walked on the wrong path earned anger and they became lost. We are afraid that we might somehow walk on the wrong path. The wrong path is the path of Shaitān. Allāh (swt) punished those who walked on the wrong path. Therefore, we pray to Allāh (swt) to guide us away from walking on the wrong path.

Words to know:

الفَاتِحَه: The Opening, the first sūrah in the Qur'an. فَتَحَ: to open, to give victory. مِفتَح: keys, treasure.

الفَتَّاح: Supreme Judge, one of the excellent names of Allāh.

رَحمَن: most Kind. رَحِمَ: to love, to have mercy. رَحِيم: most Rewarding. رَحمَةٌ: mercy.

مَرحَمَة: compassion.

مَالِك: Master, Lord. مَلَك: king. مَلَكَ: to own. مَلَكَت: has owned. مَلَكٌ: angel. مَلَا ئِك: angels.

مُستَقِيم: straight, shortest, smooth, right. قَام: to stand, to rise. أَقِيمُوا: you follow, you do.

مَقَامٌ: place where one stands. قِيَامَة: rising up, resurrection.

أَنعَمتَ: You have favored. نَعَمَ: to enjoy comfort. إِنعَام: favor. اَلنِعمَت: blessing.

مَغضُوب: who earned anger or wrath. غَضَبَ: to be angry. غَضَب: anger, wrath.

Sūrah Al-Fātihah
Word-by-word meaning

بِسمِ	ٱللَّهِ	ٱلرَّحمَٰنِ	ٱلرَّحِيمِ ۝
In the name of	Allāh	the most Kind	the most Rewarding

ٱلحَمدُ	لِلَّهِ	رَبِّ	ٱلعَٰلَمِينَ ۝
The Praise	for Allāh	the Rabb	the worlds.

ٱلرَّحمَٰنِ	ٱلرَّحِيمِ ۝	مَٰلِكِ	يَومِ
most Kind	most Rewarding.	The Master	day

وَإِيَّاكَ	نَعْبُدُ	إِيَّاكَ	ٱلدِّينِ ٤
and You alone	we worship	You alone	judgment, religion
ٱلْمُسْتَقِيمَ ٦	ٱلصِّرَاطَ	ٱهْدِنَا	نَسْتَعِينُ ٥
Right, straight.	the path	Guide us	we seek for help.
عَلَيْهِمْ	أَنْعَمْتَ	ٱلَّذِينَ	صِرَاطَ
upon them.	You have favored	those who	Path
وَلَا	عَلَيْهِمْ	ٱلْمَغْضُوبِ	غَيْرِ
and not	upon them	those who earned wrath	Other than

ٱلضَّآلِّينَ ٧

who are lost.

For additional reading, students may read "An Analysis of Fātihāh" and "Fātihāh versus the Lord's Payer" in the Islamic Studies Level 10 book published by Weekend Learning Publishers.

Juz Tabārak

Sūrah 67

Part A

Revealed in Makkah

The Dominion

Introduction:

This sūrah was revealed during the middle of the Makkan period as the opposition to Islam was escalating. The sūrah preaches the infinite power of Allāh (swt). It begins by asking people to examine the divine laws operating in nature. The existence of a uniform law without fault in it is a clear indication of one sovereign being in control of every aspect of life. However, those who reject the signs of Allāh (swt) and do not believe in His authority, will suffer punishment in blazing fire. In order to guide people, Allāh (swt) sent messengers during all periods of time. If people only listened to His messengers and applied their reasoning, they would not suffer in blazing fire. On the contrary, those who listened to and obeyed the messengers, would have earned Allāh's (swt) forgiveness and a great reward.

بِسْمِ ٱللَّهِ ٱلرَّحْمَٰنِ ٱلرَّحِيمِ

In the name of Allāh, the most Kind, the most Rewarding.

تَبَٰرَكَ ٱلَّذِى بِيَدِهِ ٱلْمُلْكُ وَهُوَ عَلَىٰ كُلِّ شَىْءٍ قَدِيرٌ ۝

1. Blessed is He in Whose hand is the Sovereignty, and He is the Possessor of power over all things,

ٱلَّذِى خَلَقَ ٱلْمَوْتَ وَٱلْحَيَوٰةَ لِيَبْلُوَكُمْ أَيُّكُمْ أَحْسَنُ عَمَلًا ۚ وَهُوَ ٱلْعَزِيزُ ٱلْغَفُورُ ۝

2. Who created Death and Life that He may test you—which of you is the best in deeds? And He is the Exalted in Might, the Forgiving,

ٱلَّذِى خَلَقَ سَبْعَ سَمَٰوَٰتٍ طِبَاقًا ۖ مَّا تَرَىٰ فِى خَلْقِ ٱلرَّحْمَٰنِ مِن تَفَٰوُتٍ ۖ فَٱرْجِعِ ٱلْبَصَرَ هَلْ تَرَىٰ مِن فُطُورٍ ۝

3. Who has created the seven heavens one above another. You cannot see in the creation of the Rahman any inconsistency. Then turn again the gaze. Do you see any crack?

ثُمَّ ٱرْجِعِ ٱلْبَصَرَ كَرَّتَيْنِ يَنقَلِبْ إِلَيْكَ ٱلْبَصَرُ خَاسِئًا وَهُوَ حَسِيرٌ ﴿٤﴾

4. And then turn again to search once more, the eyesight will return to you defeated, and it will be fatigued.

وَلَقَدْ زَيَّنَّا ٱلسَّمَاءَ ٱلدُّنْيَا بِمَصَٰبِيحَ وَجَعَلْنَٰهَا رُجُومًا لِّلشَّيَٰطِينِ ۖ وَأَعْتَدْنَا لَهُمْ عَذَابَ ٱلسَّعِيرِ ﴿٥﴾

5. And We have certainly adorned the nearest heaven with lamps, and We have made them conjectures for the Evil-ones, and We have prepared for them the chastisement of burning Fire.

وَلِلَّذِينَ كَفَرُواْ بِرَبِّهِمْ عَذَابُ جَهَنَّمَ ۖ وَبِئْسَ ٱلْمَصِيرُ ﴿٦﴾

6. And for those who do not believe in their Rabb, there is the chastisement of Hell. And it is a horrid journey!

إِذَآ أُلْقُواْ فِيهَا سَمِعُواْ لَهَا شَهِيقًا وَهِىَ تَفُورُ ﴿٧﴾

7. When they are cast in it, they will hear it roaring, and it will boil,

تَكَادُ تَمَيَّزُ مِنَ ٱلْغَيْظِ ۖ كُلَّمَآ أُلْقِىَ فِيهَا فَوْجٌ سَأَلَهُمْ خَزَنَتُهَآ أَلَمْ يَأْتِكُمْ نَذِيرٌ ﴿٨﴾

8. almost bursting with fury. Every time a group is thrown into it, its guardians will ask them: "Did not a warner come to you?"

قَالُواْ بَلَىٰ قَدْ جَآءَنَا نَذِيرٌ فَكَذَّبْنَا وَقُلْنَا مَا نَزَّلَ ٱللَّهُ مِن شَىْءٍ إِنْ أَنتُمْ إِلَّا فِى ضَلَٰلٍ كَبِيرٍ ﴿٩﴾

9. They will say: "Yes, a warner of course came to warn us, but we belied and said— 'Allāh has not revealed anything; you are in nothing but a great straying'."

وَقَالُواْ لَوْ كُنَّا نَسْمَعُ أَوْ نَعْقِلُ مَا كُنَّا فِىٓ أَصْحَٰبِ ٱلسَّعِيرِ ﴿١٠﴾

10. And they will say: "Had we but listened or applied reason, we would not have been among the fellows of the burning Fire!"

فَٱعْتَرَفُواْ بِذَنۢبِهِمْ فَسُحْقًا لِّأَصْحَٰبِ ٱلسَّعِيرِ ﴿١١﴾

11. Thus they will confess their sins; so "Begone!" for the fellows of the flame!

إِنَّ ٱلَّذِينَ يَخْشَوْنَ رَبَّهُم بِٱلْغَيْبِ لَهُم مَّغْفِرَةٌ وَأَجْرٌ كَبِيرٌ ﴿١٢﴾

12. Surely those who fear their Rabb in secret, for them is forgiveness and a great reward.

وَأَسِرُّواْ قَوْلَكُمْ أَوِ ٱجْهَرُواْ بِهِۦٓ ۖ إِنَّهُۥ عَلِيمٌۢ بِذَاتِ ٱلصُّدُورِ ﴿١٣﴾

13. And whether you hide your statements or expose it, surely He knows what is inside the hearts.

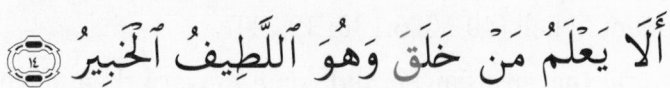

14. Does He not know Who created? And He is the Knower of Subtleties, all-Aware.

أَلَا يَعْلَمُ مَنْ خَلَقَ وَهُوَ ٱللَّطِيفُ ٱلْخَبِيرُ ۝

Explanation:

1. The name of this Juz is derived from the first word, *tabārak*, in this āyah. The title of the sūrah is derived from the key word *al-mulk* (the dominion, sovereignty), also used in this āyah. The word *tabāraka* is used here to exalt the almightiness and eternal nature of Allāh (swt) (23:14; 25:1; 40:64; 43:85). The word "blessed" implies glorification or praise of the Almightiness that is manifested throughout His dominion over everything. He has authority and Lordship over all of creation— both visible and invisible. This authority is said to be in His hands (*yad*). If something is in one's hand, it can be said that he or she owns it and is in control of that thing. Therefore, when Allāh (swt) says He has supreme power in His "hands," it means He has full control over everything, as can be seen in āyāt 3:26,73; 5:64; 36:71; 39:67; and 48:10.

2. The blessedness of Allāh's abiding and everlasting existence is contrasted with the life and death of the creations. In this āyah, death is said to have been created. Death is not a state of "non-existence," rather it is an inanimate stage just as life is a stage of existence. Both stages were created to test each human being to reveal who ultimately excels in his or her deeds.

3-4. The dominion of Allāh (swt) over all things is illustrated by the example of creation of the universe. In Arabic literary style, seven (*sab'a*) often denotes "several" or "many." The creation of the entire universe, or any other creation for that matter, was not undertaken in a careless, inconsistent manner. The perfect order of the universe is proof, not only of Allāh's existence, but also of His unity. If perfect order were not maintained, everything would break its laws and violate the measures. This āyah challenges ordinary observers, as well as accomplished scientists, to find any inconsistencies in the mechanism of nature. The emphasis on observing once, observing again and observing a third time implies employing ordinary knowledge as well as undertaking detailed research, again and again, in order to understand the mechanism behind the origin, creation and operation of every animate and inanimate object in the universe. The uniformity in the laws of nature in the universe points to a single Supreme Being in control of everything. Regarding the word *tibāqan* (layers), see 71:15.

5. The universe is so vast that we can only see a tiny fragment of it with our eyes. This fragment is mentioned as the lower heaven. The lamps in the lower heaven refer to stars and planets in the visible sky (37:6; 41:12). The term *shayātīn,* in this instance, is used to characterize people with satanic tendencies—the soothsayers and astrologers—who predict good and evil outcomes based on planetary positions (15:16–17; 37:6–10). The word *rajm* (plural, *rujum*) is a noun indicating an object that is used for stoning. Shaitān was chased away by stoning. The word also means false guesses about the unknown, speaking hypothetically or making something the object of guesswork.

6-8. Those who do not believe or reject their Rabb will suffer punishment in Fire. Ordinary fire does not roar unless it is fierce and destructive. The word *shahaqa* means loud breathing, such as that of a donkey or horse. It also means something that is roaring, causing a loud sound. This fire of Hell is also bursting with ferocity. The extent of this ferocity is indicated by the word *tafūr* (derived from *fāra*), meaning something that is boiling over. Every time sinners are brought to the Fire, the angels who are guarding the gates of Hell will ask them questions (43:77; 66:6). For example, during earthly life, did not a warner come warning you about punishment in hell (40:50; 6:130; 39:71)?

9–11. Before entering the Fire, the sinners will admit that messengers did come to warn them during their earthly lives, but they rejected their message. Then they will admit a very important thing: they did not apply reasoning. If they had applied reasoning, they would not be in the burning fire today. This demonstrates that if people apply their reasoning properly, it should lead them to the realization of Allāh's (swt) existence. In Islam, rational thinking is intended to synchronize with faith. Islam is not afraid of challenging man's intellect or rational thinking. The question is whether realization of Allāh's existence is everything. The answer is no. For that reason, people need divine guidance in order to follow the right path. The messengers do this precisely by acting as the medium for transmitting Allāh's revelations.

12. The purpose of fearing Allāh (swt) is not to run away from Him, but to fear doing anything that would displease Him. The phrase *rabbahum bil'ghaybi* can be interpreted to mean "Rabb in secret" or "Rabb the Unseen." The former interpretation implies that fear of Allāh (swt) should be kept in mind even when no one is watching (21:49; 50:33). This interpretation is reasonable based on the next āyah in which Allāh (swt) says He is aware of man's innermost thoughts and inclinations.

13–14. Allāh (swt) is aware of everything, both obvious and secretive. Nothing is hidden from His knowledge. Hiding or publishing one's word (*qawl*) indicates either hiding or declaring one's faith. The āyah then asserts a qualifying attribute of Allāh: He is *al-Latīf* (gracious, sharp-sighted, one who understands mysteries). This qualifying name of Allāh (swt) highlights some of His attributes that are incomprehensible and imperceptible to the five senses (6:103; 12:100; 22:63; 33:34; 67:14). The term *latīf* denotes something that is extremely subtle, therefore, it is boundless and unintelligible.

Words to know:

بَرَكَ: be honored and respected. مُبَارَكٌ: blessed one. تَبَارَكَ: highly exalted, far removed from, possessing abundant good, blessed. بَرَكَاتٌ: blessings.

مَلَكَ: to possess, to become owner, to rule, to have authority. مَالِكٌ: Master, Sovereign, Owner, Lord. يَمِلِكُ: he has power to prevail. مَلَكُوت: Dominion, kingdom.

قَدَرَ: to be able to do, to have power over. قَادِرٌ: one who is able to or has power over. قَادِرٌ: law, power, knowledge, measure, majesty. تَقْدِير: decree, disposition, measuring. مُقْتَدِر: all-powerful.

خَسِرَ: to wander about, to suffer loss. خُسْرٌ: loss. خَاسِرُون: loser.

رَجَمَ: to stone, to stone to death. رَجُومٌ: guesswork, conjecture, missile. رُجُومٌ: shooting star. رَجِيم: one thrown off, rejected.

لَقِيَ: to meet, to experience, to suffer. اَلْقَت: cast forth. لِقَاءٌ: meeting.

نَذَرَ: to admonish, to caution. نَذِير: warner. مُنْذِرٌ: warner.

ضَنَب: to make a tale, to track. ضَنب: crime, fault, sin.

خَشِيَ: to awe, to awe with reverence. يَخْشَى: be careful. خَشْيَةٌ: Fear, awe.

اَجَرَ: to reward. اَجْرٌ: reward. اُجُورٌ: dowries.

صَدَرَ: to return, to commence. صَدْرٌ: bosom, chest.

لَطُف: to be delicate, graceful. اَللَّطِف: All subtle being, unfathomable, incomprehensible.

Sūrah Al-Mulk
Word-by-word meaning

ٱلرَّحِيمِ	ٱلرَّحْمَـٰنِ	ٱللَّهِ	بِسْمِ
the most Rewarding	the most Kind	Allāh	in the name of
ٱلْمُلْكُ	بِيَدِهِ	ٱلَّذِى	تَبَـٰرَكَ
is the dominion	in Whose hand	He	Blessed is
شَىْءٍ	كُلِّ	عَلَىٰ	وَهُوَ
things	all	over	and He is
ٱلْمَوْتَ	خَلَقَ	ٱلَّذِى	قَدِيرٌ ﴿١﴾
Death	has created	Who	possessor of power
أَحْسَنُ	أَيُّكُمْ	لِيَبْلُوَكُمْ	وَٱلْحَيَوٰةَ
is best	which of you	that He may test you	and life
ٱلْغَفُورُ ﴿٢﴾	ٱلْعَزِيزُ	وَهُوَ	عَمَلًا
the oft-Forgiving	the Almighty	and He is	in deeds
سَمَـٰوَٰتٍ	سَبْعَ	خَلَقَ	ٱلَّذِى
heavens	the seven	has created	Who
فِى	تَرَىٰ	مَّا	طِبَاقًا
in	you can see	not	one above another
تَفَـٰوُتٍ	مِن	ٱلرَّحْمَـٰنِ	خَلْقِ
fault	any	the most Merciful	the creation of
تَرَى	هَلْ	ٱلْبَصَرَ	فَٱرْجِعِ
you see	can	the sight	so repeat again

ٱرۡجِع repeat	ثُمَّ then	فُطُورٍ ۝ rifts, cracks	مِن any
إِلَيۡكَ to you	يَنقَلِبۡ will return	كَرَّتَيۡنِ and yet again	ٱلۡبَصَرَ the sight
حَسِيرٌ ۝ is worn out, fatigued	وَهُوَ and it	خَاسِئًا defeated	ٱلۡبَصَرُ the sight
ٱلدُّنۡيَا the nearest	ٱلسَّمَآءَ the heaven	زَيَّنَّا We have adorned	وَلَقَدۡ and indeed
لِّلشَّيَـٰطِينِ for the devils	رُجُومًا conjectures	وَجَعَلۡنَـٰهَا and We have made them	بِمَصَـٰبِيحَ with lamps
ٱلسَّعِيرِ ۝ blazing fire	عَذَابَ chastisement of	لَهُمۡ for them	وَأَعۡتَدۡنَا and We have prepared
عَذَابُ is the torment of	بِرَبِّهِمۡ in their Rabb	كَفَرُواْ do not believe	وَلِلَّذِينَ and for those who
إِذَآ when	ٱلۡمَصِيرُ ۝ destination	وَبِئۡسَ and it is the worst	جَهَنَّمَ hell
لَهَا of its	سَمِعُواْ they will hear	فِيهَا in it	أُلۡقُواْ they are cast
تَكَادُ almost	تَفُورُ ۝ boils, blazes forth	وَهِىَ as it	شَهِيقًا roaring
كُلَّمَآ every time	ٱلۡغَيۡظِ fury	مِنَ from, with	تَمَيَّزُ bursting with

ألْقِىَ	فِيهَا	فَوْجٌ	سَأَلَهُمْ
is cast	in it	a group	will ask them
خَزَنَتُهَآ	أَلَمْ	يَأْتِكُمْ	نَذِيرٌ ۸
its keepers	did not	come to you	a warner
قَالُواْ	بَلَىٰ	قَدْ	جَآءَنَا
they will say	yes	indeed	did come to us
نَذِيرٌ	فَكَذَّبْنَا	وَقُلْنَا	مَا
a warner	but we denied (him)	and we said	not
نَزَّلَ	ٱللَّهُ	مِن	شَىْءٍ
sent down	Allāh	any	thing
إِنْ	أَنتُمْ	إِلَّا	فِى
but	you are	only	in
ضَلَلٍ	كَبِيرٍ ۹	وَقَالُواْ	لَوْ
error	great	and they will say	if
كُنَّا	نَسْمَعُ	أَوْ	نَعْقِلُ
we had	listened	or	applied reasoning
مَا	كُنَّا	فِى	أَصْحَبِ
not	we would have been	among	fellows of
ٱلسَّعِيرِ ۱۰	فَٱعْتَرَفُو	بِذَنْبِهِمْ	فَسُحْقًا
the burning fire	thus they will confess	their sins	so away with
لِّأَصْحَبِ	ٱلسَّعِيرِ ۱۱	إِنَّ	ٱلَّذِينَ
for the fellows of	the burning fire	surely	those who
تَخْشَوْنَ	رَبَّهُم	بِٱلْغَيْبِ	لَهُم
fear	their Rabb	in secret	for them

وَأَسِرُّوا

and whether you keep secret

كَبِيرٌ ۱۲

a great

وَأَجْرٌ

and reward

مَغْفِرَةٌ

forgiveness

بِهِۦ

it

ٱجْهَرُوا

disclose

أَوِ

or

قَوْلَكُمْ

your sayings

ٱلصُّدُورِ ۱۳

the breasts

بِذَاتِ

of what is in

عَلِيمٌ

the all-Knower

إِنَّهُۥ

Surely He is

خَلَقَ

created

مَنْ

Who

يَعْلَمُ

He know

أَلَا

does not

ٱلْخَبِيرُ ۱٤

all Aware

ٱللَّطِيفُ

the knower of all subtleties

وَهُوَ

and He is

A few applications of the message:

This sūrah draws attention to the laws of nature operating throughout the entire universe. The uniform laws of nature are a sign of Allāh's mercy, power and wisdom that we can see all around us. We can comprehend the signs of Allāh (swt) only through the application of reasoning. The sūrah teaches that those who reject the signs will be the companions of fire. Allāh (swt) sent messengers during all periods of time so that we could listen to and obey their teachings. As long as we remain obedient to the true teachings of our Rasūl (S) and follow the teachings of the Qur'ān, we should have no fear. We will earn the forgiveness of Allāh and earn a great reward. We should not compromise our lives in the Hereafter by becoming disloyal to Allāh (swt).

Questions:

1. Explain the significance of the word *yad* (hand) used in the first āyāt of sūrah al-Mulk.

2. Why is it impossible to find any inconsistencies in the creations of Allāh (swt)? What does this indicate?

3. How many times did Allāh (swt) ask us to investigate heaven in order to find possible inconsistencies in the laws of nature? What would be the final result of such investigations?

4. Can the position of the stars and planets foretell the future? Explain your answer.

5. What will the gatekeepers of hell ask people? What does their question confirm?

6. What confession will people in hell admit to regarding the messengers who came to warn them during their earthly lives?

Sūrah 67 | *Al-Mulk*

Revealed in Makkah

Part B | **The Dominion**

Introduction:

The previous section of the sūrah explained the uniformity of Allāh's (swt) laws and stated that those who reject the warnings will be in hell-fire. In this section, Allāh (swt) cautions all of us to be fearful of His punishment, which can occur anytime in any manner. Allāh (swt) explains how He made the earth suitable for life. He saves us from earthquakes and hurricanes. He provides us food and water. He has given us the five senses and faculties of understanding and reasoning. Yet many of us do not give thanks to Him, and We deviate from the right path. This sūrah provides the parable of a believer and a non-believer. Finally, the sūrah cautions us about the Day of Judgment. On that day, the sinners will have no choice but to confess their sins and face the consequences of their actions.

بِسۡمِ ٱللَّهِ ٱلرَّحۡمَـٰنِ ٱلرَّحِيمِ

In the name of Allāh, the most Kind, the most Rewarding.

هُوَ ٱلَّذِى جَعَلَ لَكُمُ ٱلۡأَرۡضَ ذَلُولًا فَٱمۡشُواْ فِى مَنَاكِبِهَا وَكُلُواْ مِن رِّزۡقِهِۦ ۖ وَإِلَيۡهِ ٱلنُّشُورُ ۝

15. He it is Who has made the earth calm for you, so that you walk in its ways; and you eat its provisions. And toward Him is the rising up.

ءَأَمِنتُم مَّن فِى ٱلسَّمَآءِ أَن يَخۡسِفَ بِكُمُ ٱلۡأَرۡضَ فَإِذَا هِىَ تَمُورُ ۝

16. What! do you feel secure from Him Who is overhead, lest He will cause the earth to swallow you up? Then lo! it will shake!

أَمۡ أَمِنتُم مَّن فِى ٱلسَّمَآءِ أَن يُرۡسِلَ عَلَيۡكُمۡ حَاصِبًا ۖ فَسَتَعۡلَمُونَ كَيۡفَ نَذِيرِ ۝

17. Or do you feel secure from Him Who is overhead, lest He will send you a hurricane! Then soon you will know how was My warning!

وَلَقَدۡ كَذَّبَ ٱلَّذِينَ مِن قَبۡلِهِمۡ فَكَيۡفَ كَانَ نَكِيرِ ۝

18. And indeed those before them belied! Then how was My reprobation!

أَوَلَمْ يَرَوْا۟ إِلَى ٱلطَّيْرِ فَوْقَهُمْ صَٰٓفَّٰتٍ وَيَقْبِضْنَ مَا يُمْسِكُهُنَّ إِلَّا ٱلرَّحْمَٰنُ ۚ إِنَّهُۥ بِكُلِّ شَىْءٍۭ بَصِيرٌ ۝

19. What! Do they not see the birds above them spreading out their wings and folding them in? They are held up by no one except the *Rahman.* Surely He is the Seer of all things.

أَمَّنْ هَٰذَا ٱلَّذِى هُوَ جُندٌ لَّكُمْ يَنصُرُكُم مِّن دُونِ ٱلرَّحْمَٰنِ ۚ إِنِ ٱلْكَٰفِرُونَ إِلَّا فِى غُرُورٍ ۝

20. Well, who is that can be an army for you that will help you besides the *Rahman?* The non-believers are in nothing but delusion.

أَمَّنْ هَٰذَا ٱلَّذِى يَرْزُقُكُمْ إِنْ أَمْسَكَ رِزْقَهُۥ ۚ بَل لَّجُّوا۟ فِى عُتُوٍّ وَنُفُورٍ ۝

21. Well, who is there that will feed you, if He should withhold His provision? Of course, they persist in rebellion and aversion.

أَفَمَن يَمْشِى مُكِبًّا عَلَىٰ وَجْهِهِۦٓ أَهْدَىٰٓ أَمَّن يَمْشِى سَوِيًّا عَلَىٰ صِرَٰطٍ مُّسْتَقِيمٍ ۝

22. Well then, is he who walks upon his face groveling better guided, or one who walks upright on the Right Path?

قُلْ هُوَ ٱلَّذِىٓ أَنشَأَكُمْ وَجَعَلَ لَكُمُ ٱلسَّمْعَ وَٱلْأَبْصَٰرَ وَٱلْأَفْـِٔدَةَ ۖ قَلِيلًا مَّا تَشْكُرُونَ ۝

23. Say: "He it is Who has evolved you, and made hearing and sight and the hearts for you. Little it is what you thank!"

قُلْ هُوَ ٱلَّذِى ذَرَأَكُمْ فِى ٱلْأَرْضِ وَإِلَيْهِ تُحْشَرُونَ ۝

24. Say: "He it is Who has spread you in the earth, and you will be gathered toward Him."

وَيَقُولُونَ مَتَىٰ هَٰذَا ٱلْوَعْدُ إِن كُنتُمْ صَٰدِقِينَ ۝

25. And they say: "When will this promise be? If you are truthful."

قُلْ إِنَّمَا ٱلْعِلْمُ عِندَ ٱللَّهِ وَإِنَّمَآ أَنَا۠ نَذِيرٌ مُّبِينٌ ۝

26. You say: "Surely the knowledge is with Allāh; and I am only a plain warner."

فَلَمَّا رَأَوْهُ زُلْفَةً سِيٓـَٔتْ وُجُوهُ ٱلَّذِينَ كَفَرُوا۟ وَقِيلَ هَٰذَا ٱلَّذِى كُنتُم بِهِۦ تَدَّعُونَ ۝

27. But when they will see it approaching, the faces of those who do not believe will turn sad, and it will be said: "This is what you have been asking for."

قُلْ أَرَءَيْتُمْ إِنْ أَهْلَكَنِىَ ٱللَّهُ وَمَن مَّعِىَ أَوْ رَحِمَنَا فَمَن يُجِيرُ ٱلْكَٰفِرِينَ مِنْ عَذَابٍ أَلِيمٍ ۝

28. Say: "Have you thought if Allāh were to destroy me and those with me, or have mercy on us, who will then rescue the Unbelievers from a painful punishment?"

قُل هُوَ ٱلرَّحْمَٰنُ ءَامَنَّا بِهِۦ وَعَلَيْهِ تَوَكَّلْنَا ۖ فَسَتَعْلَمُونَ مَنْ هُوَ فِى ضَلَٰلٍ مُّبِينٍ ۝

29. Say: "He is the most Merciful,—We believe in Him and we rely upon Him. So you will soon know who is he— in manifest straying."

قُلْ أَرَءَيْتُمْ إِنْ أَصْبَحَ مَآؤُكُمْ غَوْرًا فَمَن يَأْتِيكُم بِمَآءٍ مَّعِينٍ ۝

30. Say: "Have you seen—if your water should disappear to morrow, who will then bring you flowing water?"

Explanation:

15. After continuing with Allāh's almightiness, this āyah says the earth was made calm for us so that we might walk on it and eat its provisions. The āyah draws our attention to the topographical features of the earth during the time of its formation, when it was a bubbling-hot mass of fire. Subsequently it cooled down over billions of years, and thus, became conducive to early life forms emerging.

16–17. The phrase *man fis-samāi'* (one who is in heaven) is metaphorically used to indicate Allāh's omnipresence, authority and power encompass everything. We may feel safe on earth because Allāh (swt) made it safe and suitable for our survival; however, if we defy Allāh (swt), then we do not have any protection against His punishment. These two āyāt indicate that He might let the earth "swallow" people using the hazards of nature. Alternatively He might make the earth shake in an earthquake, hurricane or other turmoil created by human beings. It is estimated that about 1,000 earthquakes over the magnitude of 4 Richter scale occur every year. Several of them are greater than a 7 point magnitude. Allāh (swt) saves us from calamities of nature. We have to think—who, other than Allāh (swt), could keep people secure?

18. The entire passage directs our attention to the history of the downfall of earlier nations and communities. They were destroyed because they rejected the truth. Today, from the perspective of readers of the Qur'ān, these communities include all those nations originating in the recent past and dating back thousands of years in human history.

19. The inquisitive mode of the āyah indicates the non-believers do not take notice of a common signs in nature. One of the signs is the adaptation of birds to fly in the air. Their physique, feathers, bone and muscle structure is a divine gift that allows them to fly. The metaphor of birds in the sky is presented to supplement the laws of nature mentioned previously in āyāt 3 and 4.

20. After narrating some of the almighty ways of Allāh (swt), this āyah prompts non-believers to think about their possible helpers besides Allāh (swt). Truly, there are no helpers besides Allāh. The use of the word *jund* (army, force, troops) scorns the collective efforts of any group or power that seems to help the non-believers against Allāh (swt). The term *ghurūr* (useless thing, vain hope) implies being mislead or lured into false vanity or deceptive promises. As a result of self-delusion, people mistakenly assume falsehood as a valid norm and harmful things as beneficial.

21. The term provision (*rizk*) includes every tangible and intangible blessing from Allāh (swt). For example, this includes rain and suitable climatic conditions for farming as well as water and air.

22. The āyah contrasts two types of people: those who walk on the Straight Path and those who walk on the evil path. Groveling on one's face (*mukibb,* derived from *kabba*) means one who throws his face downward, thus, only seeing what is below his feet and totally unaware in which direction he is

walking. As a result, such a person is prone to stumbling and falling on his face. This metaphor is used to show the spiritual deficiency of a person who only sees the boundaries of his or her immediate earthly motives.

23. In order to attain higher ethical and spiritual standards, a person is required to use the faculties of perceiving, understanding and thinking—all of which are Allāh's special gifts to human beings. Yet many of us use these faculties for negative purposes or use them sparingly or do not use them at all. As a result, these faculties are sealed for them (2:18,171; 7:179; 8:22; 17:97). Such abuse or misuse is a reflection of our ingratitude toward Allāh (swt).

24–26. Allāh (swt) created and multiplied people from a single *nafs* (4:1). Ultimately, every one of us will be gathered unto Him on the Day of Awakening. The non-believers are skeptical about this promise. They want to know when, if ever, this promise will be fulfilled. In response, it is clarified that only Allāh (swt) knows about the timing of the Awakening. The duty of the Rasūlullāh (S) was not to speculate about the timing, rather to warn about the inevitable day.

27. The non-believers used to laugh and ask about the promise of the Day of Awakening (āyah 25). When the promise of the Day is fulfilled, the non-believers will realize that they were terribly wrong about the Day. Their faces will reflect their innermost feelings and thoughts at that very moment (3:106).

28. In this life, when calamity strikes, it may destroy both good and bad people. However, the question is not whether good people are destroyed in a calamity. The question is what will happen to the non-believers. The consequence will, nonetheless, be the same: they will receive a painful punishment.

29. In the previous āyah, two possible endings for Rasūlullāh (S) and the believers are mentioned—they might be destroyed or rescued. Of the two possibilities, this āyah now assures that when the real accounting of human deeds and values are ultimately determined, everyone will learn who was wrong and who was right. The āyah then assures that Allāh (swt) is the most gracious, and whom all believers must trust.

30. The sūrah ends with yet another reminder of the almightiness of Allāh (swt). Throughout this sūrah, various earth-related metaphors are used to prompt non-believers to reflect on the truth. The sinking or disappearing of water into the earth is yet another metaphor that connects to other metaphors such as the steadying of the earth in āyah 15, the swallowing of the earth in āyah 16, groveling on the face in āyah 22, and multiplying of life forms on the earth in āyah 24. Just as the constant flow of water is indispensable for life forms, so is the constant flow of Allāh's inspiration and guidance essential for the spiritual and moral improvement of people. Allāh (swt) could withdraw the inspiration altogether and let human civilization undergo disintegration. Or He may let human beings regain their spiritual liveliness after letting all obsolete and rejected values disappear completely.

Words to know:

ذَلَّ: to be low, to make submissive, to humble. تَذْلِيلًا within easy reach. ذَلُولٌ: meekness, submissiveness. ذَلُولٌ: made subservient, broken. أَذَلُّوا: meanest, lowest.

مَشَى: to walk, to go. يَمْشِي: he walks.

نَكَبَ: to go a side, to swerve from. نَاكِبُون: they are deviators. مَنَاكِب: spacious path, regions.

نَكِرَ: to dislike, to disown. نُكْرًا: awful, dreadful. مُنكَر: false, something strange to human nature.

صَفَّ: to set in order, to arrange in rows. صَافٌّ: extending its wings. صَفًّا: rank, row.

قَبَضَ: to contract, to seize, to grasp, to withdraw. يَقْبِضُوا: received, withdraws.

مَسَكَ: to take hold of, to grasp. أَمْسَكَ: withhold, keep back. مَسَّكَ: to perfume with musk.

غَرَّ: to beguile, to deceive. لَايَغُرَّنَّ: let not deceive. غُرُور: deceiving, beguiling.

نَشَأَ: to grow up be produced. أَنْشَأَ: to create, to produce. مُنْشِئِ: we raise, we bring up.

ذَرَّ: to scatter. ذَرَّةٌ: atom. ذُرِّيَات: progeny, children.

Sūrah Al-Mulk
Word-by-word meaning

ٱلرَّحِيمِ	ٱلرَّحْمَٰنِ	ٱللَّهِ	بِسْمِ
the most Rewarding	the most Kind	Allāh	In the name of
لَكُمُ	جَعَلَ	ٱلَّذِى	هُوَ
for you	has made	Who	He it is
فِى	فَٱمْشُوا	ذَلُولاً	ٱلْأَرْضَ
in	so that you walk	subservient	the earth
رِّزْقِهِ	مِن	وَكُلُوا	مَنَاكِبِهَا
its provision	of	and eat	its paths
مَّن	ءَأَمِنتُم	ٱلنُّشُورُ ⑮	وَإِلَيْهِ
(from) He who is	do you feel secure	is the resurrection	and to Him
تَخْسِفَ	أَن	ٱلسَّمَآءِ	فِى
He will cause to sink	that	(in) heaven	over
هِىَ	فَإِذَا	ٱلْأَرْضَ	بِكُمُ
it	so when	the earth	with you
مَّن	أَمِنتُم	أَمْ	تَمُورُ ⑯
He who is	do you feel secure from	or	will shake

فِى	ٱلسَّمَآءِ	أَن	يُرْسِلَ
over	the heaven	that	He sends

عَلَيْكُمْ	حَاصِبًا	فَسَتَعْلَمُونَ	كَيْفَ
against you	a hurricane	then you will know	how was

نَذِيرِ ١٧	وَلَقَدْ	كَذَّبَ	ٱلَّذِينَ
My warning	and indeed	denied, belied	those who

مِن قَبْلِهِمْ	فَكَيْفَ	كَانَ	نَكِيرِ ١٨
before them	then how	was	my punishment

أَوَلَمْ	يَرَوْاْ	إِلَى	ٱلطَّيْرِ
do they not	see	at, to	the birds

فَوْقَهُمْ	صَٰفَّٰتٍ	وَيَقْبِضْنَ	مَا
above them	spreading their wings	and folding them in	no one

يُمْسِكُهُنَّ	إِلَّا	ٱلرَّحْمَٰنُ	إِنَّهُۥ
holds them	except	the most Merciful	surely He is

بِكُلِّ	شَىْءٍ	بَصِيرٌ ١٩	أَمَّنْ
of every	things	the all-Seer	who is

هَٰذَا	ٱلَّذِى	هُوَ	جُندٌ
this	that can	be	an army

لَّكُمْ	يَنصُرُكُم	مِّن دُونِ	ٱلرَّحْمَٰنِ
to you	to help you	besides	the most Merciful

إِن	ٱلْكَٰفِرُونَ	إِلَّا	فِى
nothing	the disbelievers (are in)	but	in

غُرُورٍ ٢٠	أَمَّنْ	هَٰذَا	ٱلَّذِى
delusion	who is	this	that

رِزْقَهُۥ	أَمْسَكَ	إِنْ	يَرْزُقُكُم
His provision	He should withhold	if	can provide for you
عُتُوٍّ	فِى	لَّجُّوا۟	بَل
pride	be in	they continue to	but, of course
مُكِبًّا	يَمْشِى	أَفَمَن	وَنُفُورٍ ۲۱
bent down without seeing	walks	is he who	and flee
أَمَّن	أَهْدَىٰٓ	وَجْهِهِۦٓ	عَلَىٰ
or he who	more rightly guided	his face	on
صِرَٰطٍ	عَلَىٰ	سَوِيًّا	يَمْشِى
way	on	upright	walks
ٱلَّذِى	هُوَ	قُلْ	مُّسْتَقِيمٍ ۲۲
Who	(is it) He	say	straight
ٱلسَّمْعَ	لَكُمُ	وَجَعَلَ	أَنشَأَكُمْ
hearing	for you	and made	has created you
مَّا	قَلِيلًا	وَٱلْأَفْـِٔدَةَ	وَٱلْأَبْصَـٰرَ
(is) that	little	and hearts	and seeing
ٱلَّذِى	هُوَ	قُلْ	تَشْكُرُونَ ۲۳
who	it is He	say	you give thanks
وَإِلَيْهِ	ٱلْأَرْضِ	فِى	ذَرَأَكُمْ
and unto Him	the earth	in	has created you
هَـٰذَا	مَتَىٰ	وَيَقُولُونَ	تُحْشَرُونَ ۲۴
will this	when	and they say	you shall be gathered
صَـٰدِقِينَ ۲۵	كُنتُمْ	إِن	ٱلْوَعْدُ
truthful	you are	if	promise be

عِندَ	ٱلْعِلْمُ	إِنَّمَا	قُلْ
with	the knowledge	is only	say
نَذِيرٌ	أَنَا۠	وَإِنَّمَآ	ٱللَّهِ
a warner	I am	and only	Allāh
زُلْفَةً	رَأَوْهُ	فَلَمَّا	مُّبِينٌ ۝
approaching	they see it	but when	plain
كَفَرُواْ	ٱلَّذِينَ	وُجُوهُ	سِيٓـَٔتْ
disbelieve	those who	the faces of	will be displeased
كُنتُم	ٱلَّذِى	هَـٰذَا	وَقِيلَ
you were	which	this is	and it will be said
أَرَءَيْتُمْ	قُلْ	تَدَّعُونَ ۝	بِهِۦ
have you seen	say	asking for	for it
وَمَن	ٱللَّهُ	أَهْلَكَنِىَ	إِن
and those	Allāh	destroys me	if
فَمَن	رَحِمَنَا	أَوْ	مَّعِىَ
Who	have mercy on us	or	with me
عَذَابٍ	مِنْ	ٱلْكَـٰفِرِينَ	تُجِيرُ
punishment	from	the non-believers	can save
ٱلرَّحْمَـٰنُ	هُوَ	قُلْ	أَلِيمٍ ۝
the most Merciful	He is	say	a painful
تَوَكَّلْنَا	وَعَلَيْهِ	بِهِۦ	ءَامَنَّا
we put our trust	and in Him	in Him	we believe
فِى	هُوَ	مَنْ	فَسَتَعْلَمُونَ
in	that is	who is it	so you will soon know

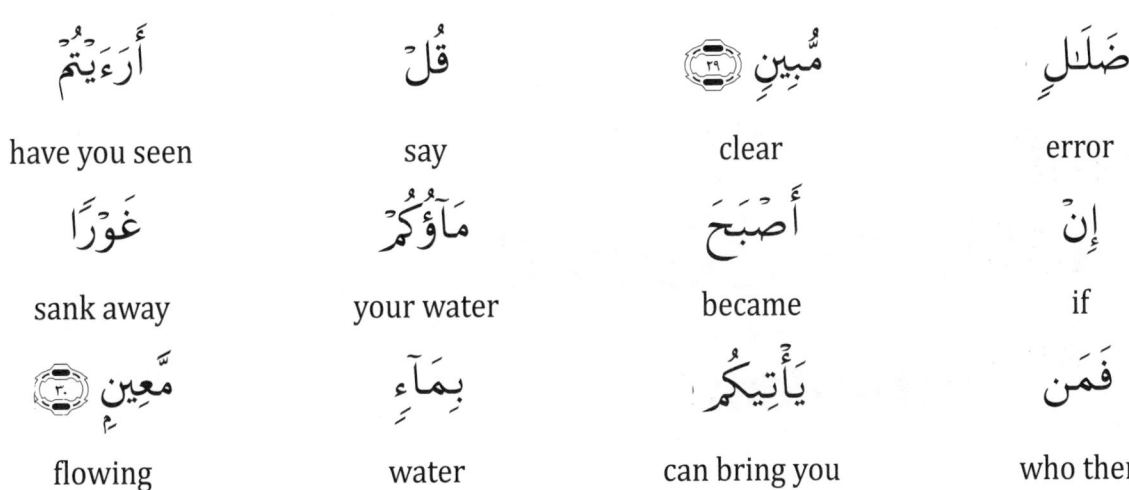

أَرَءَيْتُمْ	قُلْ	مُّبِينٍ ۞	ضَلَلٍ
have you seen	say	clear	error
غَوْرًا	مَاؤُكُمْ	أَصْبَحَ	إِنْ
sank away	your water	became	if
مَّعِينٍ ۞	بِمَاءٍ	يَأْتِيكُم	فَمَن
flowing	water	can bring you	who then

A few applications of the message:

Throughout the sūrah, Allāh (swt) draws our attention to His almightiness. We believe in Him and follow His commands. Sometimes we forget His commands and follow the wrong path. As soon as we realize our mistake, we should seek His forgiveness. We should never attempt to defy Him. We should remember that if Allāh (swt) were to destroy us and those with us, there is no one who can rescue us. The question is: why would He destroy us? The answer is: He would destroy us only if we rebel against Him and reject His commands.

Throughout the Qur'ān, Allāh (swt) mentions several familiar historical accounts of past communities that rejected Him, and as a consequence, suffered terrible punishment. We should learn the lessons from these historical accounts. We should remember that if we continue doing wrong, we run the same risk of suffering severe punishment. We should always remember that Allāh (swt) can punish us anytime, anywhere, in any manner. We must pay attention to His warnings and remain faithful to His commands.

We should never lose hope of receiving Allāh's mercy. He teaches us to say: "He is the most Merciful—we believe in Him and upon Him do we rely." As long as we remain faithful to Him and follow His commands carefully, we do not have to worry.

Questions:

1. What are some of the natural calamities that Allāh (swt) can apply to punish sinners?

2. What does the example of birds in āyah 19 of sūrah al-Mulk indicate?

3. What is the meaning of the parable mentioned in āyah 22 of sūrah al-Mulk?

4. When the non-believers questioned about the timing of the Day of Judgment, what answers were given to them?

5. What three senses are mentioned in sūrah al-Mulk? What is the reason for mentioning these senses?

6. Explain why water is vital for life forms on earth. What could happen to human civilization if entire world experiences water scarcity?

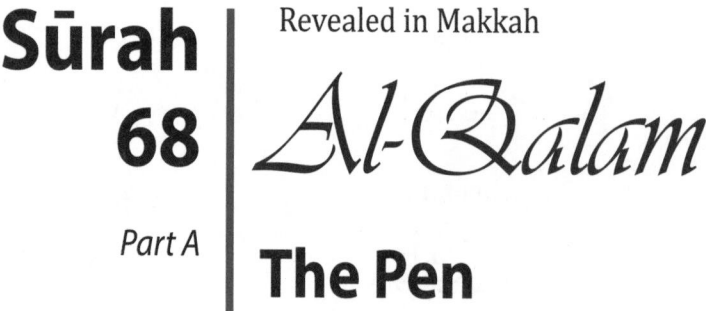

Sūrah 68
Part A

Revealed in Makkah

Al-Qalam

The Pen

Introduction:

In the first part of sūrah al-Qalam, two major themes are presented. The Makkan people wanted to undermine Nabi Muhammad's (S) mission by claiming that he was insane. The sūrah first defends Nabi Muhammad (S) as a person with outstanding moral character and then states that he was not insane. People who raise such false accusations have several notorious character traits. They will be humiliated and punished in this life and in the Hereafter. The second theme involves some wealthy farmers who were determined to deprive poor people from getting a share of their harvest. Their greed and determination to deprive the poor caused them to suffer a total loss. Using this parable, the Qur'ān cautions the wealthy Quraish that if they abuse and harm the poor believers, they could suffer a similar loss.

بِسْمِ ٱللَّهِ ٱلرَّحْمَٰنِ ٱلرَّحِيمِ

In the name of Allāh, the most Kind, the most Rewarding.

نٓ ۚ وَٱلْقَلَمِ وَمَا يَسْطُرُونَ ۝	1. NUN! Consider the pen and what they write.
مَآ أَنتَ بِنِعْمَةِ رَبِّكَ بِمَجْنُونٍ ۝	2. You are not, by the favor of your Rabb, a madman.
وَإِنَّ لَكَ لَأَجْرًا غَيْرَ مَمْنُونٍ ۝	3. And surely for you there is indeed a never-exhausting reward.
وَإِنَّكَ لَعَلَىٰ خُلُقٍ عَظِيمٍ ۝	4. And truly you, indeed have outstanding morals.
فَسَتُبْصِرُ وَيُبْصِرُونَ ۝	5. And you will soon see, and they will see—
بِأَييِّكُمُ ٱلْمَفْتُونُ ۝	6. which of you is demented.

إِنَّ رَبَّكَ هُوَ أَعْلَمُ بِمَن ضَلَّ عَن سَبِيلِهِۦ وَهُوَ أَعْلَمُ بِٱلْمُهْتَدِينَ ۝

7. Surely your Rabb, He knows best who has gone astray from His way, and He knows best the guided ones.

فَلَا تُطِعِ ٱلْمُكَذِّبِينَ ۝

8. Therefore do not yield to the belying ones.

وَدُّوا۟ لَوْ تُدْهِنُ فَيُدْهِنُونَ ۝

9. They wish that you would slacken, so that they might slacken.

وَلَا تُطِعْ كُلَّ حَلَّافٍ مَّهِينٍ ۝

10. And do not yield to any oath-monger, a degraded—

هَمَّازٍ مَّشَّآءٍ بِنَمِيمٍ ۝

11. any backbiter—a walker with slander,

مَّنَّاعٍ لِّلْخَيْرِ مُعْتَدٍ أَثِيمٍ ۝

12. any forbidder of good, transgressor, sinner,

عُتُلٍّ بَعْدَ ذَٰلِكَ زَنِيمٍ ۝

13. any insolent who is in addition illegitimate—

أَن كَانَ ذَا مَالٍ وَبَنِينَ ۝

14. because he possesses wealth and children.

إِذَا تُتْلَىٰ عَلَيْهِ ءَايَٰتُنَا قَالَ أَسَٰطِيرُ ٱلْأَوَّلِينَ ۝

15. When Our Messages are recited to him, he says: "Fables of the ancients."

سَنَسِمُهُۥ عَلَى ٱلْخُرْطُومِ ۝

16. We shall soon brand him on the nose.

إِنَّا بَلَوْنَٰهُمْ كَمَا بَلَوْنَآ أَصْحَٰبَ ٱلْجَنَّةِ إِذْ أَقْسَمُوا۟ لَيَصْرِمُنَّهَا مُصْبِحِينَ ۝

17. Now We shall try them as We tried the owners of the garden, when they vowed that they would surely gather the crops by morning;

وَلَا يَسْتَثْنُونَ ۝

18. and they made no reservations.

فَطَافَ عَلَيْهَا طَآئِفٌ مِّن رَّبِّكَ وَهُمْ نَآئِمُونَ ۝

19. So a visitation from your Rabb occurred it while they were asleep.

فَأَصْبَحَتْ كَٱلصَّرِيمِ ۝

20. Therefore, in the morning, it became a harvested land.

21. Then they called up each other in the morning,

فَتَنَادَوْاْ مُصْبِحِينَ ۝

22. saying: "Go early to your field, if you are going to reap."

أَنِ ٱغْدُواْ عَلَىٰ حَرْثِكُمْ إِن كُنتُمْ صَٰرِمِينَ ۝

23. So they departed while they were whispering together,

فَٱنطَلَقُواْ وَهُمْ يَتَخَٰفَتُونَ ۝

24. "Let no poor enter it today against you."

أَن لَّا يَدْخُلَنَّهَا ٱلْيَوْمَ عَلَيْكُم مِّسْكِينٌ ۝

25. So in the morning they went determined to their purpose.

وَغَدَوْاْ عَلَىٰ حَرْدٍ قَٰدِرِينَ ۝

26. But when they saw it, they said: "Surely we have gone astray."

فَلَمَّا رَأَوْهَا قَالُوٓاْ إِنَّا لَضَآلُّونَ ۝

27. "Obviously, we have been deprived."

بَلْ نَحْنُ مَحْرُومُونَ ۝

28. The worthiest of them asked: "Did I not say to you—'Why do you not glorify?'"

قَالَ أَوْسَطُهُمْ أَلَمْ أَقُل لَّكُمْ لَوْلَا تُسَبِّحُونَ ۝

29. They said: "Glory be to our Rabb, surely we were unjust."

قَالُواْ سُبْحَٰنَ رَبِّنَآ إِنَّا كُنَّا ظَٰلِمِينَ ۝

30. Then some of them advanced upon the others reproaching one another.

فَأَقْبَلَ بَعْضُهُمْ عَلَىٰ بَعْضٍ يَتَلَٰوَمُونَ ۝

31. They said: "O woe to us! We were surely immoderate.

قَالُواْ يَٰوَيْلَنَآ إِنَّا كُنَّا طَٰغِينَ ۝

32. "Maybe our Rabb will exchange something better than this for us; surely we are entreating to our Rabb."

عَسَىٰ رَبُّنَآ أَن يُبْدِلَنَا خَيْرًا مِّنْهَآ إِنَّآ إِلَىٰ رَبِّنَا رَٰغِبُونَ ۝

33. Such is the punishment. And surely the chastisement of the Hereafter is greater; did they but know!

كَذَٰلِكَ ٱلْعَذَابُ وَلَعَذَابُ ٱلْءَاخِرَةِ أَكْبَرُ لَوْ كَانُواْ يَعْلَمُونَ ۝

Explanation:

1. The opening letter *nun* appears to be the first occurrence of abbreviated letters (*al-muqatta'at*) at the beginning of a sūrah. The true meaning and significance of these abbreviations are not clear; however, commentators express various opinions about their intended meaning and use. Many scholars think the letter *nun* is not an abbreviation, but an actual word. According to one opinion, supported by Ibn 'Abbās, the letter *nun* is a noun that means "fish," mentioned in āyah 48 of this sūrah as well as in āyah 21:87. According to another opinion, the letter itself is a word meaning "inkstand," if we relate it to pen (*qalm*) mentioned in the same āyah. The reference of pen connects to the first set of revelations where pen is mentioned (96:1–5).

2. Frequently the Makkans taunted Rasūlullāh (S) as a madman (*majnūn*) when his preaching appeared to counter the tribal social order, idolatrous religious faith, and economic imbalance. This accusation was strongly condemned in many āyāt (7:184; 15:6; 34:8; 37:36; and 52:29). The āyah not only rejects such taunting comments as untrue, but it also testifies to the generations to come that Muhammad's (S) message and teachings did not represent those of a mad person.

3–4. Due to his painstaking work and utmost dedication to establish Islam, Rasūlullāh (S) would receive never-ending blessings and rewards—in this life and in the Hereafter. The term *khuluq* (natural disposition, manner, habit) means a person's character, moral uprightness, temperament or personality. Much earlier than the revelation of the Qur'ān, the Quraish recognized the excellent moral character of Muhammad (S), as they fondly addressed him as *al-Amin* (the trustworthy, 10:16; 33:21).

5–6. Allāh (swt) assured Rasūlullāh (S) that he would soon find out whether it was he or his opponents who were manic. This is a prophecy of Rasūlullāh's (S) glorious success as opposed to his opponents' wretched end, which would be carried out in his lifetime and continue thereafter. The letter *sa* is a prefix to *basara* (to see) indicating the prophecy will be fulfilled very soon. In response to the accusation of *majnūn* in āyah 2, this āyah uses the word *maftūn,* which also indicates craziness or madness. The word is derived from the root word *fatana*, which means "to cause affliction," "to persecute," or "to test." Thus, the craziness of the non-believers would occur as a result of suffering from an affliction, undergoing a trial, and facing hardship.

7. Allāh (swt) knows who is on the Right Path and who has gone astray. The word *muhtadīn* (those who have been guided) indicates that Allāh (swt) Himself guided the righteous. Whereas the word *dalla* (to go astray) is used as a verb without any modification, indicating Allāh (swt) is not to be blamed for disbelief, the non-believers themselves are to be blamed for their lack of belief.

8. Allāh (swt) advises the righteous people not to obey or be influenced by those who continuously lie and falsify truth. Their influence can be distracting and harmful to the believers. They have to remain steadfast against all provocations. In sūrah Bani Isrā'īl, āyah 17:74, it says, "And had We not made you firm, surely you might have inclined toward them a little bit." Thus we see that if believers preserve ties with habitual liars, there is a risk of being influenced by them.

9. One risk of obeying habitual liars, as mentioned in the previous āyah, is clarified here. They want the believers to soften their approach or faith. They want the believers to compromise their morals during times of hardship. Their objective is to misguide the believers. The āyat also refers to a point in Rasūlullāh's (S) career when opponents wanted to reach a compromise. They wanted Rasūlullāh (S) not to speak against their social and religious practices in such strong words. In return they would decrease their opposition to him (see 10:15; 17:73). Rasūlullāh (S) rejected this compromise offer.

10–12. In āyah 8, Rasūlullāh (S) and the believers are cautioned about the people who habitually and knowingly reject the truth. In this set of āyāt, some of the negative traits of these people are mentioned. These traits are: (1) frequently making oaths in order to deceive, (2) backbiting, (3) spreading slander, (4) forbidding good, (5) transgressing, and (6) sinning. These āyāt not only denounce these traits, but they also advise true believers that the likes and dislikes of people with such traits should not influence them. Among some of the obvious negative traits in āyah 10, oath-mongers (*hallaf*, meaning one who swears, and *mahin*, meaning despised, weak, miserable) are mentioned because they take shelter under the cloak of an oath with the intention of not carrying out the promise.

13–14. A person possessing the traits mentioned above is said to be cruel (*'utulin*) and notoriously mischievous. The word *zanim* means a person who is notoriously mischievous or a person of low birth-rank. The reason for his cruelty and notoriety is due to his wealth and having a large number of children. Possessing wealth and children gave the Arabs false pride and power, which was the root of their tribal dominance and rivalry. Even though the context may have changed today, these statutes still impart similar pride and power in modern society.

15. Many of the Qur'ān's moral teachings are illustrated through references of familiar accounts known to Arabs at the time of revelation. The non-believers argued that these narrations typically resembled ideas that they already knew; therefore, these ideas could not be divine revelations.

16. The word *khurtum* (snout, nose) is used to draw attention to a significant feature of one's personality. The shape of one's nose often indicates his or her personality. In many writings, including classical Arabic, raising one's nose implies false pride and vanity. Branding the nose is a metaphor for being subjected to utter disgrace. As mentioned in āyah 5 note, the letter *sa* is a prefix for *nasimu* (to brand with a hot metal), indicating the prophecy will be fulfilled very soon. Also see āyah 9:35 where sinners would be branded on the forehead—implying the sinners would be subjected to a similar disgrace. Also see āyah 96:15, where it says sinners will be dragged by their forelock, that is the hair above the forehead. To drag someone by the forelock is a big humiliation.

17. Allāh's (swt) trials and tribulations (*balā*) are completed using affluence and paucity. The word *balā* does not signify an ordinary trial, but a harsh and severe trial, conducted publicly and openly so that it becomes an example for others. The Makkans, as well as the people who had some of the denounced traits (āyāt 10–14), would be tried by Allāh (swt)—possibly by giving them abundant wealth. This proposition appears reasonable because their trial would be like the trial of certain gardener who had abundant crops in his field, but did not share them with the poor.

18–23. In this set of āyāt, the trial of a certain gardener is mentioned. In āyah 17, the gardener vowed without stating the customary phrase, "if God wills," or *insha-Allāh*. Furthermore, the gardener did not intend to allocate a share of the harvest to the poor, although it was a common practice in many societies to grant a share to the poor. Due to the bad intention of the gardener, before the harvest could take place, a visitation (*tāfa*) utterly destroyed the crops, flattening the harvest to the ground and rendering it unusable. The standing crops of the previous day then looked as if they had been harvested the following day. The specific detail of the visitation is not important to the moral of the story; therefore, the Qur'ān is silent about the details. The gardener apparently did not know anything about the visitation, and he was very hopeful about the harvest.

24–27. It was customary for affluent landlords to offer a share of the harvest to the poor. The Qur'ān also requires that on the day of the harvest, dues should be paid to the poor (6:141). In this parable, the rich landlords not only showed the greediness of their hearts, but they also expressed their determination to deprive the poor of their due share. The lesson of this parable applies to people during all times, particularly to the wealthy who have a moral responsibility to share their riches with the poor through compulsory giving (*zakah*), as well as through voluntary charity, but fail to recognize their social obligations toward the poor.

28–31. Among the gardeners, there was one who understood the destruction of the crops was a divine punishment because they had been unjust and greedy. In āyah 28, the root word *wasat* means "the midmost," "the middle one," "between two extremes," or "justly balanced." Therefore, the meaning of *awsat* is one who demonstrates these qualities. The person mentioned in the āyah was the just one, the best one, the right-minded one or the worthiest one; however, his realization was a little too late.

32–33. The right-minded gardener hoped that his Rabb might give them something better. There are various possible meanings of the phrase, one of which is Allāh's (swt) forgiveness. Another meaning could be guidance to not make this type of misjudgment. Allāh's (swt) punishment is often settled during our lifetimes, as exemplified by the episode of the gardener narrated previously. However, Allāh's (swt) punishment in the Hereafter is even worse unless forgiveness was sought from Him and granted.

Words to know:

جَنَّ: to be dark, to cover, to conceal. مَجنُون: man, insane. جَنَّة: garden, paradise. جِن: genious, any hidden thing, evil spirit.

مَمنُون: diminish. مَنَّ: favor, gift, anything obtained without trouble.

خُلُق: character, nature, moral. خَلَقَ: He created. خَالِقٌ: Creator.

طَاعَ: to obey. يُطِيعُ: He obeys. مُطَاعٌ: obeyed.

هَمَذَ: to backbite. هَمَّاذ: backbiter, defamer. هُمَذَةٍ: slanderer, backbiter.

مَنَعَ: to deny a thing. مُنِعَ: protector. مَنُوعًا: one who holds back.

عَدَا: to transgress, to turn aside. عَدُوَّةٌ: enemy. عَادُونَ: transgressors

تَلَا: to follow, to walk behind. تَلَوتُ: I recited. تِلَاوَةٌ: recitation.

سَطَرَ: to write, to inscribe. أَسَاطِير: fables, stories. مُسَيطِر: warden, manager.

نَسِمُ: we shall brand. وَسَمَ: to brand, to stamp, to impress.

يَستَثنُونَ: they made no exception. ثَنَى: to bend, to double. إِثنَين: two. مَثَان: oft-repeated.

طَافَ: to go about, to walk about. طُوفَان: overpowering rain, flood. طَائِفٌ: calamity, visitation.

صَرَمَ: to cut off, to pluck. صَرِيم: garden whose fruits have been plucked.

انطَلَقُ: to go about, to set out. طَلَّقَ: to divorce.

خَفَتَ: to speak in low voice. يَتَخَافَتُونَ: they talked to one another in a hushed voice.

مَحرُوم: deprived. حَرَمَ: to forbid, to prohibit.

Sūrah Al-Qalam
Word-by-word meaning

ٱلرَّحِيمِ	ٱلرَّحْمَٰنِ	ٱللَّهِ	بِسْمِ
the most Rewarding	the most Kind	Allāh	In the name of
يَسْطُرُونَ ۝	وَمَا	وَٱلْقَلَمِ	نٓ
they (angels) write	and what	by the pen	Nun
رَبِّكَ	بِنِعْمَةِ	أَنتَ	مَآ
your Lord	by the Grace of	you are	not
لَأَجْرًا	لَكَ	وَإِنَّ	بِمَجْنُونٍ ۝
will be a reward	for you	and verily	a madman
خُلُقٍ	لَعَلَىٰ	وَإِنَّكَ	غَيْرَ مَمْنُونٍ ۝
standard of character	on	and verily you are	an endless
بِأَيِّكُمُ	وَيُبْصِرُونَ ۝	فَسَتُبْصِرُ	عَظِيمٍ ۝
which of you	and they will see	so you will see	an exalted
هُوَ	رَبَّكَ	إِنَّ	ٱلْمَفْتُونُ ۝
He	your Lord	verily	is afflicted with madness
عَن	ضَلَّ	بِمَن	أَعْلَمُ
from	has gone astray	who	knows better
بِٱلْمُهْتَدِينَ ۝	أَعْلَمُ	وَهُوَ	سَبِيلِهِۦ
those who are guided	knows better	and He	His path
وَدُّوا۟	ٱلْمُكَذِّبِينَ ۝	تُطِعِ	فَلَا
they wish	the deniers	obey	so do not
وَلَا	فَيُدْهِنُونَ ۝	تُدْهِنُ	لَوْ
and not	so they would compromise	you should compromise	that

مَّهِينٍ ۝	حَلَّافٍ	كُلَّ	تُطِعْ
and is considered worthless	who swears much	everyone	obey
مَّنَّاعٍ	بِنَمِيمٍ ۝	مَّشَّاء	هَمَّازٍ
hinderer of	with calumnies	going about	a slanderer
عُتُلٍّ	أَثِيمٍ ۝	مُعْتَدٍ	لِّلْخَيْرِ
cruel	sinful	transgressor	the good
أَن	زَنِيمٍ ۝	ذَٰلِكَ	بَعْدَ
because	wicked	all that	after
وَبَنِينَ ۝	مَالٍ	ذَا	كَانَ
and children	wealth	had	he
ءَايَٰتُنَا	عَلَيْهِ	تُتْلَىٰ	إِذَا
Our verses	to him	are recited	when
سَنَسِمُهُ	ٱلْأَوَّلِينَ ۝	أَسَٰطِيرُ	قَالَ
We shall brand him	the men of old	tales of	he says
بَلَوْنَٰهُمْ	إِنَّا	ٱلْخُرْطُومِ ۝	عَلَى
shall try them	verily We	the nose	over
ٱلْجَنَّةِ	أَصْحَٰبَ	بَلَوْنَا	كَمَا
the garden	the people of	We tried	as
مُصْبِحِينَ ۝	لَيَصْرِمُنَّهَا	أَقْسَمُوا	إِذْ
by the morning	surely gather crop of it	they swore	when
عَلَيْهَا	فَطَافَ	يَسْتَثْنُونَ ۝	وَلَا
on it	then there passed by	they made reservation	and not
وَهُمْ	رَّبِّكَ	مِّن	طَآئِفٌ
while they	your Rabb	from	a visitation

فَتَنَادَوْا۟ then they called out to one another	كَٱلصَّرِيمِ ﴿٢٠﴾ it became like harvested land	فَأَصْبَحَتْ so in the morning	نَآيِمُونَ ﴿١٩﴾ were asleep
عَلَىٰ to	ٱغْدُوا۟ go early	أَنِ (saying) to	مُّصْبِحِينَ ﴿٢١﴾ in the morning
صَٰرِمِينَ ﴿٢٢﴾ pluck the fruits.	كُنتُمْ you would	إِن if	حَرْثِكُمْ your tilth
أَن (saying) that	يَتَخَٰفَتُونَ ﴿٢٣﴾ whispering together	وَهُمْ and they (were)	فَٱنطَلَقُوا۟ so they departed
عَلَيْكُم upon you	ٱلْيَوْمَ today	يَدْخُلَنَّهَا shall enter into it	لَّا not
حَرْدٍ a strong intention	عَلَىٰ with	وَغَدَوْا۟ and they went in the morning	مِّسْكِينٌ ﴿٢٤﴾ any poor person
قَالُوا۟ they said	رَأَوْهَا they saw it	فَلَمَّا but when	قَٰدِرِينَ ﴿٢٥﴾ they have powers
نَحْنُ we	بَلْ nay indeed	لَضَآلُّونَ ﴿٢٦﴾ have gone astray	إِنَّا verily we
أَلَمْ did not	أَوْسَطُهُمْ the best among them	قَالَ said	مَحْرُومُونَ ﴿٢٧﴾ are deprived
تُسَبِّحُونَ ﴿٢٨﴾ glorify Allāh	لَوْلَا why do you not	لَّكُمْ you	أَقُل I tell
إِنَّا verily	رَبِّنَآ our Lord	سُبْحَٰنَ glory to	قَالُوا۟ they said
بَعْضُهُمْ some	فَأَقْبَلَ so they turned	ظَٰلِمِينَ ﴿٢٩﴾ been wrongdoers.	كُنَّا we have

قَالُوٓاْ	يَتَلَوَمُونَ	بَعْضٍ	عَلَىٰ
they said	in blaming	others	to
طَٰغِينَ	كُنَّا	إِنَّا	يَٰوَيْلَنَآ
transgressors	we were	verily	woe to us
يُبْدِلَنَا	أَن	رَبُّنَآ	عَسَىٰ
He will exchange for us	that	our Rabb	we hope (maybe)
إِلَىٰ	إِنَّا	مِّنْهَآ	خَيْرًا
to	truly	than this	something better
ٱلْعَذَابُ	كَذَٰلِكَ	رَٰغِبُونَ	رَبِّنَا
the punishment	such is	we turn	our Rabb
لَوْ	أَكْبَرُ	ٱلْأَخِرَةِ	وَلَعَذَابُ
if	is greater	the Hereafter	and truly the punishment of
		يَعْلَمُونَ	كَانُوٓاْ
		but knew	they

A few applications of the message:

This sūrah cautions us not to be like the people who refuse truth and go astray. These people refused to accept the moral teachings of the Qur'ān because, to them, these teachings seem like stories from the past. The Qur'ānic moral teachings do not inspire them; as a result, they remained in spiritual darkness. Their wealth and possessions made them adopt a morally wrong course in life. They are the liars, slanderers, transgressors, and sinners. They suffer punishment in this world, and they will also suffer greater punishment in the Hereafter. The Qur'ān advises us not become like them and follow the wrong path.

The parable in this sūrah illustrates that greedy gardeners suddenly lost their crops because they were conspiring to deprive the poor. As a result, they suffered in this world and more sufferings are in store for them in the Hereafter. The moral of the parable is to never be unjust when dealing with people. We may profess our faith, but faith alone will not suffice. Our actions will determine our final destination in the Hereafter. In this parable, it is clear that the gardeners believed in their Rabb, but they were selfish people. Their actions caused the loss of their crops. We should learn a lesson from the parable and not behave the same way. We should encourage goodness, obey the Messenger (S), and uphold the truth.

Questions:

1. Why did the Quraish accuse Muhammad (S) of being an insane person?

2. In response to the accusation that Muhammad (S) was insane, how did Allāh (swt) reject this accusation?

3. How did the Quraish want to compromise with Rasūlullāh (S)?

4. How many traits of a wicked person are mentioned in sūrah al-Qalm? What are these traits?

5. What did the gardener want to do on the day of the harvest?

6. What happened to the garden on the night before the gardeners were ready to harvest?

7. What did the wisest gardener realize after witnessing the loss of the crops?

Sūrah 68 | *Al-Qalam*

Revealed in Makkah

Part B | **The Pen**

Introduction:

The second part of sūrah al-Qalam explains that the righteous servants of Allāh (swt) will be in the Garden of Delight. They will not face the same consequences that the sinners will face. The sinners think that Allāh (swt) will treat them in the manner they choose for themselves. However, this is a baseless hope. How can they avoid punishment knowing that they deny the Qur'ān and refuse to submit to Allāh (swt)? They rejected the Messenger (S) without any valid reason. In conclusion, the Messenger (S) was asked to have patience until Allāh's judgment arrives. He was advised not be become impatient in his mission. The example of Yūnus (A) illustrates that he suffered in the past because he was impatient.

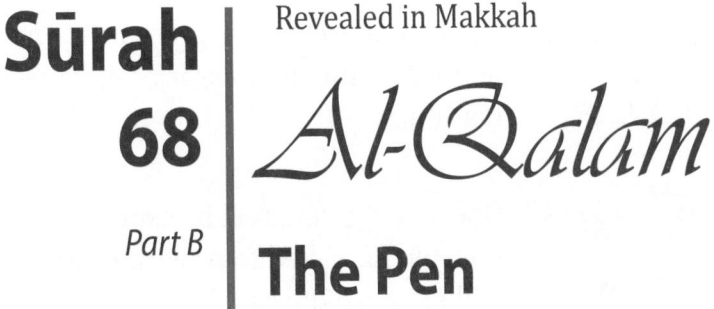

In the name of Allāh, the most Kind, the most Rewarding.

إِنَّ لِلْمُتَّقِينَ عِندَ رَبِّهِمْ جَنَّـٰتِ ٱلنَّعِيمِ ۝	34. Surely for the pious there are Gardens of Delight with their Rabb.
أَفَنَجْعَلُ ٱلْمُسْلِمِينَ كَٱلْمُجْرِمِينَ ۝	35. Shall We then treat the submitting ones as the guilty?
مَا لَكُمْ كَيْفَ تَحْكُمُونَ ۝	36. What is the matter with you? How do you judge?
أَمْ لَكُمْ كِتَـٰبٌ فِيهِ تَدْرُسُونَ ۝	37. Or is there a scripture for you from which you read,
إِنَّ لَكُمْ فِيهِ لَمَا تَخَيَّرُونَ ۝	38. that for you, there is certainly whatever you choose?
أَمْ لَكُمْ أَيْمَـٰنٌ عَلَيْنَا بَـٰلِغَةٌ إِلَىٰ يَوْمِ ٱلْقِيَـٰمَةِ إِنَّ لَكُمْ لَمَا تَحْكُمُونَ ۝	39. Or is there for you covenants upon Us—extending up to the Day of the Awakening—that for you there will surely be whatever you judge?

سَلْهُمْ أَيُّهُم بِذَٰلِكَ زَعِيمٌ ﴿٤٠﴾

40. You ask them as to which of them will vouch for that?

أَمْ لَهُمْ شُرَكَآءُ فَلْيَأْتُوا۟ بِشُرَكَآئِهِمْ إِن كَانُوا۟ صَٰدِقِينَ ﴿٤١﴾

41. Or is it that they have associates? Then let them bring their associates, if they be truthful.

يَوْمَ يُكْشَفُ عَن سَاقٍ وَيُدْعَوْنَ إِلَى ٱلسُّجُودِ فَلَا يَسْتَطِيعُونَ ﴿٤٢﴾

42. One day the shin will be exposed, and they will be called to prostrate, but they will not have the capability.

خَٰشِعَةً أَبْصَٰرُهُمْ تَرْهَقُهُمْ ذِلَّةٌ ۖ وَقَدْ كَانُوا۟ يُدْعَوْنَ إِلَى ٱلسُّجُودِ وَهُمْ سَٰلِمُونَ ﴿٤٣﴾

43. Their looks will be cast down, ignominy will cover them up because they were called upon to prostrate themselves, while they were safe.

فَذَرْنِي وَمَن يُكَذِّبُ بِهَٰذَا ٱلْحَدِيثِ سَنَسْتَدْرِجُهُم مِّنْ حَيْثُ لَا يَعْلَمُونَ ﴿٤٤﴾

44. Therefore leave Me alone, and whoever belies this discourse. We shall draw them gradually, from whence they do not know.

وَأُمْلِي لَهُمْ إِنَّ كَيْدِى مَتِينٌ ﴿٤٥﴾

45. Yet I bear with them. My plan is certainly firm.

أَمْ تَسْـَٔلُهُمْ أَجْرًا فَهُم مِّن مَّغْرَمٍ مُّثْقَلُونَ ﴿٤٦﴾

46. Or do you ask them for a fee so that they were burdened with debt?

أَمْ عِندَهُمُ ٱلْغَيْبُ فَهُمْ يَكْتُبُونَ ﴿٤٧﴾

47. Or is the unseen with them so that they can write it down?

فَٱصْبِرْ لِحُكْمِ رَبِّكَ وَلَا تَكُن كَصَاحِبِ ٱلْحُوتِ إِذْ نَادَىٰ وَهُوَ مَكْظُومٌ ﴿٤٨﴾

48. Therefore you persevere for the judgment of your Rabb, and do not be like the Companion of the Fish. Behold! he cried while he was in distress.

لَّوْلَآ أَن تَدَٰرَكَهُۥ نِعْمَةٌ مِّن رَّبِّهِۦ لَنُبِذَ بِٱلْعَرَآءِ وَهُوَ مَذْمُومٌ ﴿٤٩﴾

49. Had the favor of his Rabb not reached him, he would surely have been thrown on a barren shore, and be blamed.

فَٱجْتَبَٰهُ رَبُّهُۥ فَجَعَلَهُۥ مِنَ ٱلصَّٰلِحِينَ ﴿٥٠﴾

50. But his Rabb chose him, so He made him to be among the righteous.

وَإِن يَكَادُ ٱلَّذِينَ كَفَرُوا۟ لَيُزْلِقُونَكَ بِأَبْصَٰرِهِمْ لَمَّا سَمِعُوا۟ ٱلذِّكْرَ وَيَقُولُونَ إِنَّهُۥ لَمَجْنُونٌ ﴿٥١﴾

51. And those who have not believed would almost smite you with their looks when they hear the Reminder; and they say: "Surely he is mad indeed."

وَمَا هُوَ إِلَّا ذِكْرٌ لِّلْعَالَمِينَ ٥٢   52. And it is nothing but a Reminder of all the worlds.

Explanation:

34. The word *muttaqīn* (the reverent, the pious) refers to those who have the highest level of faith. This word is used in contrast to the arrogant non-believers mentioned earlier in this sūrah (āyāt 10–13). The God-fearing, pious people will be in the Garden of Delight where the atmosphere will be full of satisfaction.

35. In this āyah, the term *muslimīn*, in its original sense, implies those who surrender to Allāh (swt), including all true followers of the earlier prophets during their respective periods. The followers of many of the earlier prophets were called *muslimun* (3:52, 67), and they certainly qualified to enter the Garden of Delight. In the post-Qur'ānic period, the term Muslim (singular) has widely and rather inaccurately been used to exclusively mean the followers of Muhammad (S). The question is: "Shall We then treat the submitting ones (Muslims) as We treat the guilty?" Allāh (swt) speaks in first person because He is the one Who will reward or punish. The answer to the question is: No, they will not be treated the same. The Muslims are compared to the *mujrimīn*. A *mujrim* is one who has been convicted of a crime and sentenced guilty. The sinners are mentioned as *mujrimīn* because they are accountable for their deeds and face judgment.

36–38. This passage deals with the discourse of the disbelievers, so the question raised in this āyah is addressed to them. They are asked to reveal the basis of their sinful conduct and the justification for their wrongful worshipping. Do they have divine approval for whatever they do? Will they not be held accountable for their behavior? Do they have this approval granted to them in their scripture?

39–41. A covenant is a mutual agreement between two parties. In this case, the parties are Allāh (swt) on one side and the people on the other side. Rasūlullāh (S) was asked to question the sinners: Do they have an everlasting covenant from Allāh (swt) stating that whatever is convenient for them would continue to be granted to them? If not, do they have any leaders among them who approved of these wrongdoings and guaranteed them Allāh's (swt) approval? In āyah 41, the term associate (*shurakāa*) alludes to the religious leaders and false gods who endorse and promote the views subscribed to by the people.

42. The shin bone is the larger and stronger of the two bones in the leg below the knee. The phrase the "shin (bone) will be exposed" implies their personal secrets, inclinations, thoughts, motives, and all concealed bad deeds will be exposed. If the phrase is taken literally, the exposed shin bone will cause the sinners pain and make it difficult to kneel down before Allāh (swt). They will be asked to prostrate, but their inability to do so would be a reflection of their past attitude not to bow down to Allāh (swt). In their earthly lives, they were rebellious, disrespectful, uncommitted, and doubtful about Allāh (swt). Prostration is the highest form of respect. It shows our complete submission because during prostration, we lower our forehead to the ground—the forehead that houses our cerebrum—the part of our brain that made us superior to all of creation.

43. On the Day of Judgment, when punishment awaits the sinners, their looks will be downcast. Their faces will be covered with shame and humiliation upon realizing that they were reluctant to prostrate before Allāh (swt) when they were free and safe, meaning when they were living their earthly lives.

44. The āyah indicates that Allāh (swt) alone has the right to deal with sinners in a manner He deems appropriate. To leave Allāh (swt) and the sinners alone precludes anybody from interfering with judgment, let alone promising salvation based on his or her faith. Allāh's (swt) master plan will draw the sinners toward their suffering and punishment in a manner that they will not be able to understand but they will be forced to face His judgment.

45. Even though Allāh's (swt) plan will draw sinners toward their suffering and punishment, He will give them the time and opportunity to rectify and amend their sins. This is implied by the phrase, "yet I bear with them." The term *kayd* (a plot, a stratagem), when related to Allāh (swt), means He planned or devised; His plan is not only unchangeable, but it is also certain to happen.

46. Although the question is posed to Rasūlullāh (S), the non-believers are asked: Did he, that is, Muhammad (S) ask people to pay him an honorarium for his preaching of Islam? If he did, then the people might have felt a burden to pay the honorarium in order to receive divine guidance. In that case, people who did not pay remained outside of Islam. The purpose of the question is to allow the rejecters of truth to justify their reasons for showing such a strong apathy toward Rasūlullāh's (S) teachings.

47. Continuing with the previous question, do the non-believers have knowledge of the unseen with them so that they do not feel necessity to listen to Rasūlullāh's (S) message?

48. The phrase "Companion of the Fish" refers to prophet Yūnus (A) (Jonah) who abandoned his community and ran away because they would not listen to his teachings (21:87; 37:141–142). Rasūlullāh (S) is asked to persevere when things around him became challenging to his mission. He is urged not to give up his mission due to despair or anger at the community that largely rejected his teachings.

49–50. The āyāt illustrate a glorious example of how Allāh's (swt) endless mercy saved a person from imminent death only because he cried earnestly to his Rabb while in distress. Even though Yūnus (A) abandoned his mission, and thus clearly defied Allāh's (swt) command, he soon realized his costly mistake and turned back to Allāh (swt) before it was too late. The moral of the story illustrates that Allāh's (swt) mercy is not inaccessible by any means. Rather it is available for anyone who turns to Him and expresses earnest remorse.

51–52. Regarding the allegation of Rasūlullāh's (S) madness, see āyah 2 above. Even though the local Arabs, at the time of revelation of the Qur'ān, maliciously looked upon the mission of Rasūlullāh (S), Allāh (swt) assures them that the Qur'ān is a reminder not only for them, but also for the entire world.

Words to know:

تَخَيَّرُون: you may select. خَارَ: to choose, to select. خِيَارَةٌ: choice, selection. خَيِر: good.

أَيْمَن: right, blessed. أَيْمَانٌ: oaths. مَيْمَنَة: people of right-hand.

زَعَمَ: to speak, to assert, to imagine. زَعَمَتَ: you claimed. زَعَمٌ: assertion. زَعِيم: guarantee.

كَشَفَ: to remove, to lay open, to uncover. كَاشِفٌ: one who removes.

خَاشِعَهُ: in the state of humility. خُشُوع: humility. خُشَّعًا: downcast.

رَهِقَ: to cover, to follow closely. تَرهَقُ: will cover. رَهَقٌ: arrogance, conceit.

مَغرَم: undue debt, forced loan. غَرِم: be in debt. غَرَامًا: continuous torment.

مَكظُوم: oppressed and depressed with grief. كَظَمَ: to choke, to suppress.

Sūrah Al-Qalam
Word-by-word meaning

بِسْمِ	ٱللَّهِ	ٱلرَّحْمَٰنِ	ٱلرَّحِيمِ
In the name of	Allāh	the Most Kind	the Most Rewarding
إِنَّ	لِلْمُتَّقِينَ	عِندَ	رَبِّهِمْ
verily	for the pious	with	their Lord
جَنَّٰتِ	ٱلنَّعِيمِ ﴿٣٤﴾	أَفَنَجْعَلُ	ٱلْمُسْلِمِينَ
are garden of	delight	shall We then treat	the Muslims
كَٱلْمُجْرِمِينَ ﴿٣٥﴾	مَا لَكُمْ	كَيْفَ	تَحْكُمُونَ ﴿٣٦﴾
like the criminals	what is the matter with you?	how	do you judge?
أَمْ	لَكُمْ	كِتَٰبٌ	فِيهِ
or	have you	a Book	through which
تَدْرُسُونَ ﴿٣٧﴾	إِنَّ	لَكُمْ	فِيهِ
you learn	that	you shall have	in it
لَمَا	تَخَيَّرُونَ ﴿٣٨﴾	أَمْ	لَكُمْ
all that	you choose?	or	have you
أَيْمَٰنٌ	عَلَيْنَا	بَٰلِغَةٌ	إِلَىٰ
oaths	from us	reaching	to
يَوْمِ	ٱلْقِيَٰمَةِ	إِنَّ	لَكُمْ
the Day of	Resurrection	that	yours will be
لَمَا	تَحْكُمُونَ ﴿٣٩﴾	سَلْهُمْ	أَيُّهُم
what	you judge?	ask them	which of them
بِذَٰلِكَ	زَعِيمٌ ﴿٤٠﴾	أَمْ	لَهُم
for that	will vouch	or	they have

شُرَكَآءُ	فَلْيَأْتُواْ	بِشُرَكَآئِهِم	إِن
partners	then let them bring	their partners	if
كَانُواْ	صَٰدِقِينَ ٤١	يَوْمَ	يُكْشَفُ
they are	truthful	the Day which	shall be uncovered
عَن	سَاقٍ	وَيُدْعَوْنَ	إِلَىٰ
from	the shin	and they shall be called	to
ٱلسُّجُودِ	فَلَا	يَسْتَطِيعُونَ ٤٢	خَٰشِعَةً
prostrate	but shall not	they be able to do so	will be cast down
أَبْصَٰرُهُمْ	تَرْهَقُهُمْ	ذِلَّةٌ	وَقَدْ
their eyes	will cover them	humiliation	and indeed
كَانُواْ	يُدْعَوْنَ	إِلَى	ٱلسُّجُودِ
they used to	be called	to	prostrate
وَهُم	سَٰلِمُونَ ٤٣	فَذَرْنِي	وَمَن
and they were	healthy and secure	then leave Me alone	and whoever
يُكَذِّبُ	بِهَٰذَا	ٱلْحَدِيثِ	سَنَسْتَدْرِجُهُم
denies	this	discourse	We shall draw them gradually
مِّن	حَيْثُ	لَا	يَعْلَمُونَ ٤٤
from	where	not	they perceive
وَأُمْلِي	لَهُمْ	إِنَّ	كَيْدِى
yet I bear	to them	surely	My Plan
مَتِينٌ ٤٥	أَمْ	تَسْـَٔلُهُمْ	أَجْرًا
is strong	or is it that	you ask them	a wage
فَهُم	مِّن	مَّغْرَمٍ	مُّثْقَلُونَ ٤٦
so they	from	debt	are heavily burdened?

أَمْ	عِندَهُمُ	ٱلْغَيْبُ	فَهُمْ
or that	is with them	the unseen	so they
يَكْتُبُونَ ٤٧	فَٱصْبِرْ	لِحُكْمِ	رَبِّكَ
can write it down	so wait with patience	for the Decision of	your Rabb
وَلَا	تَكُن	كَصَاحِبِ	ٱلْحُوتِ
and not	be	like the companion of	the fish
إِذْ	نَادَىٰ	وَهُوَ	مَكْظُومٌ ٤٨
when	he cried out	while he (was)	restrained, suppressed
لَّوْلَآ	أَن	تَدَارَكَهُ	نِعْمَةٌ
had not	that	reached him	a Grace
مِّن	رَّبِّهِ	لَنُبِذَ	بِٱلْعَرَآءِ
from	his Rabb	he would indeed have been cast off	on the barren shore
وَهُوَ	مَذْمُومٌ ٤٩	فَٱجْتَبَـٰهُ	رَبُّهُ
while he	was to be blamed	but chose him	his Rabb
فَجَعَلَهُ	مِنَ	ٱلصَّـٰلِحِينَ ٥٠	وَإِن
and made him	of	the righteous	and surely
يَكَادُ	ٱلَّذِينَ	كَفَرُوا	لَيُزْلِقُونَكَ
would almost	those who	disbelieve	make you slip
بِأَبْصَـٰرِهِمْ	لَمَّا	سَمِعُوا	ٱلذِّكْرَ
with their eyes	when	they hear	the Reminder
وَيَقُولُونَ	إِنَّهُ	لَمَجْنُونٌ ٥١	وَمَا
and they say	surely he	is a madman	and not
هُوَ	إِلَّا	ذِكْرٌ	لِّلْعَـٰلَمِينَ ٥٢
it is	but	a reminder	to all the worlds

A few applications of the message:

The main theme of this part of the sūrah is admonition for the guilty ones. However, this admonition is a reminder for us because we may sometimes behave like the guilty ones.

Allāh (swt) guarantees that Paradise is exclusively reserved for the righteous people. We must do everything possible to qualify ourselves as righteous people. Righteousness is not a label that we may place on ourselves. We become righteous people by adopting the truth and demonstrating our faith through righteous conduct. Guilty people do whatever they want, thinking that Allāh (swt) will treat them in the manner they choose. However, they are wrong. Allāh (swt) causes their gradual loss in every aspect of their lives in a manner they cannot perceive. They will experience more losses, suffering and humiliation in the Hereafter.

One of the reasons for the losses and suffering of guilty people is they did not prostrate to Allāh (swt). Prostration is not only physically bowing down, as in salāt, but also showing full obedience to the Almighty. If we neglect to prostrate to Allāh (swt), that is, if we ignore our salāt, then it is certain that we will suffer punishment.

As we read this part of the sūrah, we must caution ourselves never to associate with Allāh (swt), never disobey the divine teachings, always perform salāt, and always persevere and have patience to receive Allāh's (swt) judgment.

Questions:

1. Regarding the judgment of Allāh (swt), what are some of the false hopes of the guilty ones?

2. What is the significance of the "shin" becoming exposed?

3. Why will the guilty people not be able to prostrate on the Day of Judgment?

4. What did the "Companion of the Fish" do? Why was he in distress?

5. What message do we learn from the example of the "Companion of the Fish?"

Sūrah 69
Part A

Revealed in Makkah

Al-Haqqah

The Inevitable

Introduction:

The word *al-Haqqah* refers to the Awakening, but it literally means "absolute reality." The absolute reality is Allāh's (swt) way of bringing the guilty people and the nation to justice. They cannot continue to sin and transgress without facing the consequences on earth. Such justice occurred in the past with several large and powerful nations and it can happen again. More importantly, justice will happen on a large scale during the Day of Judgment. The Day of Judgment is also an absolute reality from which no one can escape. Those who will be given their book of accounts in their right hands will be very pleased as they will enter Paradise. This will be a sign of approval of their faith and deeds. Those who will be given their book of accounts in their left hands will suffer punishment. This will be a sign of disapproval of their faith and deeds. They belied the truth, rejected their messengers, did not urge to help and support the poor, and transgressed in many other matters.

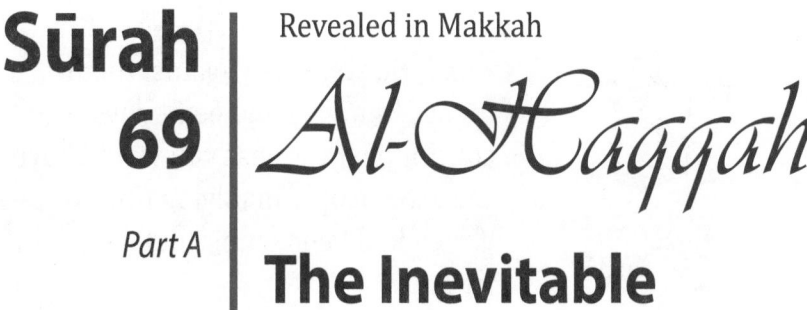

بِسْمِ ٱللَّهِ ٱلرَّحْمَٰنِ ٱلرَّحِيمِ

In the name of Allāh, the most Kind, the most Rewarding.

ٱلْحَآقَّةُ ۝	1. The sure Event!
مَا ٱلْحَآقَّةُ ۝	2. What is the sure event?
وَمَآ أَدْرَىٰكَ مَا ٱلْحَآقَّةُ ۝	3. Ha! What could make you realize what the Sure Event is?
كَذَّبَتْ ثَمُودُ وَعَادٌ بِٱلْقَارِعَةِ ۝	4. Thamūd and 'Ād denied the striking calamity.
فَأَمَّا ثَمُودُ فَأُهْلِكُوا بِٱلطَّاغِيَةِ ۝	5. Then as to Thamūd—they were then destroyed by a violent blast.

وَأَمَّا عَادٌ فَأُهْلِكُوا بِرِيحٍ صَرْصَرٍ عَاتِيَةٍ ۝

6. And as to 'Ād—they were then destroyed by a roaring, fierce hurricane,

سَخَّرَهَا عَلَيْهِمْ سَبْعَ لَيَالٍ وَثَمَانِيَةَ أَيَّامٍ حُسُومًا فَتَرَى ٱلْقَوْمَ فِيهَا صَرْعَىٰ كَأَنَّهُمْ أَعْجَازُ نَخْلٍ خَاوِيَةٍ ۝

7. which He subjected against them for seven nights and eight days, continuously, so that you would have seen the people in it lying prostrate—as if they had been trunks of fallen palm trees.

فَهَلْ تَرَىٰ لَهُم مِّنۢ بَاقِيَةٍ ۝

8. Now, can you see any remnant of them?

وَجَآءَ فِرْعَوْنُ وَمَن قَبْلَهُۥ وَٱلْمُؤْتَفِكَٰتُ بِٱلْخَاطِئَةِ ۝

9. And Fir'awn, and who were before him, and the Overthrown Cities committed sins.

فَعَصَوْا۟ رَسُولَ رَبِّهِمْ فَأَخَذَهُمْ أَخْذَةً رَّابِيَةً ۝

10. And they disobeyed the rasul of their Rabb; so He seized them with a severe grasp.

إِنَّا لَمَّا طَغَا ٱلْمَآءُ حَمَلْنَٰكُمْ فِى ٱلْجَارِيَةِ ۝

11. Surely when the water rose high, We bore you in the Ark,

لِنَجْعَلَهَا لَكُمْ تَذْكِرَةً وَتَعِيَهَآ أُذُنٌ وَٰعِيَةٌ ۝

12. that We might make it an admonition for you and that the listening ear might listen.

فَإِذَا نُفِخَ فِى ٱلصُّورِ نَفْخَةٌ وَٰحِدَةٌ ۝

13. So when blowing will be done into the trumpet by a single blowing,

وَحُمِلَتِ ٱلْأَرْضُ وَٱلْجِبَالُ فَدُكَّتَا دَكَّةً وَٰحِدَةً ۝

14. and the earth and the mountains are lifted up and then they are crushed down with a single crushing—

فَيَوْمَئِذٍ وَقَعَتِ ٱلْوَاقِعَةُ ۝

15. then on that Day the Event will occur.

وَٱنشَقَّتِ ٱلسَّمَآءُ فَهِىَ يَوْمَئِذٍ وَاهِيَةٌ ۝

16. And the sky will cleave asunder, and it will that Day be fragile;

وَٱلْمَلَكُ عَلَىٰٓ أَرْجَآئِهَا وَيَحْمِلُ عَرْشَ رَبِّكَ فَوْقَهُمْ يَوْمَئِذٍ ثَمَٰنِيَةٌ ۝

17. and the angels will be on its sides, and above them on that Day, eight will bear the Throne of Power of your Rabb.

18. On that Day you will be exposed—the secret will not remain secret from you.

يَوْمَئِذٍ تُعْرَضُونَ لَا تَخْفَىٰ مِنكُمْ خَافِيَةٌ ﴿١٨﴾

19. Then as to him whose book is given in his right hand, he will then say: "Come! read this book!

فَأَمَّا مَنْ أُوتِيَ كِتَٰبَهُۥ بِيَمِينِهِۦ فَيَقُولُ هَآؤُمُ ٱقْرَءُوا۟ كِتَٰبِيَهْ ﴿١٩﴾

20. "Surely I knew that I was going to meet this account."

إِنِّى ظَنَنتُ أَنِّى مُلَٰقٍ حِسَابِيَهْ ﴿٢٠﴾

21. So he will be in a well-pleased life—

فَهُوَ فِى عِيشَةٍ رَّاضِيَةٍ ﴿٢١﴾

22. in a highly placed Garden,

فِى جَنَّةٍ عَالِيَةٍ ﴿٢٢﴾

23. the fruits of which are close at hand.

قُطُوفُهَا دَانِيَةٌ ﴿٢٣﴾

24. "You eat and drink joyfully for what you advanced in bygone days."

كُلُوا۟ وَٱشْرَبُوا۟ هَنِيٓـًٔا بِمَآ أَسْلَفْتُمْ فِى ٱلْأَيَّامِ ٱلْخَالِيَةِ ﴿٢٤﴾

25. And as to him whose book is delivered in his left hand, he will then say: "O my misfortune! That I had never been given my book,

وَأَمَّا مَنْ أُوتِيَ كِتَٰبَهُۥ بِشِمَالِهِۦ فَيَقُولُ يَٰلَيْتَنِى لَمْ أُوتَ كِتَٰبِيَهْ ﴿٢٥﴾

26. "and I had never known what my account was!

وَلَمْ أَدْرِ مَا حِسَابِيَهْ ﴿٢٦﴾

27. "O would that it had made an end!

يَٰلَيْتَهَا كَانَتِ ٱلْقَاضِيَةَ ﴿٢٧﴾

28. "My wealth does not avail me anything;

مَآ أَغْنَىٰ عَنِّى مَالِيَهْ ﴿٢٨﴾

29. "my authority is perished from me."

هَلَكَ عَنِّى سُلْطَٰنِيَهْ ﴿٢٩﴾

30. "Seize him and tie him up,

خُذُوهُ فَغُلُّوهُ ﴿٣٠﴾

ثُمَّ ٱلْجَحِيمَ صَلُّوهُ ۝

31. "then throw him into the fierce Fire,

ثُمَّ فِى سِلْسِلَةٍ ذَرْعُهَا سَبْعُونَ ذِرَاعًا فَٱسْلُكُوهُ ۝

32. "and then let him pass through a chain the length of which is seventy cubits.

إِنَّهُ كَانَ لَا يُؤْمِنُ بِٱللَّهِ ٱلْعَظِيمِ ۝

33. "Surely he was not given to believing in Allāh, the Mighty,

وَلَا يَحُضُّ عَلَىٰ طَعَامِ ٱلْمِسْكِينِ ۝

34. "nor did he urge the feeding of the poor.

فَلَيْسَ لَهُ ٱلْيَوْمَ هَـٰهُنَا حَمِيمٌ ۝

35. "There is therefore no warm friend for him on this day,

وَلَا طَعَامٌ إِلَّا مِنْ غِسْلِينٍ ۝

36. "nor food except from the washing—

لَّا يَأْكُلُهُ إِلَّا ٱلْخَـٰطِئُونَ ۝

37. "no one eats it except the sinful."

Explanation:

1. The title of the sūrah is derived from the word *al-hāqqah*, which is mentioned in the first three āyāt. The root word *haqq* means "true," "just" and "that which is right." When the particle "*al-*" is attached to the word, the meaning emphasizes the certainty of an event. The event will invariably take place, and its occurrence is so certain that there can be no doubt. The event is the onset of the Hour—the Awakening. On that day, full manifestation of the triumph of Truth and the annihilation of falsehood will take place. To use a word that literally means "the truth," but to imply its meaning as "the Awakening," and importantly, to begin a sūrah with this key word, indicates that people denied this event would occur. However, their denial will not prevent it from happening.

2–3. When we hear a novel word, sometimes we wonder about the word. Sometimes, we do not pay enough attention to the word. Therefore, he word is repeated. Repetition of the word *al-hāqqah* creates curiosity, suspense and tension. The repetition also shows that we do not have full knowledge about the realities of the events indicated by the word. We do not have the necessary faculties to fully comprehend these aspects of the unknown. Therefore, this passage explains it in great detail and provides examples from past communities.

Āyah 3 mentions *wa mā adrāka* meaning "what could make you understand." Grammatically the word *adrāka* is in the past tense. If it was in the present or future tense, it would read *udrīka*.

Whenever the Qur'ān uses the past tense for a word, the āyāt that follow the word usually elaborate on the word in detail. On the other hand, whenever the present or future tense is used, Allāh (swt) does not provide details, allowing readers to ponder the word.

The question is: "what could make you realize what the Sure Event is?" People will not fully realize what will happen when the sure event takes place, so in the following āyāt, a few examples are mentioned in order to illustrate the realities of *al-hāqqah*.

4. The first example of *al-hāqqah* occurs in the reference of a familiar account of the tribes of Thamūd and 'Ād. Of the two tribes, the 'Ād lived in the Hadhramawt region and the Thamūd lived in the Hijāz region of Arabia. Both tribes reached the pinnacle of glory during their respective periods, but they subsequently became sinners. They received guidance from their rasūls, but they rejected the truth. The use of the word *kadhdhabat* indicates that they continuously belied the truth. When punishment eventually fell upon them, it was strikingly stunning and devastatingly fierce. The word *qāriatun* indicates this punishment was not a simple, ordinary one—it was an extraordinary punishment that usually occurs all of a sudden and destroys large numbers of the population or even an entire nation. Their history serves as an example of what *al-hāqqah* could mean for future generations. All these calamities are recognized by their unpredictable beginning followed by their severity, magnitude and terrible aftermath.

5. The Thamūd, known as the Second 'Ād, belied their rasūl Sālih (A), hamstrung a she-camel (7:75–77; 11:65; 26:157; 54:29; and 91:14) and consequently suffered utter destruction by an earthquake and a violent blast of volcanic eruption (7:78; 11:67; 26:158; and 41:13, 17). It is important to understand why the killing of a she-camel was viewed as a serious crime. The camel was not a sacred animal, but Sālih (A) had declared the owner-less camel was a sign for the tribe, and they were asked not to harm her. By showing cruelty toward the camel, the Thamūd sent a message that they did not care about the divine command. The word *taghā* means to transgress, to exceed the boundary. The same root word is used to describe their punishment. The word *tāghiyatun* means a violent blast accompanied by loud thunder and lightening.

6. The 'Ād, known as the First 'Ād, were a great nation praised in the Qur'ān for their extraordinary skill in building rock-carved dwellings. Their cultural and industrial supremacy did not come without blessings from Allāh (swt); however, over time they began to worship four different idols (7:70). They rejected their rasūl Hūd (A), and the teachings he brought to them, and consequently were destroyed by a roaring, fierce hurricane (41:16; 54:19). The combination of the word *ātiyah* (harsh, exceedingly violent) with *rihin sarsar* (a loud roaring and furious wind) indicates that it was some type of tropical cyclone or hurricane.

7–8. The word *husūm* means a succession of unlucky nights or successive and complete disaster. Date palms are well-rooted, firm trees that do not get uprooted by any ordinary storm. The metaphor of uprooted date palms is used to stress the severity of the storm and utter ruin of the community (54:20). The destruction of these two tribes was so extensive that by the end of the hurricane, the remnants of these tribes were difficult to find.

9–10. References to Fir'awn and the overthrown cities are specifically mentioned, however, before Fir'awn there were many other generations who committed sins. These overthrown cities are Sodom and Gomorrah, where Lūt (A) and his people lived (9:70; 11:69–83; 15:73–74; 29:34–35). All of these cities received divine guidance through their respective messengers, but they rejected the guidance and disobeyed their messengers. As a consequence, all of these cities were punished. The references to these past nations stress the breadth and expanse of Allāh's (swt) judgment across different geographic locations and time periods.

11. A reference is made here to Nūh (A) and his safe escape from a great deluge aboard an ark (7:64; 11:42; 23:27; 25:37; and 26:119–120). The pronoun "you" (plural, indicated by the suffix -kum in hamalnākum) implies "your ancestors," but its use stresses Allāh's (swt) protection of all righteous believers.

12. The well-known account of the rescue of Nūh (A) is considered an admonition for all of us. The word used here is tadhkirah, which means "ultimate reminder." It is a wake-up call intended to make us realize why Allāh (swt) sent messengers and why we are obligated to accept their teachings. We are required to remember this admonition carefully. The word wa'aya means "to keep in mind" and "to preserve in memory." It also means a sack or bag in which one can place objects and close the top so that the contents are safe. In the same sense, the word wa'aya indicates the admonition must be listened to and preserved in our memory. Interestingly, this word is used after the accounts of Thamūd, 'Ād, Fir'awn and Lūt (A) to indicate that the narratives of all past nations should serve as an admonition. We need to listen to the admonition attentively and never forget it, so that we do not face a similar fate.

13–15. After narrating the punishments of some of the past communities, the theme changes to the Awakening. Why? The reason is to point out that punishment in this world is not the end of suffering, but there are more in store in the Hereafter. The end of powerful nations is only the beginning of more punishment in the Hereafter. For this reason, the Day of Judgment is described in terrifying visual details. The Sure Event (al-haqqah) will begin on a day when several things will happen. First, a loud trumpet will blow with a single note (6:74; 20:102; 36:51). In the past, people used to blow a trumpet to announce something. On the day of the Sure Event, some kind of loud "announcement," will take place. The earth and the mountains will be lifted up and smashed with a single crush. It seems that some kind of super volcanic eruption will be followed by a massive earthquake; however, nobody can tell for sure what is intended by the tremendous event.

16. The heavens (samā) being rent asunder is particularly mentioned in many other āyāt in order to highlight the terror stricken day (25:25; 55:37; 77:9; 78:19; and 84:1). The sky is not a physical structure to break apart or become fragile. Therefore, it is evidently an allusion to possible havoc in the atmospheric or cosmic system, or breakdown of the usual orderliness of the sky.

17. Allāh (swt) does not have a physical body and does not sit down on a physical throne. Nothing can limit Him and His glory is limitless. The Throne of Power signifies the absolute almightiness of Allāh (swt). The imagery of angels bearing the Throne is a metaphorical allusion to their continued obedience and glorification of Allāh (swt). The āyah does not declare to whom or what the "eight" refer. Most early and later commentators maintain the "eight" refers to eight angels (Ibn Kathīr). Others have suggested that it could mean eight specified or unspecified attributes of Allāh (swt) that would predominantly reflect His almightiness on the Day of Awakening.

18. On this day, each individual will be exposed for his or her actions—whether small or large, known or forgotten, and intentional or unintentional. The secret or hidden realities of each person's actions, intentions, commissions and omissions will be disclosed, and he or she will be given an objective view of his or her past (6:28; 17:13; 18:49; 50:22; 79:35).

19–20. The allusion to receiving the book of deeds in "right hand" or in the "left hand" indicates divine approval or disapproval of one's deeds. In the Qur'an, the allusion of "right," "right side" and "right hand," or "left," "left side" and "left hand," is used to denote the virtue and vice, or righteousness and wickedness of a person (56:8–9, 27–40; 74:39–40; and 90:18–19). Righteous people will receive their book in their right hand as symbolic of the divine approval of their deeds (see 17:71; 84:7). They will like to read their book, because during earthly life, they knew that they would be held accountable for their deeds. This led them to perform more righteous deeds. On the Day of Judgment, they will be able to recognize and freely admit their deeds.

21–24. The lofty or highly raised Garden alludes to the elevated status of the righteous people in Paradise. Clusters of fruits hanging low and within easy reach implies abundant and easy access to all the pleasures and satisfaction of heaven. It also implies all their needs are easily met and effortlessly achieved.

25–27. The left hand mentioned in this āyah is used as a contrast to the right hand mentioned in āyah 19. Unlike the righteous person who will enjoy seeing his or her book of accounts, a sinner will wish that no such account existed, or that a distance be created between him or her and the book (3:30). The sinner will express a vain wish to die rather than read from the book, thereby disclosing all the evils committed, and face the impending punishment (25:14; 43:77).

28–29. During earthly life, the sinner was obsessed with wealth and power, thinking that these qualities would make him abide. But in the Hereafter, he or she will realize that wealth cannot buy the soul's ransom and no earthly powers can avert his or her punishment.

30–32. The Qur'ān often mentions the sinners will be linked together in chains or *silsila* (14:49; 25:13; 40:71–72; 73:12; and 76:4). Tying people together in chains indicates not only their humiliating condition, but also their inescapable destiny—the punishment of Fire. The number seven or seventy is often used in classical Arabic to imply a large number or quantity. Here seventy cubits' length of the chain indicates inescapably long interlinked shackle. The sinners would be tied (*usluku*, meaning bind, string) with it it. Alternately, the sinners would be made to pass through (*salaka*, meaning to cause to flow, to cause to go along, to tread a pathway) the chain as a mark of life long evil deeds.

33–34. In this set of āyah, we are given two reasons why the sinners will be given their books in their left hand and be chained together to suffer punishment. One of the reasons has to do with faith, and the other has to do with service to humanity. These two reasons are: (1) not believing in the oneness of Allāh (swt) and consequently not obeying His commands, and (2) not feeding the poor. The word "urge" (*hadda*) implies carrying out a duty with energy and enthusiasm. Neglecting the poor and not taking the initiative to provide them with food shows human greed, selfishness and possessiveness. In several āyāt in the Qur'ān, Allāh (swt) strongly criticizes this kind of attitude (89:18; 107:3).

35–37. During earthly life, a sinner hurt many people with cruelty and injustice. Therefore, on the Day of Judgment, there will be no warm friend for support, consolation or pleading his or her case. The person did not purify his or her wealth by giving zakāh. His or her wealth remained impure on earth, so his or her food will also remain impure in the Hereafter. The word "washing" (*ghislin*) means the water that has been washed from something, therefore, the water is dirty and impure. *Ghislin* also means the liquid that comes out of an open, infectious wound.

Words to know:

دَرَكَ: to overtake, to follow up. أَدْرَكَ: to perceive, overtook. يُدْرِكُ: he overtakes.
دَرَكٌ: abyss, lowest point.

كَذَبَ: to lie, to fabricate. كَذَّابٌ: one given to lying. كَذَّبَ: to belie outright, to continuously belie. كَاذِبًا: liar. مَكْذُوب: falsified.

طَغَى: to transgress, to exceed the bound. طَاغِيَةٌ: severe storm of thunder and lightening.
أَطْغَى: most notorious in wickedness. طَاغُوت: transgressor, powers of evil, one who leads to evil.

أَهْلَكَ: caused to perish. هَلَكَ: to die, to perish, be lost. مُهْلِكِين: those who are dead.

سَخَّرَ: to compel to work without payment, to make subservient. مُسَخَّر: one subjugated.
مُسَخَّرَات: those who are made subservient.

قَارِعَة: great calamity. قَرَعَ: to strike, to strike severely.

بَاقِيَةٌ: remainder, residue, legacy of good. بَقِيَ: to remain, continue. أَبْقَى: the lasting one.

عَصَى: to rebel, to disobey, to oppose. عِصْيَانٌ: transgression. عِصِيًّا: disobedient.

أَرْجَا: borders, sides. رَجَا: to hope, to expect. أَرْجِ: put off, wait a while. مَرْجُوّ: one hoped for.

تَعْرَضُونَ: you shall be exposed. عَرَضَ: to take place, to happen, to show, to expose.
عُرْضَةٌ: excuse, hindrance. عَرْضٌ: width, extensiveness, expanse.

دَنَا: to be near, come near. أَدْنَى: nearest, baser, worse. دُنْيَا: this world (because it is within reach)

أَسْلَفْتُم: you did in past. سَلَفَ: he is past, to be in past. سَلَف: ancestor, predecessor.

سُلْطَان: authority, argument, power, demonstration. سَلَّطَ: to give power, make victorious.

يَحُضُّونَ: to urge, to incite one another. حَضَّ: to incite, to instigate.

حَمِيم: near relative or warm friend, very hot or very cold water. حَمَّ: to heat, to melt.

Sūrah Al-Haqqah
Word-by-word meaning

بِسْمِ	ٱللَّهِ	ٱلرَّحْمَٰنِ	ٱلرَّحِيمِ
In the name of	Allāh	the most Kind	the most Rewarding

ٱلْحَاقَّةُ ۚ	مَا	ٱلْحَاقَّةُ ۚ	وَمَآ
the reality	what is	the reality	and what

أَدْرَىٰكَ	مَا	ٱلْحَاقَّةُ ۚ	كَذَّبَتْ
will make you know	what is	the reality	denied

فَأَمَّا	بِٱلْقَارِعَةِ ٤	وَعَادٌ	ثَمُودُ
as for	the calamity	and Ad people	Thamūd
وَأَمَّا	بِٱلطَّاغِيَةِ ٥	فَأُهْلِكُوا۟	ثَمُودُ
and as for	by the awful cry	they were destroyed	Thamūd
صَرْصَرٍ	بِرِيحٍ	فَأُهْلِكُوا۟	عَادٌ
a furious	by wind	they were destroyed	ʿĀd
سَبْعَ	عَلَيْهِمْ	سَخَّرَهَا	عَاتِيَةٍ ٦
for seven	on them	which Allāh imposed	violent
حُسُومًا	أَيَّامٍ	وَثَمَٰنِيَةَ	لَيَالٍ
in succession	days	and eight	nights
صَرْعَىٰ	فِيهَا	ٱلْقَوْمَ	فَتَرَى
lying overthrown	in it	the people	so that you could see
خَاوِيَةٍ ٧	نَخْلٍ	أَعْجَازُ	كَأَنَّهُمْ
hollow.	date palms	trunks of	as if they were
مِّنْ	لَهُمْ	تَرَىٰ	فَهَلْ
any	of them	you see	so do
وَمَن	فِرْعَوْنُ	وَجَآءَ	بَاقِيَةٍ ٨
and those	Pharaoh	and brought	remnants.
فَعَصَوْا۟	بِٱلْخَاطِئَةِ ٩	وَٱلْمُؤْتَفِكَٰتُ	قَبْلَهُۥ
and they disobeyed	committed sin	and the cities	before him
أَخْذَةً	فَأَخَذَهُمْ	رَبِّهِمْ	رَسُولَ
seizing	so He grasped them	their Rabb's	Messenger
طَغَا	لَمَّا	إِنَّا	رَّابِيَةً ١٠
rose beyond limits	then	indeed we	a strong.

ٱلْمَآءُ	حَمَلْنَٰكُمْ	فِى	ٱلْجَارِيَةِ ⓫
the water	We carried you	in	the floating
لِنَجْعَلَهَا	لَكُمْ	تَذْكِرَةً	وَتَعِيَهَآ
that We might make it	for you	a remembrance	and may understand it
أُذُنٌ	وَٰعِيَةٌ ⓬	فَإِذَا	نُفِخَ
an ear	keen	then when	will be blown
فِى	ٱلصُّورِ	نَفْخَةٌ	وَٰحِدَةٌ ⓭
in	the Trumpet	with blowing	one
وَحُمِلَتِ	ٱلْأَرْضُ	وَٱلْجِبَالُ	فَدُكَّتَا
and shall be removed	the earth	and the mountains	and crushed
دَكَّةً	وَٰحِدَةً ⓮	فَيَوْمَئِذٍ	وَقَعَتِ
crushing	with a single	then on that Day	shall befall
ٱلْوَاقِعَةُ ⓯	وَٱنشَقَّتِ	ٱلسَّمَآءُ	فَهِىَ
the sure event	and will split asunder	the heaven	so it
يَوْمَئِذٍ	وَاهِيَةٌ ⓰	وَٱلْمَلَكُ	عَلَىٰ
on that Day	be fragile	and the angels	will be on
أَرْجَآئِهَا	وَتَحْمِلُ	عَرْشَ	رَبِّكَ
its sides	and will bear	the Thrones of	your Rabb
فَوْقَهُمْ	يَوْمَئِذٍ	ثَمَٰنِيَةٌ ⓱	يَوْمَئِذٍ
above them	that Day	eight	that Day
تُعْرَضُونَ	لَا	تَخْفَىٰ	مِنكُمْ
shall you be exposed	not	will be hidden	of you
خَافِيَةٌ ⓲	فَأَمَّا	مَنْ	أُوتِىَ
a secret	then as for	him who	will be given

هَآؤُمُ take	فَيَقُولُ will say	بِيَمِينِهِۦ in his right hand	كِتَٰبَهُۥ his record
ظَنَنتُ did believe	إِنِّى surely I	كِتَٰبِيَهْ ۱۹ my record	ٱقْرَءُوا۟ read
فَهُوَ so he shall be	حِسَابِيَهْ ۲۰ my account	مُلَٰقٍ shall meet	أَنِّى that I
فِى in	رَّاضِيَةٍ ۲۱ well-pleasing	عِيشَةٍ a life	فِى in
دَانِيَةٌ ۲۳ are close at hand	قُطُوفُهَا the fruits of which	عَالِيَةٍ ۲۲ a lofty	جَنَّةٍ Paradise
بِمَآ for that which	هَنِيٓـًٔا at ease	وَٱشْرَبُوا۟ and drink	كُلُوا۟ eat
ٱلْخَالِيَةِ ۲۴ past	ٱلْأَيَّامِ days	فِى in	أَسْلَفْتُمْ you have sent on
كِتَٰبَهُۥ his record	أُوتِىَ will be given	مَنْ him who	وَأَمَّا but as for
لَمْ not	يَٰلَيْتَنِى I wish	فَيَقُولُ will say	بِشِمَالِهِۦ in his left hand
أَدْرِ I had known	وَلَمْ and that not	كِتَٰبِيَهْ ۲۵ my record	أُوتَ I had been given
كَانَتِ had been	يَٰلَيْتَهَا If only it	حِسَابِيَهْ ۲۶ my account	مَا what is
عَنِّى me	أَغْنَىٰ has availed	مَآ not	ٱلْقَاضِيَةَ ۲۷ my end.

سُلْطَانِيَهْ ۳۹	عَنِّى	هَلَكَ	مَالِيَهْ ۲۸
my authority	from me	have gone	my wealth.
ٱلْجَحِيمَ	ثُمَّ	فَغُلُّوهُ ۳۰	خُذُوهُ
in the blazing Fire	then	and fetter him	seize him
سِلْسِلَةٍ	فِى	ثُمَّ	صَلُّوهُ ۳۱
a chain	in	then	burn him
فَٱسْلُكُوهُ ۳۲	ذِرَاعًا	سَبْعُونَ	ذَرْعُهَا
fasten him	cubits	is seventy	whereof the length
يُؤْمِنُ	لَا	كَانَ	إِنَّهُ
believe	not	used to	surely he
تَحُضُّ	وَلَا	ٱلْعَظِيمِ ۳۳	بِٱللَّهِ
he urged	and not	the Most Great	in Allāh
فَلَيْسَ	ٱلْمِسْكِينِ ۳٤	طَعَامِ	عَلَىٰ
so not	the poor.	the feeding of	on
حَمِيمٌ ۳٥	هَٰهُنَا	ٱلْيَوْمَ	لَهُ
friend	here	this Day	has he
مِنْ غِسْلِينٍ ۳٦	إِلَّا	طَعَامٌ	وَلَا
filth from the washing of wounds	except	any food	nor
ٱلْخَاطِئُونَ ۳۷	إِلَّا	يَأْكُلُهُ	لَا
the sinners	except	will eat it	none

A few applications of the message:

The Qur'ān reminds us of the "Sure Event," which is a striking calamity that will fall upon people or nations that do not follow the divine message and rebel against their Creator. In the past, several eminent nations and rulers disobeyed Allāh (swt) and the teachings of their messengers. References to these past nations stress the breadth and expanse of Allāh's (swt) judgment across different geographic locations and time periods.

What moral should we learn from the history of these eminent nations? The moral is this: if we disobey Allāh (swt) and His messenger, our end will be similar to those who suffered a striking calamity. In the Hereafter, the punishment will be even more severe.

However, if we pay attention to the divine teachings and follow their commands, it is guaranteed that we will be in the Garden of Paradise, living a well-pleased life. We want our final destination to be joyous. We know that each one of us will receive an account of our earthly deeds. We do not want our books to contain any records of bad deeds. We can erase the bad deeds by sincerely asking Allāh (swt) for forgiveness and avoiding the sins for which we sought forgiveness.

Small but frequent righteous deeds will benefit us immensely in the long run. For example, feeding poor and needy people carries tremendous value in Allāh's (swt) sight. We should never ignore such small but meritorious deeds. We should take every opportunity to perform such deeds that will earn us immense rewards.

Questions:

1. Explain the nature of the calamity that destroyed the tribe of Thamūd.

2. What type of calamity destroyed the tribe of 'Ād? Use several of the key words in āyāt 6 and 7 to explain your answer.

3. Who were the people of the cities that were destroyed?

4. Based on sūrah al-Haqqah, describe a few events that will occur after the "trumpet" is blown.

5. Based on sūrah al-Haqqah, describe some of the experiences of those who will receive their books in their right hand.

6. Those who will receive their books in their left hand will realize their mistakes. What will they say after they realize their mistakes?

7. What did the guilty people not do during their earthly lives? Explain your answer based on sūrah al-Haqqah.

Sūrah 69
Al-Haqqah

Revealed in Makkah

Part B

The Inevitable

Introduction:

Non-believers reject the message of the Qur'ān because they think it is not the words of Allāh (swt) but the work of a poet foretelling the future. They are reminded that the Qur'ān is not the work of a poet or soothsayer, but it is a divine revelation. They are also told that if Muhammad (S) had forged any part of the Qur'ān, Allāh (swt) would have severely punished him. A description of the severe punishment is mentioned. Since no such punishment was inflicted upon Muhammad (S), therefore, the conclusion is this: the Qur'ān is a divine revelation and a reminder for the pious.

بِسْمِ ٱللَّهِ ٱلرَّحْمَـٰنِ ٱلرَّحِيمِ

In the name of Allāh, the most Kind, the most Rewarding.

فَلَآ أُقْسِمُ بِمَا تُبْصِرُونَ ۝

38. But no! I swear by what you see,

وَمَا لَا تُبْصِرُونَ ۝

39. and by what you do not see,

إِنَّهُ لَقَوْلُ رَسُولٍ كَرِيمٍ ۝

40. it is surely the word of an honorable Rasul,

وَمَا هُوَ بِقَوْلِ شَاعِرٍ قَلِيلًا مَّا تُؤْمِنُونَ ۝

41. and it is not the word of a poet. Little it is what you believe!—

وَلَا بِقَوْلِ كَاهِنٍ قَلِيلًا مَّا تَذَكَّرُونَ ۝

42. nor is it the word of a soothsayer. Little it is what you mind!

تَنزِيلٌ مِّن رَّبِّ ٱلْعَـٰلَمِينَ ۝

43. It is the revelation from the Rabb of all the worlds.

وَلَوْ تَقَوَّلَ عَلَيْنَا بَعْضَ ٱلْأَقَاوِيلِ ۝

44. And had he fabricated against Us certain sayings,

لَأَخَذْنَا مِنْهُ بِٱلْيَمِينِ ۝

45. We would invariably have seized him by the right hand,

ثُمَّ لَقَطَعْنَا مِنْهُ ٱلْوَتِينَ ۝

46. and then We would have certainly cut through his aorta.

فَمَا مِنكُم مِّنْ أَحَدٍ عَنْهُ حَٰجِزِينَ ۝

47. Then not one of you could have stopped from him.

وَإِنَّهُ لَتَذْكِرَةٌ لِّلْمُتَّقِينَ ۝

48. And surely it is a Reminder for the pious.

وَإِنَّا لَنَعْلَمُ أَنَّ مِنكُم مُّكَذِّبِينَ ۝

49. And, indeed, We know for certain that among you are the deniers.

وَإِنَّهُ لَحَسْرَةٌ عَلَى ٱلْكَٰفِرِينَ ۝

50. And certainly it is, of course, a grief to the non-believers.

وَإِنَّهُ لَحَقُّ ٱلْيَقِينِ ۝

51. And truly it is the Certain Truth.

فَسَبِّحْ بِٱسْمِ رَبِّكَ ٱلْعَظِيمِ ۝

52. Therefore glorify the name of your Rabb—the Greatest.

Explanation:

38–40. The phrase "what you can see" includes those areas of knowledge that human beings can analyze, apply and evaluate. The phrase "what you do not see" relates to those areas of knowledge that are acquired through intuition, instinct or one's conscience. It also signifies those aspects that human beings cannot see, for example, the Hereafter, jinn, angels and the hidden blessings of Allāh (swt), to name a few. Both of these knowledge bases must prove that the revelation sent to an honorable rasūl (S) included words from Allāh (swt), as clarified in āyah 43.

41–42. In ancient Arabia a *kāhin* earned great attention and awe from his audience. A *kāhin* was a title given to a person who showed strong aptitude for reciting couplets. They also made predictions about the future. Most of the predictions were derived from Shaitān or from jinn sources. The *kāhin* were often reported to fall under spells induced by devilish spirits. When the non-believers accused Rasūlullāh (S) of being a *kāhin*, they implied that he was no different from other *kāhins* in Arabia—

he was influenced by the devil, he recited couplets and he made predictions about the future. They cleverly related the prophecy made by Muhammad (S) to the predictions made by the soothsayers. Although his predictions were outwardly similar, these prophecies originated from Allāh (swt) whereas soothsaying originated from Shaitān. Common people could not tell which prediction was from Allāh and which one was a trick from Shaitān. There was another group of people who also composed couplets and poems, but they did not claim to be fortune-tellers. They simply entertained people with beautiful poems. Most of the early revelations contained some sort of strong ending rhyme and resonance, which led people to believe that Muhammad (S) was either a soothsayer or a poet.

43. If the words of the Qur'ān are not the speech of a poet or a *kāhin, then* what are they? Allāh (swt) answers this by saying these are *tanzīl*, or something that has been gradually revealed, the source of which is divine, and comes from the Rabb of all worlds.

44–47. This set of āyāt emphasize the impossibility of Rasūlullāh (S) plagiarizing or making up ideas and claiming them as divine. Alternately, he could have compromised with the non-believers to gain their confidence. Neither of these scenarios were possible. In spite of being Allāh's messenger, Muhammad (S) was not above the law. If he had invented anything in the name of Allāh (swt), he would face serious consequences. Allāh (swt) would have seized him for punishment or killed him. Seizing by right hand symbolizes Allāh's power and absolute control (5:64; 36:71; 39:67; and 48:10). If the life-giving vein of a person is slit, this would cause immediate death. If Muhammad (S) had compromised with the non-believers, they might have shown empathy for him and might have wanted to protect him, but Allāh (swt) says "not one of you could have protected him."

48–50. Many people realize that Islam is the truth and its message makes sense to them. However, they deny the truth due to selfish reasons, ego or pride. In āyah 49, Allāh (swt) speaks directly to the non-believers saying: *inna minkum mukaddhibīn* ("surely among you are deniers"). The Qur'ān serves as a reminder to those who are pious. Obviously those who belie the truth, cannot find any inspiration from it; rather the Qur'ān will serve as a source of grief for them because their suffering and defeat has been prophesized in this divine book.

51–52. The truth contained in the Qur'ān qualifies as Certain Truth (*haq-al yaqīn*) because it can be verified by all forms of rigorous tests of authenticity, completeness and perfection. Therefore, believers are advised to glorify the name of their Lord—the Greatest.

Words to know:

تَقَوَّلَ: he fabricated lies. قَالَ: to say, to speak. قُلْ: say.

أَخَذَ: he took, to receive, to accept. أَخْذَةٌ: punishment.

قَطَعَ: to cut, to separate, to cross. قُطِّعَت: cut off, torn asunder.

حَاجِزِين: withholders. حَجَزَ: to withhold, to stop, to restrain.

حَسَرَةٌ: anguishes. حَسَرَ: to get tired, fatigued. حَسِير: weary, worn out, fatigued.

سَبَّحَ: to praise, to glorify. تَسبِيح: the act of praise. سُبحَان: glory be to you (it always occurs before Allāh's name to glorify Him.)

Sūrah Al-Haqqah
Word-by-word meaning

بِسمِ	ٱللَّهِ	ٱلرَّحمٰنِ	ٱلرَّحيمِ
In the name of	Allāh	the Most Kind	the Most Rewarding

فَلَآ	أُقسِمُ	بِمَا	تُبصِرُونَ ٣٨
but no	I swear	by whatsoever	you see

وَمَا	لَا	تُبصِرُونَ ٣٩	إِنَّهُۥ
and by whatsoever	not	you see	surely this is

لَقَولُ	رَسُولٍ	كَريمٍ ٤٠	وَمَا
the word of	Messenger	an honoured	and not

هُوَ	بِقَولِ	شَاعِرٍ	قَليلًا
it is	the word of	a poet	little is

مَّا	تُؤمِنُونَ ٤١	وَلَا	بِقَولِ
that	you believe	nor is it	the word of

كَاهِنٍ	قَليلًا	مَّا	تَذَكَّرُونَ ٤٢
a soothsayer	little is	that	you remember

تَنزيلٌ	مِّن	رَّبِّ	ٱلعَالَمينَ ٤٣
this is the revelation sent down	from	Rabb of	the worlds

وَلَو	تَقَوَّلَ	عَلَينَا	بَعضَ
and if	he forged	concerning Us	some

ٱلأَقَاويلِ ٤٤	لَأَخَذنَا	مِنهُ	بِٱليَمينِ ٤٥
false sayings	We surely should have seized	him	by his right hand

ثُمَّ	لَقَطَعنَا	مِنهُ	ٱلوَتينَ ٤٦
and then	certainly We would cut	from him	the life artery

أَحَدٍ	مِّن	مِنكُم	فَمَا
one	any	of you	and not
لَتَذۡكِرَةٌ	وَإِنَّهُۥ	حَـٰجِزِينَ ۝	عَنۡهُ
is a Reminder	and surely this	could withhold	from him
أَنَّ	لَنَعۡلَمُ	وَإِنَّا	لِّلۡمُتَّقِينَ ۝
that	know	and indeed We	for the pious
لَحَسۡرَةٌ	وَإِنَّهُۥ	مُّكَذِّبِينَ ۝	مِنكُم
will be anguish	and indeed it	deniers	among you are
لَحَقُّ	وَإِنَّهُۥ	ٱلۡكَـٰفِرِينَ ۝	عَلَى
an absolute truth	and surely it is	the non-believers	for
رَبِّكَ	بِٱسۡمِ	فَسَبِّحۡ	ٱلۡيَقِينِ ۝
your Rabb	the Name of	so glorify	with certainty
			ٱلۡعَظِيمِ ۝
			the Most Great

A few applications of the message:

Allāh (swt) guarantees the authenticity of the divine message. This divine message carries the guidance that will ultimately help us to enter Paradise. However, we cannot enter Paradise if we remain careless about the divine commands. This sūrah mentions a few meritorious deeds, such as prostrating to Allāh (swt) and feeding the poor. We can perform these as well as many other meritorious deeds to qualify ourselves to enter Paradise.

Many people are simply careless about the message of the Qur'ān. They simply reject the message, saying that these are the useless words of a poet or a magician. By claiming this, they only want to justify their earthly motives. They do not realize that such negligence will become the cause of their grief in the Hereafter. We should remain cautious and not behave the same way.

Allāh (swt) tells us that the Qur'ān is a reminder for the muttaqīn—those who have the highest level of faith. Each one of us can strive to become a muttaqī. All that is required is paying full attention to the divine message and following the commands carefully.

Questions:

1. What two things did people in Makkah say about the Qur'ān to discredit its divine source?

2. How would Allāh (swt) have punished Muhammad (S) if he had fabricated anything in the Qur'ān?

3. In āyah 51, what is being mentioned as *Haqq al-Yaqeen*? What is the significance of this word?

4. What are some of the ways we can glorify the name of our Rabb?

Sūrah 70

Part A

Revealed in Makkah

Al-Ma'ārij

The Ways of Ascent

Introduction:

The non-believers made fun of the news of the Awakening and life in the Hereafter. In response to their taunting remarks and doubts, this sūrah explains some of the realities of the Awakening in very graphic detail. When the Day of Awakening begins, it will cause tremendous distress to the sinners. They will find the entire world is undergoing a tumultuous change. All forms of family relationships will be severed as each individual will be concerned with his or her own safety and security. The sinners will wish to avert their punishment by any means. But they will realize they cannot avert it. There are too many reasons for their punishment. They belied their Creator, they did not submit to Him, they did not care for the needy and the poor, they did not honor their husband-wife relationships and they did not honor their trusts and agreements. In contrast to the sinners, the righteous will be granted great honor and they will enter Paradise.

بِسْمِ ٱللَّهِ ٱلرَّحْمَـٰنِ ٱلرَّحِيمِ

In the name of Allāh, the most Kind, the most Rewarding.

سَأَلَ سَآئِلٌ بِعَذَابٍ وَاقِعٍ ۝	1. A questioner questioned about the impending falling punishment—
لِّلْكَـٰفِرِينَ لَيْسَ لَهُۥ دَافِعٌ ۝	2. for the Unbelievers, there is no one for it to avert—
مِّنَ ٱللَّهِ ذِى ٱلْمَعَارِجِ ۝	3. from Allāh—Master of the Ascending Stairways.
تَعْرُجُ ٱلْمَلَـٰٓئِكَةُ وَٱلرُّوحُ إِلَيْهِ فِى يَوْمٍ كَانَ مِقْدَارُهُۥ خَمْسِينَ أَلْفَ سَنَةٍ ۝	4. To Him ascend the angels and the Spirit, in a Day the measure of which is fifty thousand years.
فَٱصْبِرْ صَبْرًا جَمِيلًا ۝	5. Therefore you persevere a noble persevering.

6. Surely they see it far off,

 إِنَّهُمْ يَرَوْنَهُ بَعِيدًا ۝

7. but We see it nigh.

وَنَرَىٰهُ قَرِيبًا ۝

8. On that Day when the heaven will be like molten copper,

يَوْمَ تَكُونُ ٱلسَّمَآءُ كَٱلْمُهْلِ ۝

9. and the mountains will be like wool;

وَتَكُونُ ٱلْجِبَالُ كَٱلْعِهْنِ ۝

10. and a loyal friend will not inquire about a loyal friend,

وَلَا يَسْـَٔلُ حَمِيمٌ حَمِيمًا ۝

11. they will be visible to them. The guilty would wish to redeem from the chastisement of that Day by his children,

يُبَصَّرُونَهُمْ يَوَدُّ ٱلْمُجْرِمُ لَوْ يَفْتَدِى مِنْ عَذَابِ يَوْمِئِذٍ بِبَنِيهِ ۝

12. and his mate and his brother,

وَصَٰحِبَتِهِ وَأَخِيهِ ۝

13. and his relations who sheltered him,

وَفَصِيلَتِهِ ٱلَّتِى تُـْٔوِيهِ ۝

14. and whoever are in the earth altogether—that then he might rescue himself;

وَمَن فِى ٱلْأَرْضِ جَمِيعًا ثُمَّ يُنجِيهِ ۝

15. never! Surely it is a flaming Fire,

كَلَّآ إِنَّهَا لَظَىٰ ۝

16. peeling off the skins—

نَزَّاعَةً لِّلشَّوَىٰ ۝

17. calling him who turns back and runs away,

تَدْعُوا۟ مَنْ أَدْبَرَ وَتَوَلَّىٰ ۝

18. and who hoards and withholds.

وَجَمَعَ فَأَوْعَىٰ ۝

19. Indeed man is created impatient—

إِنَّ ٱلْإِنسَٰنَ خُلِقَ هَلُوعًا ۝

20. when evil touches him, full of lamentations;

إِذَا مَسَّهُ ٱلشَّرُّ جَزُوعًا ۝

وَإِذَا مَسَّهُ ٱلْخَيْرُ مَنُوعًا ۝

21. but when good touches him, miserly,

إِلَّا ٱلْمُصَلِّينَ ۝

22. excepting the performers of Salāt,

ٱلَّذِينَ هُمْ عَلَىٰ صَلَاتِهِمْ دَآئِمُونَ ۝

23. those people who are constant in their Salāts,

وَٱلَّذِينَ فِىٓ أَمْوَٰلِهِمْ حَقٌّ مَّعْلُومٌ ۝

24. and in whose wealth there is a recognized right—

لِّلسَّآئِلِ وَٱلْمَحْرُومِ ۝

25. for the beggar and the abstainer,

وَٱلَّذِينَ يُصَدِّقُونَ بِيَوْمِ ٱلدِّينِ ۝

26. and those who hold to be true the Day of Judgment,

وَٱلَّذِينَ هُم مِّنْ عَذَابِ رَبِّهِم مُّشْفِقُونَ ۝

27. and those who are themselves afraid of the chastisement of their Rabb;

إِنَّ عَذَابَ رَبِّهِمْ غَيْرُ مَأْمُونٍ ۝

28. surely the chastisement of their Rabb is not to be felt secure from—

وَٱلَّذِينَ هُمْ لِفُرُوجِهِمْ حَٰفِظُونَ ۝

29. and those who are themselves watchful over their appetites,

إِلَّا عَلَىٰٓ أَزْوَٰجِهِمْ أَوْ مَا مَلَكَتْ أَيْمَٰنُهُمْ فَإِنَّهُمْ غَيْرُ مَلُومِينَ ۝

30. except with their mates or whom their right hands possess, because then they are not to be blamed;

فَمَنِ ٱبْتَغَىٰ وَرَآءَ ذَٰلِكَ فَأُوْلَٰٓئِكَ هُمُ ٱلْعَادُونَ ۝

31. but he who seeks beyond that, they themselves are then the transgressors.

وَٱلَّذِينَ هُمْ لِأَمَٰنَٰتِهِمْ وَعَهْدِهِمْ رَٰعُونَ ۝

32. And those persons who are faithful of their trusts and their covenants,

وَٱلَّذِينَ هُم بِشَهَٰدَٰتِهِمْ قَآئِمُونَ ۝

33. and those people who are upright in their evidence,

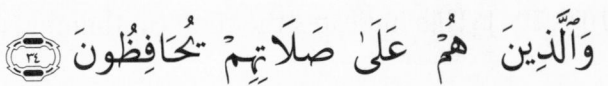

وَالَّذِينَ هُمْ عَلَىٰ صَلَاتِهِمْ يُحَافِظُونَ ﴿٣٤﴾   34. and those who themselves have been guarding their Salāts.

أُوْلَـٰٓئِكَ فِى جَنَّـٰتٍ مُّكْرَمُونَ ﴿٣٥﴾   35. These will be in Gardens, highly honored.

Explanation:

1. The identity of the questioner is irrelevant for the purpose of conveying the message in this sūrah. The significance of the question lies in the fact that the sūrah was a mid-Makkan revelation—a time when the total number of Muslims was less than one hundred. The question reflects the legitimate curiosity of the believers, who constantly witnessed non-believers violate moral, ethical and spiritual values, yet prosper in the temporal world. The non-believers, on the other hand, are least worried about any impending punishment because it is immaterial to them given that everything around them seems to work just fine. The word 'adhāb (punishment) is prefixed with letter "ba" to add additional emphasis to the word it prefixes—punishment (see examples in āyah 2:8; 29:53). Therefore, punishment is certain to happen. It is further stated to be "falling," indicated by the word waqaya. The word literally means "something that comes down or falls upon another thing and it cannot be stopped."

2. When the impending punishment truly appears, the non-believers cannot avert it. The word lahu means "for it" or "for him"—indicating "for the punishment to avert" or "for him to avert the punishment."

3. The punishment mentioned in the previous two āyāt is said to come from Allāh (swt), Whose qualification is Dhee al-Ma'ārij, that is, Possessor of Great Heights. The sūrah derives its title from the mention of al-Ma'ārij (ways that ascend, or ascending stairways), implying ways by which man is able to rise higher and higher in the spiritual realm, attain spiritual nearness to Allāh (swt) and attain an understanding of His existence. The word 'ārij means "to ascend slowly, in stages."

4. In the Qur'ān, the word rūh is used in two senses: (1) to indicate the angels, particularly angel Jibril and (2) to indicate a righteous person or a spirit of a righteous person. Here, the word rūh without a qualifier means the spirit of all the believers that are said to ascend along with the angels (Ibn Kathīr). In another opinion, since the word angels and rūh are mentioned side by side, the word rūh means angel Jibril. The equivalence of a day with 50,000 years indicates the concept of a human time scale of solar days and years is limited to the earth, but it does not apply outside of this world, and certainly not with Allāh (swt) (7:54; 22:47; 32:5).

5. In the face of mounting challenges, Rasūlullāh (S) was asked to persevere in a noble way. The more difficult his challenges became, the more nobility he was required to show. Due to such noble perseverance, the strongest opponents of Islam were eventually won over.

6–7. The word b'aīd means "that which is impossible to happen." Whether it is implied to indicate impending chastisement or Awakening, the non-believers see it as implausible and remote. In the earthly context, what appears too far away on the time scale is actually very near, although it is difficult to comprehend. In the Hereafter, when people will be given an objective view of their lives in the earth, they will think the duration of life on earth was equal to a day, whereas it will be revealed that it was less than that (10:45; 17:52; 20:103–104). This indicates the time continuum is totally different with Allāh than with human beings.

8–9. Copper has a reddish-brown color. The images of the sky resembling molten copper indicates it will assume a deep reddish-brown color. The next āyah says mountains will become like wool ('ihn). Mountains are firm structures that impart stability to the earth and act as pegs (awtād). The description of mountains becoming like wool indicates a massive explosion, like that of a super-volcanic eruption that would render the rocks into dust, thrown miles into the atmosphere. The eruption would throw the molten lava high into the air and the dust and ashes would cover an area hundreds of miles wide. They will look like lumps of wool floating around. The massive explosion would tinge the sky with a deep reddish-brown color.

10–14. The tremendous terror caused by such a blast would make everybody run for their own shelter and safety, forgetting about their good friends. When shelter is found, the guilty person (mujrim) may even let down those who gave him shelter. He will wish to redeem himself from chastisement by offering as ransom his own children, his spouse, his brother and all others who gave him shelter. On that terror-stricken day, the guilty person will try to use whoever he can and whatever resources he can find, hoping that collectively these can be traded to ensure his own rescue. In āyah 11, the person is mentioned as mujrim, which means a person who has already been proven guilty of a crime. The āyah does not say that it is a non-believer, because even a sinful Muslims could be a mujrim.

15. The participle kallā is often used to counter a statement that precedes it, and gives emphasis to what follows it (see usage in 19:79,82; 23:100; 26:15,62; 89:17). In the previous verse, the vain hope of being rescued is mentioned, but such a hope will never be possible. Instead what is stated in the next verse will be actualized. The word ladha' is one of the names for the fire of hell. It also indicates a very large flame that is so roaring with intensity that it does not contain smoke.

16–17. While four of our senses (sight, hearing, smell, and taste) are located within specific parts of the body, our sense of touch is located all over the body. The skin is the largest organ of the body. The sense of touch is felt through the skin. The sin caused by skin or touching is serious in nature. For this reason, punishment of the skin is mentioned several times in the Qur'ān (4:56; 22:20; 41:20, 22). Many scholars indicate the Qur'ānic allusion of peeling off the skin symbolizes the total disintegration of the outer personality, just as burning the bellies indicates the breakdown of inner resistance. The fire will symbolically call those turn back and run away to return to fire.

18. A characteristic of these people who will try to run away from fire are those who, during their earthly lives, turned away from guidance. The void created due to a lack of guidance was filled with wealth. You will notice that truly guided people do not hoard wealth. But the misguided people hide and stash wealth away and withhold from spending on rightful causes (2:268; 9:34; 25:67; 104:2–3). They become stingy and suffer from the anxiety of losing their wealth.

19. The word halū'ān (impatient, anxious) is used to describe an inherent characteristic of the human personality: restlessness or impatience. The tendency of impatience or restlessness is a God-given quality in human nature that may motivate one to do good deeds or incline one toward evil acts. The manner in which this quality is used will determine whether it has a constructive or destructive influence in one's life. This line of reasoning is established through the array of behavior mentioned in the following āyāt.

20–21. As long as the circumstances and the environment around some people are positive for them, they remains oblivious of Allāh (swt). But as soon as these circumstances become unfavorable for them, they suddenly become aware of God and implore Him with prayers (10:22–23; 29:65; 30:36; 41:49). When good times return, these people become oblivious of Allāh (swt) again (7:189–190; 11:9–10; 89:15–16). Although it is not mentioned here, there is another group of people who are misguided. During unfavorable conditions, these people become further distanced from Allāh (swt), and give up all hope of Allāh's mercy (6:44; 11:9; 12:87; 15:56; 17:83; 23:77).

22–23. Āyāt 22 to 34 describe eight desirable codes of conduct. If a person follows these codes, he or she will be admitted to Paradise as mentioned at the end of the passage in āyah 35. One of these codes of conduct is to perform salāt on a regular basis. The word *dāimūn* means "continuous, always." The importance of salāt is mentioned again in āyah 34, at the end of the passage, where believers are advised to protect the salāt.

24–25. The second code of conduct is to allocate a share of one's wealth so that it might benefit others. The rights (*haqq*) of the poor to the wealth of the rich is said to be known (*ma'lum*) or recognized. It is a deserving right, implying it is compulsory. These āyāt mention that two types of people deserve these benefits. The first type is the beggar, who openly begs for benefits. The second type is the abstainer (51:19). Abstainers have fallen into financial difficulties, but due to their dignity and social positions, they cannot openly beg. They have a bigger dilemma because most people do not realize that these abstainers have encountered a financial crisis. It is the duty of wealthy people to recognize both types of people and allocate a share of their wealth for both.

26. The third code of conduct is to believe in the Day of Judgment, the purpose of which is to hold everybody accountable for their deeds and to reward or punish them according to the merits of their every action. The word *yusaddiqūn* (they testify, they accept it wholeheartedly) indicates they not only believe in the Day of Judgment, but they affirm it and are fully convinced it will happen.

27–28. The fourth code of conduct is to fear punishment. The word *mushfiqūn* means "one who is fearful," or "one who is mindful," because there will be consequences. The reason the righteous people should be afraid of punishment is that nobody is perfect and everybody is susceptible to some moral wrong doing, knowingly and unknowingly. Awareness of punishment will prevent the righteous people from falling into sinful activities. Besides, no one knows which sins, if any, Allāh (swt) has forgiven and which sins will remain to be duly recompensed in this life and in the Hereafter.

29. The fifth code of conduct is to guard one's sexual desires. The word *furūj* literally means one's "private parts." The requirement to guard it means refraining from immoral and illegal expression of one's sexual appetites.

30–31. The word *zawj* refers to a pair of opposites, for a married man—his wife, and for a married woman—her husband. The phrase *mā malakat aymā nuhum* means "whom your right hand possesses." At the time of the Messenger (S), they were prisoners of war that included men as well as women. The Qur'ān addresses the issue of these captives in a manner that would be morally right, not only at the time of the Messenger (S), but during all periods in time. Islam does not allow man to hold anybody, including prisoners of war, as mistresses (4:25). Forcing anybody, including slave girls, into prostitution is strictly prohibited (24:33). To uplift the status of prisoners of war and to bring them honor and social dignity, Muslims were allowed to marry them (4:3). The permission to have intimate relations with prisoners of war was given after they were taken in marriage (4:25).

32. The sixth and seventh codes of conduct are to remain faithful to one's trust (*amānāt*) and one's covenants. The trust and covenants can be between two individuals and between an individual and Allāh (swt). Both relationships should be preserved with due care and never be violated. The word *rā'ūn* means not only "to watch over," but "to protect it from harm." A *ray'iun* is a shepherd who watches over his sheep or cattle. Similarly, people holding trust and covenants should watch and protect them like shepherds.

33. Giving truthful evidence is another core requirement of believers. False testimony can harm others and can cause unwanted and larger problems in society. One should provide evidence in a truthful manner, whether such evidence is given in a court of law or in any setting not involving a court. Evidence should not be concealed (2:140). Even if the evidence is against a close family member, one should not be afraid of upholding the truth (4:135). A person should not refuse to give testimony if he or she is called upon.

34–35. The importance of salāt is mentioned in āyāt 22 and 23, emphasizing to become *dāimūn* or "continuous in the practice." In āyah 34, we are now told to guard or protect (*hāfiz*) our salāt. To protect salāt is to maintain its sanctity by becoming attentive to salāt and by performing it at its appointed time. This passage, listing the eight core requirements to qualify for entrance into Paradise is sandwiched between the importance of salāt, mentioned in the beginning and again at the end. This shows salāt is a key component for our success in this world and in the Hereafter.

Words to know:

دَفَعَ: to push, to repel, to avert. دَافِعٌ: the act of pushing. دَافِع: Avert

عَرَجَ: to ascend, to mount. مِعرَاج: the Ascension. مَعَارِج: stairway.

قَدَرَ: to measure, to estimate, to have power over. مُقتَدِر: powerful. مِقدَار: due measure. تَقدِير: decree, disposition, measuring.

عَهَنَ: to wither, to dry, be broken. عُهُون: wool, multicolored wool.

حَمَّ: to heat, to become hot. حَمِيم: very hot or very cold. يَحمُون: warm friend.

جَرَمَ: to cut, to loop. جُرم: crime, sin, fault. مُجرِم: sinner, guilty.

فَصَلَ: to set apart, to distinguish, to set a limit. فُصِّلَت: detailed. فَصِيلَة: kinsfolk, family. مُفَصَّلاً: detailed, clearly explained.

دَبَرَ: to turn back, to flee. أَدبَرَ: turned back. يَتَدَبَّرُونَ: they ponder. مُدَبِّر: one who manages

جَزِعَ: to grow impatient, to show grief. جُزُوعَا: bewailing, full of lamentation.

مَنَعَ: to deny, to hinder, to refuse. مُنوعَا: Protector. مَنُعٌ: one who holds back.

دَامَ: to continue, to endure, to persist. دَائِمٌ: everlasting, continuous. دَائِمُونَ: one who remains steadfast.

حَرَمَ: to forbid, to prevent. مَحرُوم: deprived ones. تَحرِيم: prohibition. حَرَمَين: two sanctuaries (Makkah and Madīnah).

Sūrah Al-Ma'ārij
Word-by-word meaning

بِسْمِ	ٱللَّهِ	ٱلرَّحْمَـٰنِ	ٱلرَّحِيمِ
With the name	Allāh	the most Kind	the most Rewarding

سَأَلَ	سَآئِلٌ	بِعَذَابٍ	وَاقِعٍ ۝١
asked	a questioner	concerning a torment	about to befall.

لِّلْكَـٰفِرِينَ	لَيْسَ	لَهُ	دَافِعٌ ۝٢
upon the disbelievers	none	for it	can avert.

مِّنَ	ٱللَّهِ	ذِى	ٱلْمَعَارِجِ ۝٣
from	Allāh	the Master of	the ways of ascent.

تَعْرُجُ	ٱلْمَلَـٰئِكَةُ	وَٱلرُّوحُ	إِلَيْهِ
ascend	the angels	and the spirit	to Him

فِى	يَوْمٍ	كَانَ	مِقْدَارُهُ
in	a Day	is	the measure whereof

خَمْسِينَ	أَلْفَ	سَنَةٍ ۝٤	فَٱصْبِرْ
fifty	thousand	years.	so be patient

صَبْرًا	جَمِيلًا ۝٥	إِنَّهُمْ	يَرَوْنَهُ
patience	with a good	surely they	see it

بَعِيدًا ۝٦	وَنَرَٮٰهُ	قَرِيبًا ۝٧	يَوْمَ
far off	but We see it	near	the Day that

تَكُونُ	ٱلسَّمَآءُ	كَٱلْمُهْلِ ۝٨	وَتَكُونُ
will be	the sky	like melted lead.	and will be

ٱلْجِبَالُ	كَٱلْعِهْنِ ۝٩	وَلَا	يَسْـَٔلُ
the mountains	like flakes of wool	and not	will ask

حَمِيمٌ	حَمِيمًا ①	يُبَصَّرُونَهُمْ	يَوَدُّ
a friend	of a friend	though they shall be made to see one another	would desire
ٱلْمُجْرِمُ	لَوْ	يَفْتَدِى	مِنْ
the criminal	if	he ransom himself	from
عَذَابِ	يَوْمِئِذٍ	بِبَنِيهِ ⑪	وَصَٰحِبَتِهِ
the punishment of	that Day	by his children.	and his friends
وَأَخِيهِ ⑫	وَفَصِيلَتِهِ	ٱلَّتِى	تُؤْوِيهِ ⑬
and his brother	and his kindred	who	sheltered him
وَمَن	فِى	ٱلْأَرْضِ	جَمِيعًا
and whoever	in	the earth	all
ثُمَّ	يُنجِيهِ ⑭	كَلَّآ	إِنَّهَا
so then	it might save him.	but no means	verily it will be
لَظَىٰ ⑮	نَزَّاعَةً	لِّلشَّوَىٰ ⑯	تَدْعُوا۟
the Fire of Hell	taking away	the head skin	calling
مِنْ	أَدْبَرَ	وَتَوَلَّىٰ ⑰	وَجَمَعَ
(all) such as	turn their backs	and turn away their faces.	and hoards
فَأَوْعَىٰ ⑱	إِنَّ	ٱلْإِنسَٰنَ	خُلِقَ
and hide it.	surely	man	was created
هَلُوعًا ⑲	إِذَا	مَسَّهُ	ٱلشَّرُّ
very impatient.	when	touches him	evil
جَزُوعًا ⑳	وَإِذَا	مَسَّهُ	ٱلْخَيْرُ
distressed.	and when	touches him	good

مَنُوعًا ٢١	إِلَّا	ٱلْمُصَلِّينَ ٢٢	ٱلَّذِينَ
stingy.	except	those devoted to Salāt.	those
هُمْ	عَلَىٰ	صَلَاتِهِمْ	دَآئِمُونَ ٢٣
who	in	their Salāt	remain constant.
وَٱلَّذِينَ	فِىٓ	أَمْوَالِهِمْ	حَقٌّ
and those who	in	their wealth	is a right
مَّعْلُومٌ ٢٤	لِّلسَّآئِلِ	وَٱلْمَحْرُومِ ٢٥	وَٱلَّذِينَ
a known	for the beggar who asks	and for the deprived	and those who
يُصَدِّقُونَ	بِيَوْمِ	ٱلدِّينِ ٢٦	وَٱلَّذِينَ
believe	in the Day of	Recompense.	and those
هُم	مِّن	عَذَابِ	رَبِّهِم
who	of	the torment of	their Rabb
مُّشْفِقُونَ ٢٧	إِنَّ	عَذَابَ	رَبِّهِم
fear.	verily	the torment of	their Rabb
غَيْرُ	مَأْمُونٍ ٢٨	وَٱلَّذِينَ	هُمْ
is that before which none	can feel secure.	and those	who
لِفُرُوجِهِمْ	حَـٰفِظُونَ ٢٩	إِلَّا	عَلَىٰ
their chastity	guard.	except	with
أَزْوَاجِهِمْ	أَوْ	مَا	مَلَكَتْ
their spouses	or	what	possess
أَيْمَـٰنُهُمْ	فَإِنَّهُمْ	غَيْرُ	مَلُومِينَ ٣٠
their right hands	so they are	not	to be blamed.

فَمَنِ	ٱبْتَغَىٰ	وَرَآءَ	ذَٰلِكَ
but whoever	seeks	beyond	that

فَأُو۟لَـٰٓئِكَ	هُمُ	ٱلْعَادُونَ ۝	وَٱلَّذِينَ
then it is those	who are	transgressors.	and those

هُمْ	لِأَمَـٰنَـٰتِهِمْ	وَعَهْدِهِمْ	رَاعُونَ ۝
who	to their trust	and their covenants	they keep

وَٱلَّذِينَ	هُم	بِشَهَـٰدَٰتِهِمْ	قَآئِمُونَ ۝
and those	who	in their testimonies	stand firm.

وَٱلَّذِينَ	هُمْ	عَلَىٰ	صَلَاتِهِمْ
and those	who	over	their Salāt

يُحَافِظُونَ ۝	أُو۟لَـٰٓئِكَ	فِى	جَنَّـٰتٍ
guard well.	such	shall be in	the Gardens

مُّكْرَمُونَ ۝
highly honored.

A few applications of the message:

The message of the sūrah is about the Awakening. The sūrah describes the condition of the sinners who will not be able to avoid punishment by any means. All family relationship will be cut off as he or she will be brought before the fire. He or she will be reminded that the reasons for punishments are the negligence to fulfill the eight desirable codes of conduct.

The rest of the sūrah describes these eight codes of conduct. Although it appears that the sinners are being reminded, it is actually our own reminder. We have to learn the lessons for ourselves so that we do not end up in conditions similar to the sinners.

The eight codes of conduct are sandwiched between the mention of salāt in the beginning and at the end of the āyāt 22 ad 34. This indicates the performance of salāt is extremely important. Salāt is a personal form of worship that benefits the performer. Human beings are also social beings, and we have responsibilities to the society in which we live. Therefore, other duties include giving the beggars and needy people their due share of wealth. Charity is overly emphasized in Islam, but compared to people of other faiths, Muslims are still very reluctant to give. We must give to charity more often. The sūrah also reminds us to restrain our sexual activities. Sexual relationships are permitted only after a man and woman marry each other. As social beings, we have to honor and keep our trusts and covenants. These trusts and covenants are between individuals and between God and ourselves. We are also required to provide truthful evidence.

Allāh (swt) assures us that those who follow and respect the eight codes of conduct will enter Paradise, and they will be in an honorable position. We should always remember these codes of conduct and follow them in true spirit.

Review questions:

1. What is the significance of 50,000 years mentioned in sūrah Al Ma'arij?
2. Explain the meaning of the sky becoming molten copper and mountains becoming wool as mentioned in sūrah Al Ma'arij.
3. What will the guilty people want to use to redeem their safety?
4. Explain why Allāh (swt) used the word *mujrim* in āyah 11 and not another word to refer to those who will suffer punishment.
5. Explain the significance of the peeling of skin as mentioned in āyah 16.
6. How do sinners respond when they face good and evil in their lives?
7. Explain who the people are mentioned in ayah 25 in sūrah Al Ma'arij.
8. What is the significance of keeping trusts and covenants?

Sūrah 70
Part B

Revealed in Makkah

Al-Ma'ārij

The Ways of Ascent

Introduction:

This section of the sūrah reminds the non-believers about their insignificance as opposed to the supreme power of the Almighty. They defy their Creator yet wish to enter Paradise! They are told that unless they become righteous people, Allāh (swt) will replace them with a new generation. Instead of entering Paradise, they will stand in a humiliating condition on the Day of Judgment.

In the name of Allāh, the most Kind, the most Rewarding.

فَمَالِ ٱلَّذِينَ كَفَرُوا۟ قِبَلَكَ مُهۡطِعِينَ ۝	36. But what is the matter with those who disbelieve that they run hastening to you,
عَنِ ٱلۡيَمِينِ وَعَنِ ٱلشِّمَالِ عِزِينَ ۝	37. from the right and from the left—in groups?
أَيَطۡمَعُ كُلُّ ٱمۡرِئٍ مِّنۡهُمۡ أَن يُدۡخَلَ جَنَّةَ نَعِيمٍ ۝	38. Does every man among them covet to be admitted to the Garden of Delight?
كَلَّآ إِنَّا خَلَقۡنَـٰهُم مِّمَّا يَعۡلَمُونَ ۝	39. Never! Surely they know what We have created them from.
فَلَآ أُقۡسِمُ بِرَبِّ ٱلۡمَشَـٰرِقِ وَٱلۡمَغَـٰرِبِ إِنَّا لَقَـٰدِرُونَ ۝	40. But no! I swear by the Rabb of the Eastern Lands and the Western lands! Certainly We are Capable—
عَلَىٰٓ أَن نُّبَدِّلَ خَيۡرًا مِّنۡهُمۡ وَمَا نَحۡنُ بِمَسۡبُوقِينَ ۝	41. of replacing (them) with better than themselves, and We cannot be defeated.

فَذَرْهُمْ يَخُوضُوا۟ وَيَلْعَبُوا۟ حَتَّىٰ يُلَـٰقُوا۟ يَوْمَهُمُ ٱلَّذِى يُوعَدُونَ ۝	42. So leave them alone, let them make idle talk and let them play, till they meet their Day which they are promised—
يَوْمَ يَخْرُجُونَ مِنَ ٱلْأَجْدَاثِ سِرَاعًا كَأَنَّهُمْ إِلَىٰ نُصُبٍ يُوفِضُونَ ۝	43. the Day they will hastily come out of the graves, as if they were running toward a target—
خَـٰشِعَةً أَبْصَـٰرُهُمْ تَرْهَقُهُمْ ذِلَّةٌ ذَٰلِكَ ٱلْيَوْمُ ٱلَّذِى كَانُوا۟ يُوعَدُونَ ۝	44. their looks cast down, disgrace covering them. Such is the Day which they have been promised.

Explanation:

36–37. After stating the eight core duties of believers in āyāt 22 through 35, now a different group of people are being discussed. They are the people who distanced themselves from the truth and believe in ideologies full of weaknesses and contradictions. They are mentioned as those who disbelieve (*alladhīna kafaru*). By definition, a *kafir* is one who covers, hides, or rejects the truth. They are seen rushing madly in front of you—the Messenger (S), and in a wider context, the believers. They are said to come from every corner, symbolically mentioned as from the right and from the left. The reason they are mentioned rushing in groups is to point out that their strength arises from collective opinions, and due to the sheer numbers of their congregation, this seems to cover their inherent weaknesses and contradictions.

38. The āyah addressed those people mentioned in the previous two āyāt. They do not believe in accountability, the Awakening and the Day of Judgment. The question is: are all of them hoping to avoid judgment and enter Paradise? The answer is: never (*kallā*), mentioned in the first part of the next āyah.

39. The participle *kallā*, meaning "never," is used as an answer to the question posed in the previous āyah. Allāh (swt) does not mention the substance from which He created people, because they know it. The reference could be about insignificant germ cells from which Allāh (swt) creates new human beings. The reference could be about "dust"—the insignificant substance from which Allāh (swt) created human beings. The reference could also be about the organic and inorganic sources. Because nobody else but Allāh (swt) can create, He is speaking here in the first person, (*khalaqna*, We have created).

40. Because Allāh (swt) can create, He also has the ability to replace any of His creations. Therefore, in both instances, Allāh (swt) is speaking in the first person. However, in the beginning of the āyah, Rasulūllāh (S) is speaking on behalf of the Creator. Who is He and what are His capabilities? He is mentioned as Rabb to emphasize the inner attributes of the name—the cherisher, the creator, the evolver, the provider, the regulator, the ruler, the sustainer, to name a few. Further, He is mentioned as the Rabb of the Eastern points of sunrise or the Western points of sunrise (*mashriqi* and *maghribi*). The words are used as plurals, indicating there are multiple points of sunrise and sunset in a calendar year. This expression indicates and confirms that Allāh's (swt) dominion is not localized, but extends everywhere, including what would be known in modern times as the East and the West (55:17; 70:40; 73:9).

41. In the previous āyah, the name Rabb is used because He is capable of removing the sinful communities and nations and replacing them with better ones—an act that requires the attributes of Rabb. This is not just a warning, but history has plenty of examples when Allāh (swt) actually replaced a sinning community or nation with a better nation. We should remember that He never replaces a righteous community, but He only replaces sinning communities.

42. Rasulūllāh (S), and through him all the believers, are asked to leave these sinful people alone. They engage in idle, useless and unfounded talk to justify their blind following of a path that is not divinely approved. At other times they assume that fun and amusement are all that matters in life, thereby their spiritual objectives in life remain grossly neglected.

43–44. On the Day of Awakening, all the people who are in graves will come back to life. Those who wasted their lives in fun and amusement and never bothered to fulfill their spiritual duties will have a horrific experience. They will be rushing toward their target (*nusub*), which is nothing but a place to undergo punishment. The word *nasaba* also means difficulty, distress, or trouble. Thus, the target they will be rushing toward will also be the cause of their distress. Their looks will be downcast because they will realize they wasted their earthly lives. Disgrace will cover them from all sides. This inevitable Day was promised to them during their earthly lives and now they will meet their fate. This is the day they mockingly questioned (āyah 1), and this is the day they will ultimately face.

Words to know:

قَبِلَ: to accept, to admit. قَبْلُ: before, formerly. قِبْلَة: towards the direction of. أَقبَلَ: to come near, to rush upon.

طَمِعَ: to covet, to desire. طَمَعُ: desire, longing.

بَدَّلَ: to change, تَبدِيلًا: change, exchange, replace.

خَشَعَ: to be submissive, to humble. خُشُوعُ: humility, خَاشِعُ: one who humbles himself, desolate, lowering.

رَهِقَ: to follow closely, to cover. تَرهَقُ: she covers, will cover. رَهقٌ: arrogance, conceit.

ذَلَّ: to be low, submissive. ذُلُّ: meekness, submissiveness. أَذَلُّوا: vile, meanest.

Sūrah Al-Ma'ārij
Word-by-word meaning

ٱلرَّحِيمِ	ٱلرَّحْمَـٰنِ	ٱللَّهِ	بِسۡمِ
the Most-Rewarding	the Most-Kind	Allāh	In the name of

قِبَلَكَ	كَفَرُواْ	ٱلَّذِينَ	فَمَالِ
from you	disbelieve	those who	but what is the matter with

مُهْطِعِينَ ۳٦ — that they hasten to you. | عَنِ — from | ٱلْيَمِينِ — the right | وَعَنِ — and from

ٱلشِّمَالِ — the left | عِزِينَ ۲۷ — in groups | أَيَطْمَعُ — does hope | كُلُّ — every

آمِرِئٍ — man | مِّنْهُم — of them | أَن — to | يُدْخَلَ — be entered

جَنَّةَ — the Paradise of | نَعِيمٍ ۳۸ — delight. | كَلَّا — never | إِنَّا — surely We

خَلَقْنَـٰهُم — have created them | مِّمَّا — out of that which | يَعْلَمُونَ ۳۹ — they know. | فَلَا — so

أُقْسِمُ — I swear | بِرَبِّ — by the Rabb of | ٱلْمَشْرِقِ — Eastern Lands | وَٱلْمَغْرِبِ — and the Western Lands

إِنَّا — that surely We | لَقَـٰدِرُونَ ٤۰ — are Capable | عَلَىٰ — to | أَن — that

نُبَدِّلَ — We replace (them) | خَيْرًا — by better | مِّنْهُم — than them | وَمَا — and not

نَحْنُ — We | بِمَسْبُوقِينَ ٤۱ — are to be outrun. | فَذَرْهُمْ — so leave them | تَخُوضُوا۟ — to plunge in vain talk

وَيَلْعَبُوا۟ — and play about | حَتَّىٰ — until | يُلَـٰقُوا۟ — they meet | يَوْمَهُمْ — their day

ٱلَّذِى — which | يُوعَدُونَ ٤۲ — they are promised. | يَوْمَ — the Day when | تَخْرُجُونَ — they will come out

مِنَ — of | ٱلْأَجْدَاثِ — the graves | سِرَاعًا — quickly | كَأَنَّهُم — as if they

خَٰشِعَةً	يُوفِضُونَ ٤٣	نُصُبٍ	إِلَىٰ
lowered in fear and humility	racing.	a goal	to
ذَٰلِكَ	ذِلَّةٌ	تَرْهَقُهُمْ	أَبْصَٰرُهُمْ
that is	disgrace	covering them	with their eyes
يُوعَدُونَ ٤٤	كَانُوا	ٱلَّذِى	ٱلْيَوْمُ
promised.	they were	which	the Day

A few applications of the message:

For those who oppose Islam and remain negligent about their moral and spiritual duties, Allāh (swt) asks us to leave them alone. They are preoccupied with the idle pursuits of life and forget that one day, they will meet the Promised Day.

We should never slacken our moral and spiritual duties and never forget that we are accountable for our deeds. We cannot live like animals, one day at a time, but we must "see" the consequences of our deeds on the Day of Accounting. We must also endeavor to achieve a higher goal in the Hereafter.

The Hereafter is not the only place where we will face the consequences of our deeds. Allāh (swt) says that in this life, He can create a better nation in our place and replace us. Such replacement may not happen through a sudden calamity, but it can happen through gradual losses, which is even more painful. The only way we can prevent this from happening is by remaining aware of our relationship with Allāh (swt) and following His commands meticulously.

Review questions:

1. Can every person enter Paradise? Explain your answer based on sūrah Al Ma'arij.
2. What is the significance of Rabb of Eastern Lands and Rabb of Western Lands?
3. Why does Allāh (swt) replace some communities? What does He do after replacing them?
4. Based on sūrah Al Ma'arij, explain the condition of the guilty on the Day of Judgment.

Sūrah 71

Part A

Revealed in Makkah

Nûh

Nūh

Introduction:

The previous sūrah cautioned guilty people about the certainty of punishment. This sūrah provides an actual example of the punishment—from the life and mission of Nūh (A). The sūrah advises us to worship Allāh (swt) and lead a righteous life. It will help us avert punishment in this life and in the Hereafter. The sūrah reminds us about Allāh's (swt) grand design in making the earth habitable and helping our civilization progress.

بِسْمِ ٱللَّهِ ٱلرَّحْمَـٰنِ ٱلرَّحِيمِ

In the name of Allāh, the most Kind, the most Rewarding.

1. إِنَّآ أَرْسَلْنَا نُوحًا إِلَىٰ قَوْمِهِۦٓ أَنْ أَنذِرْ قَوْمَكَ مِن قَبْلِ أَن يَأْتِيَهُمْ عَذَابٌ أَلِيمٌ ۝

Surely We sent Nūh to his people, saying: "Warn your people before there comes to them a painful punishment."

2. قَالَ يَـٰقَوْمِ إِنِّى لَكُمْ نَذِيرٌ مُّبِينٌ ۝

He said: "O my people! certainly I am a plain warner to you—

3. أَنِ ٱعْبُدُوا۟ ٱللَّهَ وَٱتَّقُوهُ وَأَطِيعُونِ ۝

"that—'Worship Allāh and revere Him and obey me.'

4. يَغْفِرْ لَكُم مِّن ذُنُوبِكُمْ وَيُؤَخِّرْكُمْ إِلَىٰٓ أَجَلٍ مُّسَمًّى ۚ إِنَّ أَجَلَ ٱللَّهِ إِذَا جَآءَ لَا يُؤَخَّرُ ۖ لَوْ كُنتُمْ تَعْلَمُونَ ۝

"He will forgive you for some of your sins, and respite you until a fixed term. Surely the term of Allāh when it comes cannot be deferred. Would that you knew!"

5. قَالَ رَبِّ إِنِّى دَعَوْتُ قَوْمِى لَيْلًا وَنَهَارًا ۝

He said: "My Rabb! I have indeed called my people night and day,

فَلَمْ يَزِدْهُمْ دُعَآءِىٓ إِلَّا فِرَارًا ۝

6. "but my calling did not increase them in anything but aversion.

وَإِنِّى كُلَّمَا دَعَوْتُهُمْ لِتَغْفِرَ لَهُمْ جَعَلُوٓاْ أَصَـٰبِعَهُمْ فِىٓ ءَاذَانِهِمْ وَٱسْتَغْشَوْاْ ثِيَابَهُمْ وَأَصَرُّواْ وَٱسْتَكْبَرُواْ ٱسْتِكْبَارًا ۝

7. "And surely whenever I called them that You might forgive them, they put their fingers into their ears, and wrapped themselves with their clothes, and they persisted and behaved proudly with a great pride.

ثُمَّ إِنِّى دَعَوْتُهُمْ جِهَارًا ۝

8. "Then indeed I have invited them loudly,

ثُمَّ إِنِّىٓ أَعْلَنتُ لَهُمْ وَأَسْرَرْتُ لَهُمْ إِسْرَارًا ۝

9. "and indeed I made announcements to them, and I talked to them privately a private setting;

فَقُلْتُ ٱسْتَغْفِرُواْ رَبَّكُمْ إِنَّهُۥ كَانَ غَفَّارًا ۝

10. "and I told them—Ask forgiveness of your Rabb. Surely He is ever-Forgiving;

يُرْسِلِ ٱلسَّمَآءَ عَلَيْكُم مِّدْرَارًا ۝

11. "He will send down rain upon you abundantly,

وَيُمْدِدْكُم بِأَمْوَٰلٍ وَبَنِينَ وَيَجْعَل لَّكُمْ جَنَّـٰتٍ وَيَجْعَل لَّكُمْ أَنْهَـٰرًا ۝

12. "and He will increase you in wealth and children, and He will provide for you gardens and assign to you rivers.

مَّا لَكُمْ لَا تَرْجُونَ لِلَّهِ وَقَارًا ۝

13. "What is the matter with you that you do not expect greatness from Allāh,

وَقَدْ خَلَقَكُمْ أَطْوَارًا ۝

14. "while He has certainly created you by stages?

أَلَمْ تَرَوْاْ كَيْفَ خَلَقَ ٱللَّهُ سَبْعَ سَمَـٰوَٰتٍ طِبَاقًا ۝

15. "Do you not see how Allāh has created seven heavens in layers,

وَجَعَلَ ٱلْقَمَرَ فِيهِنَّ نُورًا وَجَعَلَ ٱلشَّمْسَ سِرَاجًا ۝

16. "and He has set in them the moon as a light, and has made the sun as a Lamp?

وَٱللَّهُ أَنۢبَتَكُم مِّنَ ٱلْأَرْضِ نَبَاتًا ۝

17. "And Allāh has caused you to grow out of the earth as a vegetation.

18. ثُمَّ يُعِيدُكُمْ فِيهَا وَيُخْرِجُكُمْ إِخْرَاجًا ۝

"Then He causes you to return to it, and He will bring you forth a bringing forth.

19. وَٱللَّهُ جَعَلَ لَكُمُ ٱلْأَرْضَ بِسَاطًا ۝

"And Allāh has made the earth a wide expanse for you,

20. لِتَسْلُكُوا مِنْهَا سُبُلًا فِجَاجًا ۝

"that you may go along on it on spacious paths."

Explanation:

1. The previous sūrah cautioned guilty people about the certainty of punishment. This sūrah begins with an actual example of the punishment—from the life and mission of Nūh (A). The fate of Nūh's (A) community was known to the Makkan audience, but they did not know why they were punished. The rest of the sūrah explains the reasons, but at the very beginning, the warning of punishment is mentioned for two reasons: (1) it alerts the audience because now they are learning about a specific example, (2) it establishes a principle of Allāh—He would never punish any community without first giving them guidance and warning them of the consequences.

   Nūh (A) was the first major messenger to come after Ādam (A). By then several generations had passed and the population of the world increased. Nūh (A) was sent to a community of people to guide them toward the right path and caution them about punishment if they ignored the guidance.

2-3. The first and foremost divine guidance is nothing other than a command to worship Allāh (swt) and obey the messengers. Obeying the messengers always implied paying attention to the divine message brought by them and following their sunnah (doings, examples).

   Worship and obey carry two different meanings and require different levels of response. The word *i'bud* (you worship) derived from the root word *'abada* (to worship), is a religious devotion whereby one obediently, uncritically and wholeheartedly submits to a divine being. It is a relationship involving a Master and a servant. The word *'abada* also means "to serve." The concept of "service" to Allāh (swt) lies not in mere verbal declaration of the glory of Allāh (swt) and performance of certain rites of service, for example, prayer, fasting, charity, and so forth, but it also contains the entire concept of complete obedience to Him. The concept of service to Allāh (swt) shows complete and utmost humility and submission while all along showing the utmost commitment to "serve" Him in the way He prescribed. To obey (*tā'a*)means "to follow," or "to act upon." Obedience requires following the commands or guidance of the one being obeyed. However, caution must be observed so as not to begin showing devotional submission to the person being obeyed.

4. Nūh (A) communicates to his community a key divine principle—Allāh (swt) will forgive some (*min*) of the sins. Allāh (swt) might forgive some of the sins, particularly those committed in the past, because the right and wrong actions were not defined to them prior to the divine revelations.

   Acceptance of faith would not automatically absolve them from future sins they might commit. Whether or not they will commit future sins can only be known if they were given respite. Therefore, respite (*yuakhira*, to grant reprieve) is a necessary sequel, mentioned immediately after forgiveness, to determine whether people adopt the right course and obey the divine commands.

5–6. The phrase "night and day" implies consistent preaching for a considerable period of time. In the phrase, night is mentioned before day because in the dry, arid region where Nūh (A) lived, people would generally congregate at night for community activities. That was the best time to speak to them. Besides, in Islamic concept, a new day begins with the setting of the sun. Thus, when the sun is completely below the horizon, a new calendar day has begun. No matter when Nūh (A) spoke to them, his message did not inspire anybody. Instead, they became even more opposed to listening to him, let alone obeying him.

7. In order not to listen to Nūh (A), first the people put their fingers in their ears, and then they wrapped themselves with their clothes. Putting fingers in the ears means to shut down the body and mind from listening to the truth. The use of clothing, an external object, to create a barrier is significant. Usually people believe in an ideology based on their inner call. The allegory of clothing is used, first, to indicate these people needed an external stimulus to reject the truth, and, second, in setting up a barrier, they prevented the message from reaching them. The external stimulus came from the leaders and priests. Pride is a forerunner of all sins; it cuts off a person from reality and causes him or her to become blindly attached to his or her own thoughts and beliefs.

8–10. In addition to speaking to the people night and day (āyah 5), Nūh (A) called loudly for their attention and announced to them the divine message. Sometimes private, one-on-one conversation is helpful. Nūh (A) tried that, too. The message of forgiveness appears again and again in his teachings, first in āyah 4, then in āyāt 7 and 10. This is because these people were so deeply involved in a sinful lifestyle that if they submitted to Allāh (swt), they would need some of their sins forgiven.

11. The mention of abundant rain as the first example of divine blessings is significant. In the dry, arid region where Nūh (A) and his community lived, abundant rain would rejuvenate the dead soil, bring about the growth of vegetation and help human settlement. Just as divine guidance rejuvenates dead soil, so also does divine warning bring about punishment. In this story, rainfall carries blessings of a good life. However, if the divine blessing is withdrawn, the same source can be the root of destruction. Elsewhere in the story, we can see "fountains" of the sky were let loose causing the great deluge on the community (11:40; 23:27; 54:11–12).

12. The mention of gardens and rivers, along with wealth and children, provides an imagery of overall prosperity for the believers on earth. The promise of assigning or appointing (ja'ala, to appoint, to place, to make) them rivers is significant because historically, civilizations that settled along the banks of rivers flourished and lasted longer. The gardens and rivers additionally bring to attention the heavenly happiness so often mentioned in the Qur'ān (2:25; 4:57; 13:35; 14:23).

13. Based on the sequence of the passage, it appears that Nūh (A) continued the message of āyāt 13 to 20. However, it is also possible that after briefly mentioning the account of Nūh (A), Rasūlullāh (S) mentioned this passage to his community. Regardless, the purpose of the passage is to emphasize the moral for people in every generation. Appointing gardens and rivers would herald the beginning of a new civilization and prosperity, therefore, people can expect (rajā') to achieve greatness (waqara). However, none of it will happen unless people become righteous.

14. Most of the classical commentators understand the successive stages, mentioned in this āyah, refer to embryonic development in the mother's womb, mentioned in detail in the Qur'ān. Since the āyah does not define what these successive stages of creation are, we cannot limit the interpretation to only embryonic development. It is possible the āyah is referring to the origin of human beings and their

gradual progression from a simple, humble origin to a physically perfected stage of growth (24:45; 29:20; 30:22; 53:32; 76:1).

15. The word "seven" in classical Arabic usage often denotes plurality (see 67:3). The word *tibāqān* (layers) indicates something placed one upon another, consistently, without making them scattered (see usage in 84:19).

16. The moon is compared to a light (*nūr*) and the sun is compared to a lamp (*shirāj*). In Arabic dictionary, *shirāj* refers to anything that emits light on its own. In the Qur'ān, it always refers to the sun. A full moon also emits light, but it reflects light from the sun, therefore, the moon is not *shirāj*.

17. The term *nabāt* denotes the germinating or springing up of plants, and collectively it implies vegetation produced from the ground (see 8:57). In āyah 3:37, the term is also figuratively used to denote the childhood development of Maryam. Here, in the context of human growth, the āyah seems to allude to proliferation of life forms, and the development of the human body, out of the organic and inorganic substances found on earth. The allegory of vegetation growing in stages seems to hint at human development in successive stages, from our primitive beginning to our present-day stage.

18. In the cycle of life, the same earth from which human beings were created is the same earth to which they will return upon their death when they are buried. Their next phase will begin on the Day of Awakening when Allāh (swt) will bring them out with a new life. The word *kharaja* means "to produce," "to bring something out of something." During the Awakening, dead people in their graves will be revived, therefore, the word *yukhriju* means "bringing forth at the time of the Awakening."

19–20. The phrase "spacious path" (*subulan fijājan*) carries two different meanings—both of which can be applied here. The first meaning is relative ease, implied by spaciousness of the path, which people can explore and disperse to various corners of the world. The second meaning is human beings will have the necessary avenues to advance their civilization through the application of ingenuity. Clearly, the second path, as hinted on here, brought human beings to the present-day technologically advanced stage.

Words to know:

نَذَرَ: to caution, to warn. نَذِير: a warner. نُذُور: vows, obligations. نُذُرًا: warning.

مُنْذِرٌ: (singular) a warner.

طَاعَ: to obey, to permit. طَوْعٌ: Obedient. لَا تُطِع: obey not. يَسْتَطِيعُ: he is able, he would consent.

أَخَّرَ: to put back, postpone. أَخِرَة: Hereafter. أُخْرَى: another. يُوَخِّرَ: grant respite.

فَرَّ: to flee, to run away. فِرَارًا: Fleeing. مَفَرّ: place of refuge, refugee.

كَبُرَ: to be hard, to become hard. إِستِكبَارا: to become proud. تَكَبُّر: pride, arrogance.

كِبر: pride. كِبَر: old age, advance in age. كَبِير: leader.

عَلَنَ: to be open, to become known, to make public. أَعلَنتُم: you spoke publicly. عَلَانِيَة: made public.

سَرَّ: to rejoice. سَارَّ: to speak secretly, أَسَرَار: secret, heart. سُرُرٌ: couches.

دَرَّ: to flow plentifully. دُرِّي: glittering, shining. مِدرَار: abundant rain.

طَبَقَ: to cover, to overwhelm. طِبَاقًا: one above other, in stages.

Sūrah Nūh
Word-by-word meaning

ٱلرَّحِيمِ	ٱلرَّحْمَـٰنِ	ٱللَّهِ	بِسْمِ
the most Rewarding	the most Kind	Allāh	In the name of
إِلَىٰ	نُوحًا	أَرْسَلْنَا	إِنَّآ
to	Nūh	sent	surely We
قَوْمَكَ	أَنذِرْ	أَن	قَوْمِهِۦٓ
your people	warn	(saying) to	his people
عَذَابٌ	يَأْتِيَهُم	أَن	مِن قَبْلِ
torment	comes to them	that	before
إِنِّى	يَـٰقَوْمِ	قَالَ	أَلِيمٌ ۝١
surely I am	O my people	He said	a painful
أَنِ	مُّبِينٌ ۝٢	نَذِيرٌ	لَكُمْ
that	a plain.	warner	to you
وَأَطِيعُونِ ۝٣	وَٱتَّقُوهُ	ٱللَّهَ	ٱعْبُدُواْ
and obey me	be dutiful to Him	Allāh	you should worship
ذُنُوبِكُمْ	مِّن	لَكُم	يَغْفِرْ
your sins	of	you	He will forgive
مُّسَمًّى	أَجَلٍ	إِلَىٰٓ	وَيُؤَخِّرْكُمْ
an appointed	term	to	and respite you
إِذَا	ٱللَّهِ	أَجَلَ	إِنَّ
when	Allāh	a term of	surely
لَوْ	يُؤَخَّرُ	لَا	جَآءَ
if	be delayed	cannot	it comes

كُنتُمْ	تَعْلَمُونَ ④	قَالَ	رَبِّ
you but	know.	he said	O my Rabb
إِنِّى	دَعَوْتُ	قَوْمِى	لَيْلًا
verily I	have called	my people	night
وَنَهَارًا ⑤	فَلَمْ	يَزِدْهُمْ	دُعَآءِى
and day.	but not	increased them	all my calling
إِلَّا	فِرَارًا ⑥	وَإِنِّى	كُلَّمَا
but	aversion.	and surely I	every time
دَعَوْتُهُمْ	لِتَغْفِرَ	لَهُمْ	جَعَلُوٓا
I called unto them	that you might forgive	them	they put
أَصَٰبِعَهُمْ	فِى	ءَاذَانِهِمْ	وَٱسْتَغْشَوْا
their fingers	into	their ears	covered themselves up
ثِيَابَهُمْ	وَأَصَرُّوا	وَٱسْتَكْبَرُوا	ٱسْتِكْبَارًا ⑦
with their garments	and persisted	and behaved	in pride.
ثُمَّ	إِنِّى	دَعَوْتُهُمْ	جِهَارًا ⑧
then	indeed I	called to them	openly.
ثُمَّ	إِنِّى	أَعْلَنتُ	لَهُمْ
then	indeed I	proclaimed in public	to them
وَأَسْرَرْتُ	لَهُمْ	إِسْرَارًا ⑨	فَقُلْتُ
and I secretly appealed	to them	in private.	I said
ٱسْتَغْفِرُوا	رَبَّكُمْ	إِنَّهُ	كَانَ
ask forgiveness from	your Rabb	surely He	is
غَفَّارًا ⑩	يُرْسِلِ	ٱلسَّمَآءَ	عَلَيْكُم
Oft-Forgiving.	He will send	the sky (rain)	to you

وَبَنِينَ	بِأَمْوَٰلٍ	وَيُمْدِدْكُم	مِّدْرَارًا ⑪
and children	in wealth	and increase you in	in abundance.
وَتَجْعَل	جَنَّٰتٍ	لَّكُمْ	وَتَجْعَل
and bestow	gardens	on you	and bestow
لَا	مَّا لَكُمْ	أَنْهَٰرًا ⑫	لَّكُمْ
not	what is the matter with you	rivers.	on you
وَقَدْ	وَقَارًا ⑬	لِلَّهِ	تَرْجُونَ
and surely	any respect.	for Allāh	you expect
تَرَوْا۟	أَلَمْ	أَطْوَارًا ⑭	خَلَقَكُمْ
see you	do not	in stages.	He has created you
سَبْعَ	ٱللَّهُ	خَلَقَ	كَيْفَ
the seven	Allāh	has created	how
ٱلْقَمَرَ	وَجَعَلَ	طِبَاقًا ⑮	سَمَٰوَٰتٍ
the moon	and has made	one above another	heavens
ٱلشَّمْسَ	وَجَعَلَ	نُورًا	فِيهِنَّ
the sun	and made	a light	therein
مِّنَ	أَنۢبَتَكُم	وَٱللَّهُ	سِرَاجًا ⑯
from	has brought you forth	and Allāh	a lamp.
يُعِيدُكُمْ	ثُمَّ	نَبَاتًا ⑰	ٱلْأَرْضِ
He will return you	then	as a growth.	the earth
وَٱللَّهُ	إِخْرَاجًا ⑱	وَيُخْرِجُكُمْ	فِيهَا
and Allāh	forth.	and bring you	into it
بِسَاطًا ⑲	ٱلْأَرْضَ	لَكُمْ	جَعَلَ
wide spread.	the earth	for you	has made

فِجَاجًا ٢	سُبُلًا	مِنْهَا	لِّتَسْلُكُوا
spacious	(on) roads	therein	that you may go about

A few applications of the message:

The narrative of Nūh (A) is fascinating, but the moral lesson is extremely important to remember. Allāh (swt) did not narrate the story for an academic purpose or to provide casual reading material that can be read and forgotten. Using the narrative of Nūh (A), Allāh (swt) communicated some of the key messages of Islam. We can summarize these messages in the following ways:

1. Worship Allāh (swt) and follow His messenger

2. Ask for the forgiveness of Allāh (swt) because He is ever-Forgiving.

3. Our term of life is fixed and we cannot defer it.

None of us will live forever. Our life on this earth is for a short duration and it is fixed. Within this lifetime, we have to do everything possible so that our eternal life in the Hereafter is not jeopardized. We are solely responsible for what happens to us in the Hereafter. We must take control of our lives. We can do this by worshipping Allāh (swt) and following our Messenger (S). Our lives will have many challenges and we might fall into temptation and traps. But we should always remember that Allāh (swt) is ever-Forgiving. We should never lose hope of receiving divine forgiveness. To earn His forgiveness, we must turn to Him with repentance. If Allāh (swt) forgives us, then nothing else matters—we will be admitted into Paradise.

Review questions:

1. What core message of Islam did Nūh (A) convey to his people?

2. In āyah 4, why did Nūh (A) say "some" of their sins might be forgiven?

3. Explain the preaching methodologies Nūh (A) employed to reach out to his people.

4. What were some of the blessings that Nūh (A) assured his people would be provided if they became righteous?

5. What are some of the examples Nūh (A) gave his people to explain Allāh's (swt) almightiness and His blessings for mankind?

6. What is the significance of "spacious paths" as mentioned in āyah 20?

Sūrah 71
Part B

Revealed in Makkah

Nūh

Nūh

Introduction:

Nūh (A) preached and advised his people during his entire lifetime, but very few people believed the message. Most people remained loyal to their deities and idols. The leaders mislead people and encouraged wrongdoing. Nūh (A) prayed to Allāh (swt) to save him, his parents and the believers, and destroy the evil community because it prevented people from accepting truth. As a result of this prayer, Allāh (S) destroyed the community through a massive flood.

بِسۡمِ ٱللَّهِ ٱلرَّحۡمَٰنِ ٱلرَّحِيمِ

In the name of Allāh, the most Kind, the most Rewarding.

قَالَ نُوحٌ رَّبِّ إِنَّهُمۡ عَصَوۡنِي وَٱتَّبَعُوا۟ مَن لَّمۡ يَزِدۡهُ مَالُهُۥ وَوَلَدُهُۥٓ إِلَّا خَسَارًا ۝	21. Nūh said: "My Rabb! They have indeed disobeyed me, and followed him whose wealth and children have not increased him in anything but loss.
وَمَكَرُوا۟ مَكۡرًا كُبَّارًا ۝	22. "And they have plotted a mighty plot."
وَقَالُوا۟ لَا تَذَرُنَّ ءَالِهَتَكُمۡ وَلَا تَذَرُنَّ وَدًّا وَلَا سُوَاعًا وَلَا يَغُوثَ وَيَعُوقَ وَنَسۡرًا ۝	23. And they say: "Do not forsake your deities, and do not forsake Wadd, nor Suwaʿ, neither Yaghūth and Yaʿūq and Nasr."
وَقَدۡ أَضَلُّوا۟ كَثِيرًا وَلَا تَزِدِ ٱلظَّٰلِمِينَ إِلَّا ضَلَٰلًا ۝	24. And they have already mislead many, and you will not increase the wrong doers in anything except straying!
مِّمَّا خَطِيٓـَٰٔتِهِمۡ أُغۡرِقُوا۟ فَأُدۡخِلُوا۟ نَارًا فَلَمۡ يَجِدُوا۟ لَهُم مِّن دُونِ ٱللَّهِ أَنصَارًا ۝	25. Because of their sins they were drowned, so they were admitted into Fire; then they could not find for themselves any helpers besides Allāh.

وَقَالَ نُوحٌ رَّبِّ لَا تَذَرْ عَلَى ٱلْأَرْضِ مِنَ ٱلْكَفِرِينَ دَيَّارًا ﴿٢٦﴾

26. And Nūh said: "My Rabb! Do not leave on the land any inhabitant of the Unbelievers.

إِنَّكَ إِن تَذَرْهُمْ يُضِلُّواْ عِبَادَكَ وَلَا يَلِدُوٓاْ إِلَّا فَاجِرًا كَفَّارًا ﴿٢٧﴾

27. "Because if You leave them, they will mislead Your bondsmen, and they will not procreate any except an immoral, an unbeliever.

رَّبِّ ٱغْفِرْ لِى وَلِوَٰلِدَىَّ وَلِمَن دَخَلَ بَيْتِىَ مُؤْمِنًا وَلِلْمُؤْمِنِينَ وَٱلْمُؤْمِنَتِ وَلَا تَزِدِ ٱلظَّٰلِمِينَ إِلَّا تَبَارًا ﴿٢٨﴾

28. "My Rabb! Forgive me and my parents, and whoever enters my house as a Believer, and the believing men and the believing women. And do not increase the wrongdoers in anything but destruction."

Explanation:

21–22. In this section, Nūh (A) expresses his disappointment in dealing with his people. Years of earnest effort to guide the community yielded very few results. Earlier, in āyah 7, we noted three ways people did not pay attention to Nūh (A)—they had too much pride, they put fingers in their ears and they covered themselves up with clothing—all of which were used to block out the message. Now, in āyah 21, we learn from Nūh (A) that people followed their chiefs who were powerful and influential. In the past, having wealth and children was considered to be a sign of one's prosperity and power. In the history of human civilization, influential and powerful people always controlled the belief systems of ordinary people and prevented them from accepting truth. These chiefs did not benefit ordinary people in any manner—they would only cause their moral and spiritual loss. The *makrān kubbārān* (mighty plot) refers to their plot to harm Nūh (A) in many ways, including stoning to death (26:116).

23. Each of the five gods worshipped in the past had specific features and a particular role. *Wadd* was a male deity, *Suwa'* was a female deity, *Yaghūth* was a lion-god, *Ya'ūq* was a horse-god and *Nasr* was an eagle-god. Many of these pre-Islamic ancient gods were introduced in Arabia in various denominations and seem to have existed at the time of Rasūlullāh (S). The influential and wealthy leaders controlled the belief systems of common people, and the people were told not to abandon these gods but to continue devotional dedication to them. The word *tadharuna*, derived from *wadhara* (to abandon, to neglect) is used twice in the āyat to indicate the leaders applied great pressure on the people not to abandon the idols.

24. The idols have no power to act in any manner let alone influence people. The pronoun "they" in *adhallū* (they have led astray) refers to the leaders. The wealthy, powerful and influential leaders had so much control over the belief systems of the ordinary people that even after Nūh's (A) teachings, nobody was convinced. In every generation, the leaders so successfully and so convincingly mislead their people into believing a false ideology that the more a prophet or a righteous person preached to them, the further they moved away from truth.

25. The drowning of Nūh's (A) community in a massive flood is well known to all. No details are given here, but the Qur'ān mentions it in several āyāt (7:64; 21:77; 23:27; 25:37; 26:120). After the drowning, they entered the fire. The use of past tense indicates the certainty of punishment, as if the punishment in fire already happened; therefore, there is no escape from it. Although they worshipped five idols in particular, as mentioned in āyah 23, these idols were of no help to them during the crisis. They realized that other than Allāh (swt), nobody else could have helped them.

26–27. In the concluding āyāt, two prayers of Nūh (A) are mentioned. The first prayer is for the community, and the second prayer is for his own family and close companions.

After the deluge, Nūh (A) established a new community with a few believers. The non-believers were already drowned; therefore, this prayer is forward-looking in its intention. Nūh (A) had the bitter experience of witnessing how the non-believers craftily mislead the believers and would-be believers into wrongdoing (āyah 24). So shrewd and manipulative were their arguments that if any non-believer remained among them, their children and subsequent generations would inherit the same false ideologies, and they, in turn, corrupt the believers. The prayer was, as always, granted as his teachings were given continuance for nearly a millennium (29:14).

28. In this second prayer, Nūh (A) prays particularly for his family and close companions. He begins the prayer by seeking forgiveness for any of his shortcomings (11:47). When messengers seek forgiveness, it is not because they committed a sin, but because they seek protection from committing any sin. Such prayer also shows their humbleness and their admission that human beings are likely to commit sins unknowingly. Unless they have Allāh's (swt) protection, even messengers can fall into wrongdoing. His wife and son were already drowned during the great flood because they were sinners. This prayer does not specifically include spouse and children, but includes all those who might enter the house as a believer and all believing men and women. Broadly speaking, the prayer includes spouse and children if they are believers. In this āyah, "my house" (*baytiya*) not only stands for his personal residence, but also those residences that worship Allāh (swt) and embrace the same viewpoints of Nūh (A). In an ideal society envisioned by Islam, wrongdoing of any type cannot be supported. Therefore, the prayer further seeks the destruction of all evil schemes and of evil itself, regardless of where evil originates.

Words to know:

مَكَرَ: to plan a scheme. مَكرٌ: plan, plot. مَاكِرِين: planner.

غَرِقَ: to sink. غَرَق: drowning. إِسْتَغْرَق: to exceed (the bounds).

دَارَ: to go around, to revolve. دِيَار: house, dwelling, mansion. دَيَار: inhabitants of a place.

Sūrah Nūh
Word-by-word meaning

ٱلرَّحِيمِ	ٱلرَّحۡمَـٰنِ	ٱللَّهِ	بِسۡمِ
the most Rewarding	the most Kind	Allāh	In the name of
إِنَّهُمۡ	رَّبِّ	نُوحٌ	قَالَ
surely they	my Rabb	Nūh	said
لَّمۡ	مَن	وَٱتَّبَعُوٰاْ	عَصَوۡنِي
not	one	and followed	disobeyed me
إِلَّا	وَوَلَدُهُۥ	مَالُهُۥ	يَزِدۡهُ
but	and his children	his wealth	give him increase
كُبَّارًا ٢٢	مَكۡرًا	وَمَكَرُواْ	خَسَارًا ٢١
a mighty	plot	and they have plotted	loss
ءَالِهَتَكُمۡ	تَذَرُنَّ	لَا	وَقَالُواْ
your gods	you shall leave	not	and they have said
وَلَا	وَدًّا	تَذَرُنَّ	وَلَا
nor	Wadd	shall you leave	nor
وَيَعُوقَ	يَغُوثَ	وَلَا	سُوَاعًا
not Ya'ūq	Yaghūth	nor	Suwa'
كَثِيرًا	أَضَلُّواْ	وَقَدۡ	وَنَسۡرًا ٢٣
many	they have led astray	and indeed	nor Nasr
إِلَّا	ٱلظَّـٰلِمِينَ	تَزِدِ	وَلَا
but	the wrongdoers	did increase	and not
أُغۡرِقُواْ	خَطِيٓـَٔـٰتِهِمۡ	مِّمَّا	ضَلَـٰلًا ٢٤
they were drowned	their sins	because of	error

تَجِدُواْ	فَلَمْ	نَارًا	فَأُدْخِلُواْ
they found	and not	the fire	they were made to enter
أَنصَارًا ۝	ٱللَّهِ	مِّن دُونِ	هُم
any help.	Allāh	instead of	for them
لَا	رَّبِّ	نُوحٌ	وَقَالَ
not	my Rabb	Nūh	and said
مِنَ	ٱلْأَرْضِ	عَلَى	تَذَرْ
of	the earth	on	leave
إِن	إِنَّكَ	دَيَّارًا ۝	ٱلْكَـٰفِرِينَ
if	surely you	any inhabitant.	the disbelievers
وَلَا	عِبَادَكَ	يُضِلُّواْ	تَذَرْهُمْ
and not	your slaves	they will mislead	you leave them
كَفَّارًا ۝	فَاجِرًا	إِلَّا	يَلِدُواْ
disbelievers.	wicked	but	they will beget
وَلِوَٰلِدَيَّ	لِى	ٱغْفِرْ	رَّبِّ
and my parents	me	forgive	my Rabb
مُؤْمِنًا	بَيْتِىَ	دَخَلَ	وَلِمَن
as a believer	my home	enters	and him who
تَزِدِ	وَلَا	وَٱلْمُؤْمِنَـٰتِ	وَلِلْمُؤْمِنِينَ
grant you increase	and not	women	and all the believing men
	تَبَارًا ۝	إِلَّا	ٱلظَّـٰلِمِينَ
	destruction.	but	the wrongdoers

A few applications of the message:

We should remember that the stories of past communities are narrated to us to make us better people. The punishment story of Nūh's (A) community points out the following:

1. Obeying false principles and the wrong people always causes loss in this life and in the Hereafter.

2. Allāh (swt) never punishes people without giving them a warning and time to repent.

3. When Allāh's (swt) punishment arrives, it can be very severe.

4. Allāh's (swt) punishment can take place in this world and in the Hereafter.

5. Allāh's (swt) punishment can take place all of a sudden and in ways that people cannot anticipate.

6. Allāh (swt) is ever Forgiving.

We should always remain alert not to follow false principles and the wrong people. Sometimes it may appear confusing as to which approach is right and which one is wrong. There is one easy solution to solve such confusion. Submit to Allāh (swt) wholeheartedly and seek His guidance. Stay on the course of the Messenger (S). With the help of Allāh (swt), it is always possible to avoid the wrong course in life. Our focus in this life should be to do righteous deeds. We should always remember not to do anything that would displease Allāh (swt). If we realize that we made a mistake, we should immediately seek Allāh's (swt) forgiveness and never lose hope of receiving His mercy.

Review questions:

1. What are the names of five deities Nūh's (A) people worshipped?

2. What are the ways that people did not listen to Nūh (A)?

3. Why did Nūh (A) pray to Allāh (swt) not to leave any evil people on the earth?

4. What punishment did the evil people in Nūh's (A) community suffer?

5. Explain the significance of Nūh's (A) prayer as mentioned in āyah 28.

Sūrah 72

Part A

Revealed in Makkah

Al-Jinn

The Jinn

Introduction:

Sūrah Jinn was revealed shortly after Rasūlullāh (S) returned from an unsuccessful trip to Tā'if. While the majority of the Makkan people rejected the message of Islam, and people of Tā'if scorned it, Rasūlullāh (S) found a strange group interested in the message. This group was the jinn. They listened to the Qur'ān and believed in its message. This sūrah provides clues to their identity and proceeds to describe their faith and conduct prior to their accepting Islam.

بِسْمِ ٱللَّهِ ٱلرَّحْمَـٰنِ ٱلرَّحِيمِ

In the name of Allāh, the most Kind, the most Rewarding.

1. قُلْ أُوحِىَ إِلَىَّ أَنَّهُ ٱسْتَمَعَ نَفَرٌ مِّنَ ٱلْجِنِّ فَقَالُوٓاْ إِنَّا سَمِعْنَا قُرْءَانًا عَجَبًا ۝

   SAY: "It has been revealed to me that a party of the jinn listened; so they said: 'Surely we have heard a wonderful Qur'ān,

2. يَهْدِىٓ إِلَى ٱلرُّشْدِ فَـَٔامَنَّا بِهِۦ ۖ وَلَن نُّشْرِكَ بِرَبِّنَآ أَحَدًا ۝

   'guiding toward righteousness—so we have believed in it. And we shall never associate anyone with our Rabb,

3. وَأَنَّهُۥ تَعَٰلَىٰ جَدُّ رَبِّنَا مَا ٱتَّخَذَ صَٰحِبَةً وَلَا وَلَدًا ۝

   'and that He—exalted be the Majesty of our Rabb— He has not taken a consort, nor a child,

4. وَأَنَّهُۥ كَانَ يَقُولُ سَفِيهُنَا عَلَى ٱللَّهِ شَطَطًا ۝

   'and that the foolish among us used to say against Allāh extravagant lies,

5. وَأَنَّا ظَنَنَّآ أَن لَّن تَقُولَ ٱلْإِنسُ وَٱلْجِنُّ عَلَى ٱللَّهِ كَذِبًا ۝

   'and that we thought that the men and the jinn would never speak a lie against Allāh';

وَأَنَّهُۥ كَانَ رِجَالٌ مِّنَ ٱلْإِنسِ يَعُوذُونَ بِرِجَالٍ مِّنَ ٱلْجِنِّ فَزَادُوهُمْ رَهَقًا ۝

6. "and that men from among the people used to take refuge with men of the jinn, so they increased them in evil practices;

وَأَنَّهُمْ ظَنُّوا۟ كَمَا ظَنَنتُمْ أَن لَّن يَبْعَثَ ٱللَّهُ أَحَدًا ۝

7. "and that they thought, just as you think, that Allāh would never raise up anyone;

وَأَنَّا لَمَسْنَا ٱلسَّمَآءَ فَوَجَدْنَٰهَا مُلِئَتْ حَرَسًا شَدِيدًا وَشُهُبًا ۝

8. "and that 'We had sought to pry into the heaven, but we have found it filled with strong guards, and with flames;

وَأَنَّا كُنَّا نَقْعُدُ مِنْهَا مَقَٰعِدَ لِلسَّمْعِ ۖ فَمَن يَسْتَمِعِ ٱلْءَانَ يَجِدْ لَهُۥ شِهَابًا رَّصَدًا ۝

9. 'and that we used to sit down on some of the sitting-places to listen; but whoever tries to listen, he now finds a flame in ambush for him;

وَأَنَّا لَا نَدْرِىٓ أَشَرٌّ أُرِيدَ بِمَن فِى ٱلْأَرْضِ أَمْ أَرَادَ بِهِمْ رَبُّهُمْ رَشَدًا ۝

10. 'and that we do not know whether evil is intended for those on the earth, or whether their Rabb intends right guidance;

وَأَنَّا مِنَّا ٱلصَّٰلِحُونَ وَمِنَّا دُونَ ذَٰلِكَ ۖ كُنَّا طَرَآئِقَ قِدَدًا ۝

11. 'and that some among us are the righteous, while some of us are otherwise. We are sects having different ways;

وَأَنَّا ظَنَنَّآ أَن لَّن نُّعْجِزَ ٱللَّهَ فِى ٱلْأَرْضِ وَلَن نُّعْجِزَهُۥ هَرَبًا ۝

12. 'and that we think that we can never frustrate Allāh on the earth, nor can we frustrate Him by flight;

وَأَنَّا لَمَّا سَمِعْنَا ٱلْهُدَىٰٓ ءَامَنَّا بِهِۦ ۖ فَمَن يُؤْمِنۢ بِرَبِّهِۦ فَلَا يَخَافُ بَخْسًا وَلَا رَهَقًا ۝

13. 'and that when we heard the guidance, we believed in it. So whoever believes in his Rabb, then let him not fear withholding nor injustice;

وَأَنَّا مِنَّا ٱلْمُسْلِمُونَ وَمِنَّا ٱلْقَٰسِطُونَ ۖ فَمَنْ أَسْلَمَ فَأُو۟لَٰٓئِكَ تَحَرَّوْا۟ رَشَدًا ۝

14. 'and that some among us are the submitting ones and some of us are the deviators. So whoever submits, these then seek the right way.

وَأَمَّا ٱلْقَـٰسِطُونَ فَكَانُوا۟ لِجَهَنَّمَ حَطَبًا ﴿١٥﴾

15. 'And as to the deviators, they are then the fuel of Hell.'"

وَأَلَّوِ ٱسْتَقَـٰمُوا۟ عَلَى ٱلطَّرِيقَةِ لَأَسْقَيْنَـٰهُم مَّآءً غَدَقًا ﴿١٦﴾

16. And if they keep to the path, We shall certainly provide them with abundant water,

لِّنَفْتِنَهُمْ فِيهِ ۚ وَمَن يُعْرِضْ عَن ذِكْرِ رَبِّهِۦ يَسْلُكْهُ عَذَابًا صَعَدًا ﴿١٧﴾

17. so that We may test them by it. And whoever turns away from the remembrance of his Rabb, He will thrust him into a severe punishment;

وَأَنَّ ٱلْمَسَـٰجِدَ لِلَّهِ فَلَا تَدْعُوا۟ مَعَ ٱللَّهِ أَحَدًا ﴿١٨﴾

18. and that the Masjids are for Allāh, so do not call upon anyone with Allāh;

وَأَنَّهُۥ لَمَّا قَامَ عَبْدُ ٱللَّهِ يَدْعُوهُ كَادُوا۟ يَكُونُونَ عَلَيْهِ لِبَدًا ﴿١٩﴾

19. and that when the Bondsman of Allāh stood up praying to Him, they desire to form a dense crowd over him.

Explanation:

1. This sūrah was revealed two years before Hijrah, when Rasūlullāh (S) was returning from an unsuccessful visit to Tā'if. Shortly before the trip, his wife Khadījah (ra) and uncle Abū Tālib passed away. Rasūlullāh (S) was without any tribal protection. He went to Tā'if seeking shelter and tribal protection, but the people of the city humiliated him and chased him out. On his way to Makkah, he stayed for a few days at Nakhlah, a village predominantly occupied by Arab Christians. At this village, an unusual group listened to his message and accepted faith in Islam. The sūrah provides clue to their identity.

The word *jinn* is derived from *janna*, meaning "he covered," "he concealed," "he hid." A class of invisible creatures of Allāh (swt) is known as jinn because they are concealed from human vision. The Qur'ān uses the term jinn with various shades of meaning, including the invisible creatures. The invisible creatures, jinn, antedate the creation of human beings (15:27). Ancient Arabs worshipped these invisible beings (34:41; 37:158). In common understanding, the term "jinn" became so generalized in its meaning that to most Muslim readers, it has no other meaning other than the invisible creatures. However, another sense of the word is often applied in the Qur'ān, but during casual reading, the generic meaning seems to dominate readers' minds.

In this āyah, Rasūlullāh (S) is asked to reveal that a party of jinn listened to the recitation of the Qur'ān; they concluded that it was beautiful and it contained guidance. Who were these jinn? Were they the invisible creatures? Or, is it possible that they were unknown strangers who listened to the recitation and became convinced of the truth? Based on the root meaning of *janna*, it appears that the *jinn* mentioned in this passage were strangers.

How can we justify this proposition? In sūrah al-Ahqaf, āyat 46:29–31 mentions the invisible beings and their interaction with the Qur'ān. They listened to the Qur'ān and became convinced of its authenticity. Then they returned to their own people and told them something astounding. They said that the Qur'ān confirmed what was before it, guiding everyone toward the truth and toward the right way. They invited their own people to follow Rasūlullāh (S) and believe in Allāh (swt). In āyah 2 of this sūrah, we see them confidently state that they would not associate with Allāh (swt). In āyah 3 of this sūrah, they criticize the Son-of-God theory. All these citations seem to indicate these *jinn* were not generic, invisible creatures, but the word was used to mean "strangers" belonging to some early Christian groups who followed 'Isā (A). Had these jinn in this verse been the invisible beings, their realization of Allāh's oneness, and His majesty is inconsistent, because they knew Allāh long before human beings was created. Furthermore, the Qur'ān was sent as guidance to mankind, not to the invisible beings, therefore, it is unlikely that invisible jinn would search for guidance from the Qur'ān.

2. The reason these jinn believed in the Qur'ān was because its message guided them toward righteousness. The message made sense to them. These jinn knew there were others like them who associated with Allāh (swt). Two Abrahamic faiths that do not associate partners are Judaism and Islam. The only Abrahamic faith that associates with Allāh (swt) is Christianity. The original Christians were all Jewish people, who believed in the oneness of Allāh (swt). However, as Christianity developed, the Son-of-God theory became its central theme. Then they began to associate with Allāh (swt).

3. These jinn admitted that Allāh (swt) does not have a spouse (*swāhib,* meaning spouse, wife) to give birth to a child nor has He adopted a child. Nowhere in the Qur'ān does it state that the invisible beings, jinn, believed Allāh (swt) had a consort or a child. Therefore, this statement of theirs appears odd. However, if we agree that they were strangers from the early Christian faith, the statement does not appear to be strange. It can now be explained why they criticized the Son-of-God theory—they were the early Christians who confidently rejected the Christian doctrine after realizing the truth.

4. There are two lies against Allāh (swt) that qualify to be abominable (*shatat*)—both have to do with the false belief that Allāh (swt) has a consort and a child. Any suggestion that Allāh (swt) has a child is considered to be an extreme blasphemy. The severity of such a blasphemous lie is illustrated elsewhere in the Qur'ān, in āyat 19:88–92, with an allegory of the sky bursting asunder, earth being rent into pieces and mountains crumbling down from the mere utterance of such lies.

5–6. The Qur'ān uses the term *rijal* (meaning man) to denote certain "types" of men who have an inclination towards particular activities (see usages in 4:34; 6:9; 7:46; 24:37; 33:23). The unusual mention of "man (*rijal*) from among the people" and "man (*rijal*) of jinn" indicates that "man" is the common denominator between these groups. If we consider jinn to be some early Christian group, they hoped that nobody would ever speak such blasphemous words against Allāh (swt).

In āyah 6, two groups are mentioned, both having a common alliance to propagate evil practices. One of the groups is the *gentiles*—the non-Israelite people, and the other were the Israelites who were breaking away from Judaism to start Christianity. Early Christianity expanded as more and more gentiles embraced the new religion. Both groups sought refuge with each other in order to get moral support and protection for their temporal and spiritual needs. Consequently, their mutual alliance increases nothing but confusion and evil-doing.

7. The pronoun "they" (*hum* in *wa annahum*) refers to both groups mentioned in the previous āyah—the gentiles and the Israelites, who were breaking away from Judaism to form Christianity. The pronoun

"you" (*tum* in *zanantum*) refers to the Makkan Quraish. The Quraish and other Arab tribes could not accept that Allāh (swt) had chosen an Arab man to become a prophet after Mūsā (A) and 'Isā (A). The Christians, in particular, were convinced that no new prophet would come after their own prophet. Thus, they were opposed to seeing Muhammad (S) as a prophet in the seventh century.

8. In the past, it was assumed that jinn lived in outer space from where they would try to listen to heavenly conversations. The āyah refers to the ancient practice of foretelling the future based on planetary position and predicting good and bad omens. We have to remember that for thousands of years, planetary positions inspired and shaped the beliefs of the earliest civilizations. Hundreds of years before 'Isā (A), the Greek astrological system and the Zodiac concept were adopted by ancient Egyptian, Indian and Roman civilizations. These civilizations and the people in early Christian periods tried to find cosmic meaning in the patterns of stars and planets. The Qur'ān states that heaven is filled with strong guards (*harasān shadīdan*), implying that nothing about the future can be obtained from these planetary positions, and astronomical secrets cannot be easily obtained by guesswork and ordinary observation. Any astrological attempt to understand the cosmic system will result in a worthless end, implied by *shuhabān* (flaming fire).

9. The phrase "the sitting places" (*maqāid*) alludes to ancient observatories and other centers of astrological speculation. After the advent of Islam, the group of jinn realized that the practice of divination from auspices and omen was becoming ineffective because Islam condemns blind belief and superstition. The phrase '*āna yajid* (he now finds) indicates the practice was "now" becoming ineffective.

10. The fortune tellers and soothsayers used to concentrate on the movement of the planets and stars to supposedly control and prevent bad luck. The āyah states that the evil outcomes on earth are not controlled by the soothsayers, rather through all the good and bad events Allāh (swt) intends to guide those who want to ponder the intricacies and mysteries of the universe (21:22).

11. The existence of several sects (*tarāiqun*, paths) among the group of jinn further indicates that they were a group of Christians, not the invisible beings. By the time of Rasūlullāh (S), Christianity was already divided into several branches based on the councils and churches. The righteous ones among them follow the true teachings of 'Isā (A).

12. The group of jinn further attested that they can never destroy Allāh's (swt) plan and it is not possible to escape from His judgment by running away.

13–15. When the jinn heard the recitation of the Qur'ān, some of them were able to acknowledge the truth in it and believed its divine origin. Those who were convinced accepted Islam and the rest remained deviated. The word *qāsitūn* indicates one who acts contrary to a meaning, therefore, a deviator. The deviators will end up as fuel of the fire in the Hereafter. The long report of jinn that started with āyah 1 now comes to an end in āyah 15.

16. Until this āyah, Rasūlullāh (S) narrated verbatim what the strangers—jinn—told their people and how some of them believed in the Qur'ān after listening to its recitation. The audience was the Quraish, not the jinn. In light of the experiences of the jinn, Rasūlullāh (S) now tells his people that if they followed the right path, Allāh (swt) will provide them with abundant rain. Abundant water is used as an example of Allāh's (swt) abundant sustenance. Even if it is taken literally, water is a precious resource in the desert.

17. If we consider the mention of water as the symbol of divine sustenance, Allāh (swt) will test people with it to see if they utilize it in the right manner. As a side note, we may recall that in a story about Tālūt, water is mentioned as a tool to test the Israelites (2:249). Although the story of Tālūt is not relevant here, the underlying principle of the test is the same. The moral of the āyah is: good things provided by Allāh (swt) are not always a token of reward, but they can also be a device to test whether people remain grateful to Allāh (swt) and remember their duties after being endowed with wealth and good times.

18. A masjid is a place to perform *sujud*, or prostration. People should perform prostration only to Allāh (swt), as He is the only one to whom everybody and everything prostrates. All places of prostration (plural, *masājid*), consequently all worship, is due only to Allāh (swt).

19. The person referred to in this āyah is Rasūlullāh (S). The crowding over him by others signifies collective efforts to destabilize the practice of salāt. During the Makkan period, opponents of Islam often attempted to prevent Muslims, particularly Rasūlullāh (S), from performing salāt. In sūrah 'Alaq, it is mentioned that some leaders of the Quraish were guilty of this crime (96:9–10).

Words to know:

نَفَرَ: to run away from fight, run away. إِنفِرُوا: go forth. نُفُورًا: the act of running. نَفَرٌ: people, a small group not exceeding ten. مُسْتَنْفِرَةٌ: fugitive.

رَشَدَ: to follow the right way. رُشْد: right course, true direction. رَشَاد: righteousness. : ٌ َ رَاشِدُون men of righteousness. مُرشِدٌ: director to the right path.

جَدَّ: to be of great dignity, be respectable. جَدُّ: Majesty, glory. جَدِيد: new, unexpected, newly made.

أَخَذَ: to take, to receive. أَخْذٌ: the act of taking, punishment. خُذْ: you take. آخِذٌ: overtaking, punishing, grasp.

سَفِهَ: to be foolish, ignorant. سَفَاهَةٌ: stupidity, folly. سُفَهَاء: those who are foolish.

شَطَّ: to be far off, to wrong someone. شَطَطًا: extravagant lie, exceeding. أَشَطَّ: to act unjustly. شَطَطًا: far from the truth.

ظَنَّ: to think, to assume, to imagine. ظَنَّ: thinking. ظَانِّين: entertainer of evil thoughts.

رَهِقَ: to follow closely, to cover. رَهَقَ: to oppress, to cause to suffer. رَهَقٌ: arrogance, conceit, evil nature.

بَعَثَ: to rise up, to rise up from sleep, to rise from dead. بَعْث: resurrection. مَبْعُوث: sent, raised.

وَجَدَ: to find what was lost, to obtain, to perceive. وَجَد: found.

مَلَأَ: to fill, to satisfy, to help. مُلِئَت: was filled. مِلْئٌ: full. مَلَأٌ: chiefs, leaders.

قَعَدَ: to sit down, to wait, to abstain. قُعُودٌ: the act of sitting. قَوَاعِدُ: foundations. مَقَاعِدُ: sitting places.

رَصَدَ: to watch, to lay in wait. مَرصَدٌ: place of ambush. مِرصَاد: ambush.

عَجَزَ: to lag behind, be powerless. عَجَزَ: to frustrate, be unable.

قَسَطَ: to deal unjustly, to act wrongfully. قِسْط: justice, equity. قَاسِط: one who acts unjustly. قِسطَاس: scale, balance.

Sūrah Al-Jinn
Word-by-word meaning

ٱلرَّحِيمِ	ٱلرَّحْمَٰنِ	ٱللَّهِ	بِسْمِ
the most Rewarding	the most Kind	Allāh	In the name of
أَنَّهُ	إِلَيَّ	أُوحِيَ	قُلْ
that	to me	it has been revealed	say
ٱلْجِنِّ	مِّنَ	نَفَرٌ	ٱسْتَمَعَ
jinns	of	a group	listened
قُرْءَانًا	سَمِعْنَا	إِنَّا	فَقَالُوٓاْ
Recital	have heard	surely we	they said
ٱلرُّشْدِ	إِلَى	يَهْدِىٓ	عَجَبًا ①
the Right path	to	it guides	a wonderful.
نُّشْرِكَ	وَلَن	بِهِۦ	فَـَٔامَنَّا
we shall join	and never	therein	and we believed
تَعَٰلَىٰ	وَأَنَّهُۥ	أَحَدًا ②	بِرَبِّنَآ
exalted be	and that He	anything.	with our Rabb
ٱتَّخَذَ	مَا	رَبِّنَا	جَدُّ
He has taken	not	our Rabb	the majesty of
وَأَنَّهُۥ	وَلَدًا ③	وَلَا	صَٰحِبَةً
and that	a child	nor	a wife
عَلَى	سَفِيهُنَا	يَقُولُ	كَانَ
against	the foolish among us	say	used to
ظَنَنَّآ	وَأَنَّا	شَطَطًا ④	ٱللَّهِ
thought	and that we	that which was wrong and not right	Allāh

أَن	لَّن	تَقُولَ	ٱلْإِنسُ
that	would never	say	men
وَٱلْجِنُّ	عَلَى	ٱللَّهِ	كَذِبًا ۵
and jinns	against	Allāh	a lie.
وَأَنَّهُۥ	كَانَ	رِجَالٌ	مِّنَ
and that	they were	men	among
ٱلْإِنسِ	يَعُوذُونَ	بِرِجَالٍ	مِّنَ
mankind	who took refuge	with the men	among
ٱلْجِنِّ	فَزَادُوهُمْ	رَهَقًا ۶	وَأَنَّهُمْ
the jinns	so they increased them	in evil practices	and they
ظَنُّواْ	كَمَا	ظَنَنتُمْ	أَن
thought	as	you thought	that
لَّن	يَبْعَثَ	ٱللَّهُ	أَحَدًا ۷
will never	resurrect	Allāh	anyone.
وَأَنَّا	لَمَسْنَا	ٱلسَّمَاءَ	فَوَجَدْنَـٰهَا
and we	have sought to reach	the heaven	but found it
مُلِئَتْ	حَرَسًا	شَدِيدًا	وَشُهُبًا ۸
filled with	guards	stern	and flaming fires
وَأَنَّا	كُنَّا	نَقْعُدُ	مِنْهَا
and that we	used to	we sit	there at
مَقَـٰعِدَ	لِلسَّمْعِ	فَمَن	يَسْتَمِعِ
stations	to listen	but any who	listens
ٱلْـَٔانَ	يَجِدْ	لَهُۥ	شِهَابًا
now	will find	for him	a flaming fire

نَدْرِىٓ	لَا	وَأَنَّا	رَّصَدًا ۹
know	not	and we	watching in ambush
فِى	بِمَن	أُرِيدَ	أَشَرٌّ
on	for those	is intended	whether evil
بِهِمْ	أَرَادَ	أَمْ	ٱلْأَرْضِ
for them	intends	or whether	earth
مِنَّا	وَأَنَّا	رَشَدًا ۱۰	رَبُّهُمْ
among us some that	and that	a Right Path.	their Rabb
ذَٰلِكَ	دُونَ	وَمِنَّا	ٱلصَّٰلِحُونَ
that	contrary	and of us	are righteous
وَأَنَّا	قِدَدًا ۱۱	طَرَآئِقَ	كُنَّا
and that we	different groups.	ways	we are
نُعْجِزَ	لَّن	أَن	ظَنَنَّآ
we can escape	never	that	we think
وَلَن	ٱلْأَرْضِ	فِى	ٱللَّهَ
and never	the earth	in	Allāh
لَمَّا	وَأَنَّا	هَرَبًا ۱۲	نُّعْجِزَهُۥ
when	and indeed	by flight.	we can escape Him
بِهِۦ	ءَامَنَّا	ٱلْهُدَىٰٓ	سَمِعْنَا
in it	we believed	the Guidance	we heard
فَلَا	بِرَبِّهِۦ	يُؤْمِن	فَمَن
so not	in his Rabb	believes	and whosoever
رَهَقًا ۱۳	وَلَا	بَخْسًا	يَخَافُ
any injustice	nor	any loss	have fear

وَأَنَّا	مِنَّا	ٱلْمُسْلِمُونَ	وَمِنَّا
and that	among us	are the Muslims	and among us
ٱلْقَاسِطُونَ	فَمَن	أَسْلَمَ	فَأُو۟لَٰئِكَ
deviators	so whosoever	submits	then such
تَحَرَّوْا۟	رَشَدًا ۱٤	وَأَمَّا	ٱلْقَاسِطُونَ
have sought	the Right Path.	and as for	the deviators
فَكَانُوا۟	لِجَهَنَّمَ	حَطَبًا ۱٥	وَأَلَّوِ
they shall be	for Hell	fuel	and if
ٱسْتَقَٰمُوا۟	عَلَى	ٱلطَّرِيقَةِ	لَأَسْقَيْنَٰهُم
they had stood upright	on	the Right Way	We shall provide them with
مَّآءً	غَدَقًا ۱٦	لِّنَفْتِنَهُمْ	فِيهِ
water	in abundance.	that We might try them	thereby
وَمَن	يُعْرِضْ	عَن	ذِكْرِ
and whosoever	turns away	from	the remembrance of
رَبِّهِۦ	يَسْلُكْهُ	عَذَابًا	صَعَدًا ۱۷
his Rabb	He will thrust him in	torment	a severe
وَأَنَّ	ٱلْمَسَٰجِدَ	لِلَّهِ	فَلَا
and that	the masājid are	for Allāh	so not
تَدْعُوا۟	مَعَ	ٱللَّهِ	أَحَدًا ۱۸
invoke	along with	Allāh	anyone.
وَأَنَّهُۥ	لَمَّا	قَامَ	عَبْدُ
and that	when	stood up	the slave of

يَكُونُونَ

were

كَادُوا

they almost

يَدْعُوهُ

invoking in prayer to Him

ٱللَّهِ

Allāh

لِبَدًا ۝

in a dense crowd (stifling him).

عَلَيْهِ

around him

A few applications of the message:

Through the experiences of jinn, Allāh (swt) revealed some of the important means to achieve overall success in this life and in the Hereafter. In āyah 13, one of the means is mentioned. It states that whoever believes in his Creator, he shall have no fear, either of a decrease in the reward for his good deeds or an increase in the punishment for his sins. We should remember that our belief cannot be a mere verbal declaration of faith. We must demonstrate our faith by following the guidance. Only then will the clause mentioned in ayah 13 be applicable to us.

In āyah 17, the consequence of disobeying Allāh (swt) is mentioned. It says, whoever turns away from the remembrance of Allāh (swt), He will cause him to suffer severe punishment. We must pay the utmost attention to this message. However, we should note that "remembrance of Allāh (swt)" does not mean keeping Him in our minds but ignoring to perform the duties He prescribed. Remembrance of Allāh (swt) requires us to follow His teachings, fulfill the obligations and duties, and remain within the limits. Only then can we avoid severe punishment and consequently achieve success.

Review questions:

1. After what famous incident and during which period in Rasūlullāh's (S) life was sūrah Jinn revealed?

2. After listening to the Qur'ān, the jinn admitted that Allāh (swt) does not have something. What did they specifically mention?

3. Who among the jinn say outright lies about Allāh (swt)?

4. Compare āyāt 11 and 14. What two groups of people are mentioned in both āyāt?

5. Compare āyāt 2 and 13. What common message did the jinn mention in both āyāt?

6. If jinn stay on the right path, Allāh (swt) would provide them with plenty of something and with that substance He would also test them. What substance does sūrah Jinn mention?

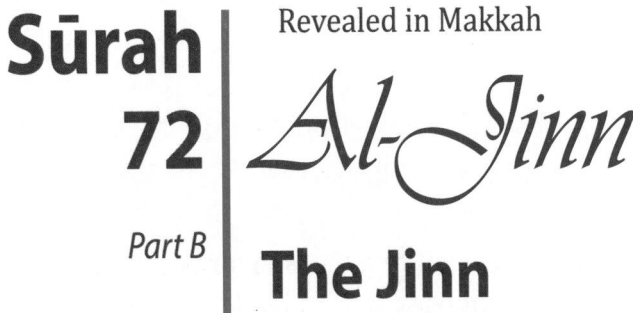

Sūrah 72 | Al-Jinn

Part B

Revealed in Makkah

The Jinn

Introduction:

Rasūlullāh (S) had gone to Tā'if seeking protection and shelter. But he had to return without accomplishing his goal. In the second part of the surah, Allāh (swt) reveals that true protection and refuge comes from Him. The enemies planned to hurt the Messenger (S), thinking that he was weak and did not have protection and helpers. But Allāh (swt) reveals that when the appointed time comes, they will realize who was weaker and who did not have helpers.

بِسْمِ ٱللَّهِ ٱلرَّحْمَـٰنِ ٱلرَّحِيمِ

In the name of Allāh, the most Kind, the most Rewarding.

قُلْ إِنَّمَآ أَدْعُواْ رَبِّي وَلَآ أُشْرِكُ بِهِۦٓ أَحَدًا ٢٠	20. Say: "I call upon only to my Rabb, and I do not associate anyone with Him."
قُلْ إِنِّى لَآ أَمْلِكُ لَكُمْ ضَرًّا وَلَا رَشَدًا ٢١	21. Say: "Surely I do not have power to hurt you nor bring you to right path."
قُلْ إِنِّى لَن يُجِيرَنِى مِنَ ٱللَّهِ أَحَدٌ وَلَنْ أَجِدَ مِن دُونِهِۦ مُلْتَحَدًا ٢٢	22. Say: "Surely no one can rescue me from Allāh, nor can I find any refuge beside Him.
إِلَّا بَلَـٰغًا مِّنَ ٱللَّهِ وَرِسَـٰلَـٰتِهِۦ وَمَن يَعْصِ ٱللَّهَ وَرَسُولَهُۥ فَإِنَّ لَهُۥ نَارَ جَهَنَّمَ خَـٰلِدِينَ فِيهَآ أَبَدًا ٢٣	23. "But a deliverance from Allāh and His Messages." And whoever disobeys Allāh and His Messenger, then for him is indeed the Fire of Hell, abiding in it for ages.
حَتَّىٰٓ إِذَا رَأَوْاْ مَا يُوعَدُونَ فَسَيَعْلَمُونَ مَنْ أَضْعَفُ نَاصِرًا وَأَقَلُّ عَدَدًا ٢٤	24. Till when they see that which is promised to them, then they will soon know who is weaker in helpers, and smaller in numbers.

قُل إِنْ أَدْرِىٓ أَقَرِيبٌ مَّا تُوعَدُونَ أَمْ يَجْعَلُ لَهُۥ رَبِّىٓ أَمَدًا ٢٥

25. You say: "I do not know whether what you are promised is nearby, or wheather my Rabb will make for it a long term."

عَـٰلِمُ ٱلْغَيْبِ فَلَا يُظْهِرُ عَلَىٰ غَيْبِهِۦٓ أَحَدًا ٢٦

26. The Knower of the unseen, so He does not divulge His secrets to anyone—

إِلَّا مَنِ ٱرْتَضَىٰ مِن رَّسُولٍ فَإِنَّهُۥ يَسْلُكُ مِنۢ بَيْنِ يَدَيْهِ وَمِنْ خَلْفِهِۦ رَصَدًا ٢٧

27. except to a messenger whom He chooses, and indeed, He causes an escort to march in front of him and behind him,

لِّيَعْلَمَ أَن قَدْ أَبْلَغُوا۟ رِسَـٰلَـٰتِ رَبِّهِمْ وَأَحَاطَ بِمَا لَدَيْهِمْ وَأَحْصَىٰ كُلَّ شَىْءٍ عَدَدًۢا ٢٨

28. so that He may know that they have delivered the Messages of their Rabb; and He encompasses what is with them, and He keeps count of all things by counting.

Explanation:

20. Rasūlullāh (S) went to Tā'if seeking shelter and protection. The people of the city refused to give him any protection; instead, they chased him out. During his return from the city, no revelation came to him to address his failure or to comfort him. But after reaching Nakhlah and meeting with a group of jinn, Rasūlullāh (S) received the following set of revelations. He could not return to Makkah without making sure his life would be safe in Makkah. Allāh (swt) consoled him that the best refuge is with Him. The opponents will soon know who is weaker in providing help and smaller in number. Although Rasūlullāh (S) was looking for external help, his true help would come from his Rabb. At that point, Rasūlullāh (S) was asked to reaffirm his position—do not associate anyone as a partner with Rabb.

21–22. As the Messenger of Allāh, Muhammad (S) had the immense responsibility to convey the divine message. But if he were to disobey Allāh (swt) or fabricate anything against Him, nobody could save him. The responsibility to convey the message does not give him any additional advantages. He has no secret power to harm those who did not believe or to guide those who want to be guided. Guidance comes only from Allāh (swt).

23. The sole duty of Rasūlullāh (S) is to deliver the message of Allāh (swt). Mere delivery will not suffice; therefore, he has to convey it to everybody. However, he cannot force anybody to believe, nor can he guide anybody. To believe or not to believe is the decision of each individual recipient of the message. Needless to say, this has its own consequences. The messenger brought the message of Allāh (swt), so to disobey the messenger amounts to disobeying Allāh (swt). It is not possible to disobey Allāh (swt) and expect to do well in the Hereafter. Those who disobey Allāh (swt) will pay the penalty in fire, abiding in it for ages (11:107; 78:23).

24. Belief in the Awakening is a core faith, but people have always wondered whether it will truly happen. They are also curious about the exact timing of the Hour. The non-believers may keep doubting the Day only to find the promise will come to reality one day. On that day, one's earthly power and support will

not benefit anyone. The non-believers will realize that they not only became weaker due to vanishing support, but they also became smaller in number due to abandoning followers.

25. In the Qur'ānic usage, the word "Hour" carries two meanings: one, the timing of some severe suffering on earth, and two, the timing of the final punishment in the Hereafter. Nobody has clue as to when the Hour will happen. The arrival of the Hour appears too far away because punishment does not always immediately happen after sin, and when it does, the sinners cannot connect it to the sins they committed earlier. Besides, when a sinner does not face punishment right away, he thinks he has averted suffering the punishment.

26–27. The human faculty of understanding has its own limitations. It can only stretch to the limits bestowed by Allāh (swt). On the contrary, Allāh's (swt) knowledge transcends time and space. Human beings cannot fathom divine knowledge; therefore, what lies beyond human reach can only be learned if divine revelations about those secrets are sent to certain individuals whom Allāh (swt) chooses. Divine protection marching in front of and behind the messengers implies that they are always guarded, temporally and spiritually.

28. Allāh (swt) has full knowledge that the messengers have properly delivered the divine message. Allāh (swt) encompasses with His knowledge all the activities of the messengers, therefore, their actions were in accordance to the divine law and divine plan (21:27). Nevertheless, Allāh (swt) keeps a record of all the actions, even if this means keeping a record of the actions of all messengers.

Words to know:

ضَرَّ: to harm, to hurt. ضَرَرٌ: hurt, inconvenience.

بَلَغَ: to arrive at, to attain. بَلَاغٌ: important message. بَالِغ: reaching.

ضَعُفَ: to be weak, feeble, infirm. ضَعْفٌ: weakness, ضَعَفَ: to exceed, twofold.

عَدَّ: to count. عَدٌّ: number. عِدَّتْ: to make up a prescribed number.

Sūrah Al-Jinn
Word-by-word meaning

ٱلرَّحِيمِ	ٱلرَّحْمَٰنِ	ٱللَّهِ	بِسْمِ
the most Rewarding	the most Kind	Allāh	In the name of
رَبِّى	أَدْعُوا۟	إِنَّمَآ	قُلْ
my Rabb	invoke	I only	say

وَلَآ	أُشْرِكُ	بِهِۦٓ	أَحَدًا ۝
and none	I associate	along with Him	as partners.
قُلْ	إِنِّى	لَآ	أَمْلِكُ
say	surely I	not	have power to cause
لَكُمْ	ضَرًّا	وَلَا	رَشَدًا ۝
you	harm	nor	to (bring you to the) Right Path.
قُلْ	إِنِّى	لَن	تُجِيرَنِى
say	surely	never	can protect me
مِن	ٱللَّهِ	أَحَدٌ	وَلَن
from	Allāh	anyone	nor
أَجِدَ	مِن دُونِهِۦ	مُلْتَحَدًا ۝	إِلَّا
can I find	except in Him	refuge.	but
بَلَٰغًا	مِّنَ	ٱللَّهِ	وَرِسَٰلَٰتِهِۦ
conveyance	from	Allāh	and His Messages
وَمَن	يَعْصِ	ٱللَّهَ	وَرَسُولَهُۥ
and whosoever	disobeys	Allāh	and His Messenger
فَإِنَّ	لَهُۥ	نَارَ	جَهَنَّمَ
then indeed	for him is	the Fire of	Hell
خَٰلِدِينَ	فِيهَآ	أَبَدًا ۝	حَتَّىٰ
they shall dwell	therein	for ages	till
إِذَا	رَأَوْاْ	مَا	يُوعَدُونَ
when	they see	that which	they are promised
فَسَيَعْلَمُونَ	مَنْ	أَضْعَفُ	نَاصِرًا
then they will know	who it is that	is weaker in	helpers

وَأَقَلُّ	عَدَدًا ۝	قُلۡ	إِنۡ
and less in	number.	say	not

أَدۡرِىٓ	أَقَرِيبٌ	مَّا	تُوعَدُونَ
I know	whether is near	what	you are promised

أَمۡ	تَجۡعَلُ	لَهُۥ	رَبِّىٓ
or whether	will appoint	for it	my Rabb

أَمَدًا ۝	عَٰلِمُ	ٱلۡغَيۡبِ	فَلَا
a distant term.	the All-Knower of	the unseen	and not

يُظۡهِرُ	عَلَىٰ	غَيۡبِهِۦٓ	أَحَدًا ۝
He reveals	on	His unseen	anyone.

إِلَّا	مَنِ	ٱرۡتَضَىٰ	مِن
except to	whom	He has chosen	of

رَّسُولٍ	فَإِنَّهُۥ	يَسۡلُكُ	مِنۡ
a Messenger	so indeed	He causes to march	from

بَيۡنَ يَدَيۡهِ	وَمِنۡ	خَلۡفِهِۦ	رَصَدًا ۝
before him	and from	behind him	an escort.

لِّيَعۡلَمَ	أَن	قَدۡ	أَبۡلَغُواْ
that He may know	that	surely	they have conveyed

رِسَٰلَٰتِ	رَبِّهِمۡ	وَأَحَاطَ	بِمَا
the messages of	their Rabb	and He surrounds	all that which is

لَدَيۡهِمۡ	وَأَحۡصَىٰ	كُلَّ	شَىۡءٍ
with them	and He keeps	of all	things

عَدَدَۢا ۝
count.

A few applications of the message:

When we encounter trouble and look for shelter and protection, we often look in and around our surroundings, hoping someone might provide the necessary protection. But we should always remember that Allāh (swt) is the ultimate protector and provider of refuge. Similarly, if Allāh (swt) intends to punish us for our wrongdoing, no one can save us.

Allāh (swt) always grants victory to the righteous. Such victories do not necessarily refer to battlefield circumstances. Victory refers to every struggle between righteousness and wickedness, between steadfastness and faltering, between obedience and disobedience. We have no knowledge of when such victory will be granted. We should not become disheartened during days of difficulty. We should trust Allāh (swt) and follow His teachings. We should never compromise our faith and never associate anyone with Him.

Review questions:

1. Rasūlullāh (S) was looking for protection and refuge. Sūrah Jinn points out a fundamental truth about refuge. What is that truth?

2. What would happen if someone disobeyed Allāh (swt) and His messenger? Write your answer based on sūrah Jinn.

3. When the promise of Allāh (swt) materializes, what will the opponents of Islam learn? Write your answer based on sūrah Jinn.

4. No one knows the secret of the unseen except some people. Who are they?

5. Is it possible that some of the messengers of Allāh (swt) died without delivering the message? Explain your answer based on sūrah Jinn.

Sūrah 73 | *Al-Muzzammil*

The One Covered Up

Introduction:

The sūrah begins with a specific command to Rasūlullāh (S) to spend part of the night in remembrance of Allāh (swt). Toward the end of the sūrah, a general command is given to all believers to be mindful of salāt and pay the obligatory zakāt. This early sūrah reminds Rasūlullāh (S) that he has a mighty job ahead, but he must patiently bear all the opposition and atrocities that are bound to come his way. Ultimately the opponents of Islam will receive their due punishment just as Pharaoh received his punishment for opposing a messenger of Allāh. The final āyat provides the believers certain codes of conduct in order to earn Allāh's (swt) forgiveness and reward.

$$ بِسۡمِ ٱللَّهِ ٱلرَّحۡمَـٰنِ ٱلرَّحِيمِ $$

In the name of Allāh, the most Kind, the most Rewarding.

يَـٰٓأَيُّهَا ٱلۡمُزَّمِّلُ ۝	1. O you covered up!
قُمِ ٱلَّيۡلَ إِلَّا قَلِيلًا ۝	2. Stand up at nighttime—except a little;
نِّصۡفَهُۥ أَوِ ٱنقُصۡ مِنۡهُ قَلِيلًا ۝	3. half of it, or lessen a little from it,
أَوۡ زِدۡ عَلَيۡهِ وَرَتِّلِ ٱلۡقُرۡءَانَ تَرۡتِيلًا ۝	4. or add thereto, and recite the Qur'ān calmly with a serene recitation.
إِنَّا سَنُلۡقِى عَلَيۡكَ قَوۡلًا ثَقِيلًا ۝	5. Surely We are going to place upon you a weighty word.
إِنَّ نَاشِئَةَ ٱلَّيۡلِ هِىَ أَشَدُّ وَطۡـًٔا وَأَقۡوَمُ قِيلًا ۝	6. Certainly the rising by the night is the firmest way to tread, and the most upright in speech.

إِنَّ لَكَ فِي ٱلنَّهَارِ سَبْحًا طَوِيلًا ۝

7. Surely you have by day prolonged occupation.

وَٱذْكُرِ ٱسْمَ رَبِّكَ وَتَبَتَّلْ إِلَيْهِ تَبْتِيلًا ۝

8. Therefore remember the Name of your Rabb and devote yourself to Him with a complete devotion.

رَّبُّ ٱلْمَشْرِقِ وَٱلْمَغْرِبِ لَآ إِلَٰهَ إِلَّا هُوَ فَٱتَّخِذْهُ وَكِيلًا ۝

9. Rabb of the East and the West, there is no deity but He; therefore, take Him as a Guardian.

وَٱصْبِرْ عَلَىٰ مَا يَقُولُونَ وَٱهْجُرْهُمْ هَجْرًا جَمِيلًا ۝

10. And persevere in spite of what they utter, and depart from them a decorous departure.

وَذَرْنِي وَٱلْمُكَذِّبِينَ أُو۟لِي ٱلنَّعْمَةِ وَمَهِّلْهُمْ قَلِيلًا ۝

11. And leave Me with the rejecters, possessors of plenty, and respite them a little.

إِنَّ لَدَيْنَآ أَنكَالًا وَجَحِيمًا ۝

12. Surely We have shackles and fierce Fire,

وَطَعَامًا ذَا غُصَّةٍ وَعَذَابًا أَلِيمًا ۝

13. and food ready to choke, and a painful punishment.

يَوْمَ تَرْجُفُ ٱلْأَرْضُ وَٱلْجِبَالُ وَكَانَتِ ٱلْجِبَالُ كَثِيبًا مَّهِيلًا ۝

14. On a day when the earth and the mountains will shake, and the mountains will become sand-hills crumbling down.

إِنَّآ أَرْسَلْنَآ إِلَيْكُمْ رَسُولًا شَٰهِدًا عَلَيْكُمْ كَمَآ أَرْسَلْنَآ إِلَىٰ فِرْعَوْنَ رَسُولًا ۝

15. We have indeed sent to you a Messenger—a witness over you, as We sent a messenger to Fir'awn.

فَعَصَىٰ فِرْعَوْنُ ٱلرَّسُولَ فَأَخَذْنَٰهُ أَخْذًا وَبِيلًا ۝

16. But Fir'awn disobeyed the messenger, so We seized him a most calamitous seizing.

فَكَيْفَ تَتَّقُونَ إِن كَفَرْتُمْ يَوْمًا يَجْعَلُ ٱلْوِلْدَٰنَ شِيبًا ۝

17. Therefore, how will you guard yourselves, if you disbelieve, on the Day which will turn children gray-headed—

ٱلسَّمَآءُ مُنفَطِرٌ بِهِۦ كَانَ وَعْدُهُۥ مَفْعُولًا ۝

18. on which the sky will be rent asunder thereby? His promise is ever-fulfilled.

إِنَّ هَٰذِهِۦ تَذْكِرَةٌ ۖ فَمَن شَآءَ ٱتَّخَذَ إِلَىٰ رَبِّهِۦ سَبِيلًا ﴿١٩﴾

19. Surely this is a Reminder; therefore, let him who pleases take a way to his Rabb.

SECTION : 2

إِنَّ رَبَّكَ يَعْلَمُ أَنَّكَ تَقُومُ أَدْنَىٰ مِن ثُلُثَيِ ٱلَّيْلِ وَنِصْفَهُۥ وَثُلُثَهُۥ وَطَآئِفَةٌ مِّنَ ٱلَّذِينَ مَعَكَ ۚ وَٱللَّهُ يُقَدِّرُ ٱلَّيْلَ وَٱلنَّهَارَ ۚ عَلِمَ أَن لَّن تُحْصُوهُ فَتَابَ عَلَيْكُمْ ۖ فَٱقْرَءُوا۟ مَا تَيَسَّرَ مِنَ ٱلْقُرْءَانِ ۚ عَلِمَ أَن سَيَكُونُ مِنكُم مَّرْضَىٰ ۙ وَءَاخَرُونَ يَضْرِبُونَ فِى ٱلْأَرْضِ يَبْتَغُونَ مِن فَضْلِ ٱللَّهِ ۙ وَءَاخَرُونَ يُقَٰتِلُونَ فِى سَبِيلِ ٱللَّهِ ۖ فَٱقْرَءُوا۟ مَا تَيَسَّرَ مِنْهُ ۚ وَأَقِيمُوا۟ ٱلصَّلَوٰةَ وَءَاتُوا۟ ٱلزَّكَوٰةَ وَأَقْرِضُوا۟ ٱللَّهَ قَرْضًا حَسَنًا ۚ وَمَا تُقَدِّمُوا۟ لِأَنفُسِكُم مِّنْ خَيْرٍ تَجِدُوهُ عِندَ ٱللَّهِ هُوَ خَيْرًا وَأَعْظَمَ أَجْرًا ۚ وَٱسْتَغْفِرُوا۟ ٱللَّهَ ۖ إِنَّ ٱللَّهَ غَفُورٌ رَّحِيمٌ ﴿٢٠﴾

20. Your Rabb indeed knows that you stand up for nearly two-thirds of the night, and half of it, or one-third of it; and also a party of those with you.

But Allāh measures the night and the day. He knows that you will not be able to do it, so He turns to you; therefore, read from the Qur'ān what is easy for you.

He knows that some of you will be sick, and others traveling on the earth seeking the grace of Allāh, and others fighting in the way of Allāh; therefore, read whatever is easy out of it; and establish the Salat and pay the Zakat, and lend to Allāh a liberal loan.

And whatever good you send forward for your souls, you will find it in the Presence of Allāh—that is better and greater in reward. And seek the forgiveness of Allāh. Allāh is of course most Forgiving, most Rewarding.

Explanation:

1. This early Makkan sūrah derives its title from the word *muzzammil* (literally, one who is covered up or enwrapped). This title, identical in meaning to *muddaththir*, used in the next sūrah, is affectionately used to address Rasūlullāh (S). The title refers to Rasūlullāh's (S) reaction after his supernatural incident in Cave Hira. While in the cave, angel Jibril brought Muhammad (S) the first set of divine revelations, but Muhammad (S) did not realize the gravity of this act. He did not realize that he was chosen to become a messenger of Allāh (swt). Due to the suddenness and supernatural nature of the incident, Rasūlullāh (S) was extremely terrified. He scurried back home, trembling due to shock and fear, and asked his wife to wrap him up in blankets to reduce his shivering. This early sūrah, fourth in the order of revelation, seems to make a loving reference to this well-known incident, particularly the fact that he asked his wife to wrap him up.

2–3. By now Muhammad (S) received a few revelations, and he was convinced that Allāh (swt) had chosen him to become a messenger. During this induction process, Rasūlullāh (S) was spending a large part of the nighttime praying to Allāh (swt), seeking His help and guidance. The āyah asks

Rasūlullāh (S) to devote parts of the night in prayer, mainly for him to gain confidence and to condition his mind to bear the tremendous responsibility of preaching the divine message. The requirement to stay awake during parts of the night is stringent, however, not inhuman because it is not unusual for people to stay awake half of the night or less than that in various pursuits. The difference with Rasūlullāh (S) was that he would spend the time in prayer and recitation.

4. Until this point in time, only four sūrahs were revealed, yet Rasūlullāh (S) was required to devote his time to careful recitation of the revelation. The purpose of this forward-looking requirement seems to be to keep Rasūlullāh (S) abreast of all the revelations that would be sent during his career. The word *tartīl*, when applied to the recitation of a text, indicates calm and measured utterance without any haste, and with due emphasis to understand the meaning (25:32).

5. After the revelation of the first five āyāt, Rasūlullāh (S) had to wait, in some accounts for nearly six months, before the second revelation was sent to him. The initial slow start was soon to be intensified by more frequent revelations. This would require Rasūlullāh (S) to start communicating the message openly to everybody rather than only to the close family members and friends whom he addressed earlier. This would put a new burden on Rasūlullāh's (S) shoulder—the burden of effectively delivering the divine message.

6. In āyah 2, the instruction is to stand up at night (*layl*). But it is not clear whether this meant to delay going to bed or to wake up later in the night, therefore, both interpretations seem to be correct. However, in this āyah, the instruction is to rise (*nasha'*) by night, indicating going to bed and then waking up later, toward the later half of the night. According to the āyah, waking up for prayer is the firmest way of devotion and to condition one's body and mind. Rising during the later half of the night, particularly to perform Tahajjud prayer, is an ideal prayer, mentioned in many of the later revelations. It is not only a requirement for Rasūlullāh (S), but it is also encouraged for all believers (17:79; 50:40; 76:26).

7–8. The official daytime prayers were not yet formalized, therefore, remembering Allāh (swt) at night was ideal. Besides, during the daytime, Rasūlullāh (S) would have a difficult job of communicating the message. During the early periods, all of Allāh's "beautiful names" (*asmā al-husna*) were yet to be revealed. The instruction to "remember the Name of your Rabb" (singular, *asma*, meaning name) does not mean to chant Allāh's name using a rosary or to adopt a rhythmic physical motion of chanting. The word *dhikr* (to remember) ideally means to show devotion with the utmost humility; preferably by praying and prostrating.

9. The āyah makes it clear that the Rabb, whom Rasūlullāh (S) was asked to remember, was not a local god, but the Lord of the East and the West (37:5; 43:38; 55:17; 70:40). In the entire universe, there is no other deity but He. He is the supreme one; therefore, believers should take Him as their guardian.

10. Rasūlullāh (S) had barely started his mission when people around him engaged in widespread mockery of his claims of being a messenger. This initial mockery would gradually turn into violent outbursts; therefore, the Qur'ān provides an appropriate response. This response would become the guiding principle for Rasūlullāh (S) and his followers—persevere when ill is uttered and avoid any confrontations in a civic manner.

11. People who reject the truth are said to be among the affluent group. The possession of wealth and power often makes people remain focused on these objects as his or her most desirable

achievements in life. As a result, they tend to shy away from spiritual objectives of life, as if, these are a repulsive and unnecessary nuisance. Little do they know that they are actually given a little respite in life before they face the consequences for staying aloof from spiritual objectives.

12. In the Hereafter, the sinners will experience a few things. As a matter of example, this āyah mentions tying them up in chains. This example is frequently mentioned in the Qur'ān (14:49; 25:13; 40:71–72; 69:30–32; 76:4). On one hand the chains reflect the inescapability of the sinners, and on the other, the chains reflect the humiliating condition of the sinners. Those who are shackled will invariably face fierce fire.

13. As a matter of another example, the sinners will be given foods that will choke them. The impossibility of consuming food indicates all earthly concern for the physical body and the urge to gratify and satiate oneself will cause a strangulating effect in the Hereafter.

14. At the end of the respite, a cataclysmic event will happen. The imagery presented in the āyah indicates a severe earthquake will happen, possibly due to an explosion of a super-volcano or some other unknown impact whereby the mountains will crumble down like sand-hills. (See also āyāt 18:47; 20:105–107; 27:88; 52:10; 56:5–6; 69:14; 70:9; 77:10; 78:20; 101:5 for similar images.)

15. After providing a short description of the Hereafter, the theme of the sūrah again reverts to Rasūlullāh (S) and his mission. His mission is now compared to that of the mission of Mūsā (A). No mention of Mūsā's (A) name is made, but the commonality between him and Muhammad (S) is pointed out in terms of their respective role—messengership. Emphasis on this commonality points to the fact that Rasūlullāh's (S) advent is nothing other than the continuation of Allāh's policy to send His messengers. This commonality also shows that Islam is not a new religion, but a continuation of the same fundamental teachings that were sent earlier.

The reference to Fir'awn is introduced for the sake of comparing him to the attitude of the Quraish mercantile community. Just as Fir'awn used his power, wealth and sense of invincibility to defy Allāh (swt) and His messenger, so also did the Quraish mercantile community use its power, wealth and supremacy to oppose Allāh (swt) and His messenger.

16. The reason for Fir'awn's exemplary punishment was he disobeyed the messenger. Once again, the name of the messenger is not mentioned in order to show the commonality in the mission of the messengers. The consequences of defying the messengers will be similar, if not identical, in every period of human civilization.

17. The terrifying events of the Hereafter are often described using metaphors of contrasting reality. The metaphor of children's hair turning gray not only provides a shocking horror, but also dissipates all hope of delegating power and wealth to subsequent generations. This metaphor is not a punishment for children because according to the teachings of the Qur'ān, children are sinless and they are not subjected to the tribulation of Judgment.

18. Regarding the sky being rent asunder, see notes in 69:16 and 77:9.

19. The word *tadhkirat* means a warning or an admonition intended to bring something to one' recollection. The sentence elliptically indicates there can be no coercion in the matter of religion.

20. The first part of the āyah addresses Rasūlullāh (S) and his followers, who used to spend long hours of the night in salāt and meditation. In the second part of the āyah, it is stated that it may

not be possible for all Muslims to follow the same example. The phrase "you will not be able to do it" refers to Muslims in general, not Rasūlullāh (S). The reading from the Qur'ān is left to the convenience of each individual; however, the preferred time is late at night, during Tahajjud Prayer prior to Fajr prayer (17:78–79). This leniency was granted for the Muslims due to varied occupations and constraints foreseeable in their lives.

The mention of *qital* in this āyah led many commentators to assume that the entire āyah was a Madinan revelation because the fighting in the way of Allāh (swt) was prescribed only after Rasūlullāh's (S) migration from Makkah to Madinah. However, since the above leniency was granted based on foreseeable future conditions (*sayakūn*, will happen in the future), it reflects the circumstances of future conditions. Therefore, the āyah was not a Madinan revelation. The phrase "lend Allāh a liberal loan" implies spending efforts on the right causes (2:245; 57:11, 18; 64:17)—that will benefit one's society, neighborhood, environment and nation.

Words to know:

نَقَصَ: to diminish, to decrease, to lessen. إِنْقُص: diminish. مَنقُص: diminished.

رَتَلَ: to set in order, to speak slowly. رَتَّلَ: to recite with a slow and distinct voice. تَرتِيلً: distinctly and thoughtfully.

لَقِيَ: to meet, to experience, to suffer from. لِقَاءٌ: meeting. لَقَّا: to cast upon. اَلقَى: to throw.

ثَقُلَ: to be heavy, weighty. ثِقل: burden. ثَقِيل: heavy. مَثقَلَة: burdened, heavily laden.

نَشَاءَ: to grow up, to rise. نَاشِئَة: rising. اَنشَاءَ: produced.

بَتَلَ: to devote, to cut off from another. تَبتِيلً: exclusive and sincere devotion.

وَكَلَ: to entrust, to dispose affairs. وَكِيل: guardian, responsible for affairs. تَوَكَّل: put your trust.

مَهَلَ: to act slowly, to act gently. اَمهِل: respite gently. مَهِّل: defer, respite.

عَصَى: to rebel, to disobey. عِصيَان: rebellion, disobedience. عِصيَانٌ: transgression.

فَضَلَ: to exceed, to excel. فَضلٌ: favor, grace, bounty.

قَرَضَ: to cut, to turn away from. اَقرِض: those who perform excellent deeds. قَرضًا: A goodly loan, a goodly gift.

Sūrah Al-Muzzammil
Word-by-word meaning

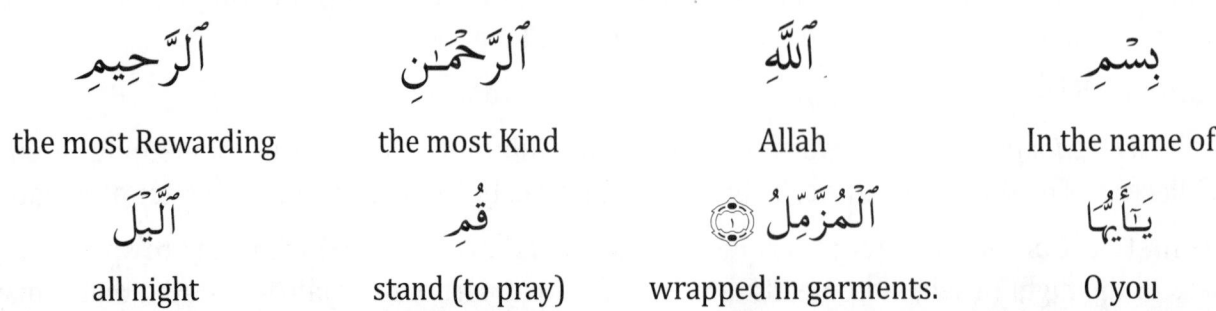

ٱلرَّحِيمِ	ٱلرَّحْمَٰنِ	ٱللَّهِ	بِسْمِ
the most Rewarding	the most Kind	Allāh	In the name of

ٱلَّيَلَ	قُمِ	ٱلْمُزَّمِّلُ	يَٰٓأَيُّهَا
all night	stand (to pray)	wrapped in garments.	O you

أَوِ	نِّصْفَهُۥ	قَلِيلًا ٢	إِلَّا
or	half of it	a little	except

أَوۡ	قَلِيلًا ٣	مِنۡهُ	ٱنقُصۡ
or	a little.	than that	less

ٱلۡقُرۡءَانَ	وَرَتِّلِ	عَلَيۡهِ	زِدۡ
the Qur'ān	and recite	to it	add

عَلَيۡكَ	سَنُلۡقِى	إِنَّا	تَرۡتِيلًا ٤
to you	shall send down	surely We	in a slow style

نَاشِئَةَ	إِنَّ	ثَقِيلًا ٥	قَوۡلًا
the rising (at)	surely	a weighty	word

وَطۡـًٔا	أَشَدُّ	هِىَ	ٱلَّيۡلِ
and most potent	very hard	is	night

لَكَ	إِنَّ	قِيلًا ٦	وَأَقۡوَمُ
for you	surely	the word.	and most suitable for

طَوِيلًا ٧	سَبۡحًا	ٱلنَّهَارِ	فِى
prolonged.	occupation with ordinary duties	day	by

وَتَبَتَّلۡ	رَبِّكَ	ٱسۡمَ	وَٱذۡكُرِ
and devote yourself	your Rabb	the Name of	and remember

ٱلۡمَشۡرِقِ	رَّبُّ	تَبۡتِيلًا ٨	إِلَيۡهِ
the East	the Rabb of	with a complete devotion.	to Him

إِلَّا	إِلَٰهَ	لَآ	وَٱلۡمَغۡرِبِ
but	true god	No	and the West

وَٱصۡبِرۡ	وَكِيلًا ٩	فَٱتَّخِذۡهُ	هُوَ
and be patient	as Guardian.	so take Him Alone	He

123

وَٱهْجُرْهُمْ	يَقُولُونَ	مَا	عَلَىٰ
and keep away from them	they say	what	with
وَٱلْمُكَذِّبِينَ	وَذَرْنِي	جَمِيلًا ۞	هَجْرًا
with the rejecters	and leave Me Alone	a good way	withdrawal.
قَلِيلًا ۞	وَمَهِّلْهُمْ	ٱلنَّعْمَةِ	أُولِى
for a little while.	and give them respite	possessor of plenty	and those who are
وَجَحِيمًا ۞	أَنكَالًا	لَدَيْنَآ	إِنَّ
and raging Fire.	are fetters	with Us	surely
وَعَذَابًا	غُصَّةٍ	ذَا	وَطَعَامًا
and torment	chokes	that	and a food
ٱلْأَرْضُ	تَرْجُفُ	يَوْمَ	أَلِيمًا ۞
the earth	will shake	on the Day when	a painful.
كَثِيبًا	ٱلْجِبَالُ	وَكَانَتِ	وَٱلْجِبَالُ
a heap of sand	the mountains	and will be	and the mountains
إِلَيْكُمْ	أَرْسَلْنَآ	إِنَّآ	مَّهِيلًا ۞
to you	have sent	indeed We	crumbling down.
كَمَآ	عَلَيْكُمْ	شَٰهِدًا	رَسُولًا
as	over you	to be a witness	a Messenger
رَسُولًا ۞	فِرْعَوْنَ	إِلَىٰ	أَرْسَلْنَآ
a Messenger.	Pharaoh	to	We did send
فَأَخَذْنَٰهُ	ٱلرَّسُولَ	فِرْعَوْنُ	فَعَصَىٰ
so We seized him	the Messenger	Pharaoh	but disobeyed
تَتَّقُونَ	فَكَيْفَ	وَبِيلًا ۞	أَخْذًا
can you avoid punishment	then how	a severe	with seizing

تَجْعَلُ	يَوْمًا	كَفَرْتُمْ	إِن
will make	in a Day that	you disbelieve	if
مُنفَطِرٌ	ٱلسَّمَآءُ	شِيبًا ۝	ٱلْوِلْدَٰنَ
will be cleft asunder	the heaven	gray-headed.	the children
مَفْعُولًا ۝	وَعْدُهُۥ	كَانَ	بِهِۦ
to be accomplished	His Promise	is (certainly)	by it
فَمَن	تَذْكِرَةٌ	هَٰذِهِۦ	إِنَّ
so whosoever	an admonition	this is	verily
رَبِّهِۦ	إِلَىٰ	ٱتَّخَذَ	شَآءَ
His Lord	to	let him take	wills
يَعْلَمُ	رَبَّكَ	إِنَّ	سَبِيلًا ۝
knows	your Lord	verily	a path.
مِن	أَدْنَىٰ	تَقُومُ	أَنَّكَ
than	a little less	stand	that you
وَثُلُثَهُۥ	وَنِصْفَهُۥ	ٱلَّيْلِ	ثُلُثَيِ
or a third of the night	or half the night	the night	two-thirds of
مَعَكَ	ٱلَّذِينَ	مِّنَ	وَطَآئِفَةٌ
with you	those	of	and so do a party
وَٱلنَّهَارَ	ٱلَّيْلَ	يُقَدِّرُ	وَٱللَّهُ
and the day	the night	measures	and Allāh
فَتَابَ	تُحْصُوهُ	أَن لَّن	عَلِمَ
so He has turned	you calculate it	that can never	He knows
تَيَسَّرَ	مَا	فَٱقْرَءُوا	عَلَيْكُمْ
may be easy for you	as much as	so recite you	to you

أَن	عَلِمَ	ٱلْقُرْءَانِ	مِنَ
that there	He knows	the Qur'an	of
وَءَاخَرُونَ	مَّرْضَىٰ	مِنكُم	سَيَكُونُ
and others	sick	some among you	will be
يَبْتَغُونَ	ٱلْأَرْضِ	فِى	يَضْرِبُونَ
seeking	the land	through	travelling
وَءَاخَرُونَ	ٱللَّهِ	فَضْلِ	مِن
so recite	of Allāh	bounty	of
ٱللَّهِ	سَبِيلِ	فِى	يُقَتِلُونَ
of Allāh	Cause (Way)	in	fighting
مِنْهُ	تَيَسَّرَ	مَا	فَٱقْرَءُواْ
of it	may be easy	as much as	so recite
ٱلزَّكَوٰةَ	وَءَاتُواْ	ٱلصَّلَوٰةَ	وَأَقِيمُواْ
Zakāt	and give	salāt	and perform
حَسَنًا	قَرْضًا	ٱللَّهَ	وَأَقْرِضُواْ
a goodly	loan	Allāh	and lend to
مِّنْ خَيْرٍ	لِأَنفُسِكُم	تُقَدِّمُواْ	وَمَا
of good	for yourselves	you send before you	and whatsoever
هُوَ	ٱللَّهِ	عِندَ	تَجِدُوهُ
it is	Allāh	with	you will find it
وَٱسْتَغْفِرُواْ	أَجْرًا	وَأَعْظَمَ	خَيْرًا
and seek Forgiveness	in reward	and greater	better
رَّحِيمٌ	غَفُورٌ	إِنَّ ٱللَّهَ	ٱللَّهَ
Most Merciful.	is Oft-Forgiving	surely Allāh	(of)Allāh

A few applications of the message:

We are busy with our earthly lives and professions. We have to go to school or work to earn our livelihood. Amid all these earthly duties, we have certain key duties toward Allāh (swt). These duties are for our own good. In ayah 20, Allāh (swt) says, "and whatever good you send forward for your own souls, you will find it in the presence of Allāh."

One of the duties is to remember the names of our Creator. Remembering His name does not mean to chant the name using a rosary or to adopt a rhythmic, physical motion of chanting. Ideally it means to emulate the essence of His names in our conduct.

This sūrah also reminds us of certain key duties we all have to perform. One of the main duties is to read the Qur'ān every day. How much we read is entirely up to us. Allāh (swt) is fully aware of human limitations, and each person has his or her own limitations. Allāh (swt) has prescribed us to read the Qur'ān, but He also advises us to read "what is easy for you." No matter what we do, we should develop a habit of reading the Qur'ān every day. Along with this duty, Allāh (swt) also reminds us to establish salāt and pay zakāt.

As we read the surah, we should once again remind us to develop these desirable habits and follow them meticulously.

Review questions:

1. Which parts of the night was Rasūlullāh (S) asked to devote in recitation of the Qur'ān?

2. What is the significance of asking Rasūlullāh (S) to recite the Qur'ān? Explain the meaning of the word *tartīl* in this context.

3. In āyah 5, the phrase "weighty word" (*qawlan thaqīl*) is mentioned. Explain the significance of the weighty word.

4. What is the significance of "Rabb of the East and the West," as mentioned in āyah 9?

5. Āyah 10 provides a code of conduct when opposition to Islam escalates and personal attacks increase. What is the code of conduct?

6. In the Hereafter, the sinners will be treated in a certain manner. What treatment is mentioned in sūrah Muzzammil?

7. On the Day of Awakening, certain things will happen to the world and the sky. Mention these specific events as stated in sūrah Muzzammil.

Sūrah 74

Part A

Revealed in Makkah

Al-Muddaththir

The One Wrapped Up

Introduction:

The first seven āyāt of sūrah Muddaththir was the second revelation sent after the first five āyāt of sūrah al-'Alaq. The first part of this sūrah has two distinct themes. The first theme is preparing Rasūlullāh (S) to openly invite people to accept Islam. The second theme is making him aware of the resistance he would face during the process of the invitation. The sūrah cautions the rejecters of truth about painful punishment in scorching fire.

بِسۡمِ ٱللَّهِ ٱلرَّحۡمَـٰنِ ٱلرَّحِيمِ

In the name of Allāh, the most Kind, the most Rewarding.

يَـٰٓأَيُّهَا ٱلۡمُدَّثِّرُ ۝	1. O you, the one wrapped up!
قُمۡ فَأَنذِرۡ ۝	2. Arise and warn.
وَرَبَّكَ فَكَبِّرۡ ۝	3. And your Rabb—do magnify!
وَثِيَابَكَ فَطَهِّرۡ ۝	4. and your garment—do purify!
وَٱلرُّجۡزَ فَٱهۡجُرۡ ۝	5. and the uncleanliness—do flee!
وَلَا تَمۡنُن تَسۡتَكۡثِرُ ۝	6. And do not bestow favors seeking to increase.
وَلِرَبِّكَ فَٱصۡبِرۡ ۝	7. And for the sake of your Rabb, you persevere.
فَإِذَا نُقِرَ فِى ٱلنَّاقُورِ ۝	8. Then when the trumpet is blown into,

فَذَٰلِكَ يَوْمَئِذٍ يَوْمٌ عَسِيرٌ ۝

9. that then will be, that day, a distressing day—

عَلَى ٱلْكَٰفِرِينَ غَيْرُ يَسِيرٍ ۝

10. for the non-believers, not at all easy.

ذَرْنِي وَمَنْ خَلَقْتُ وَحِيدًا ۝

11. Leave Me alone with him whom I have created singly,

وَجَعَلْتُ لَهُ مَالًا مَّمْدُودًا ۝

12. and whom I have given abundant riches,

وَبَنِينَ شُهُودًا ۝

13. and children abiding in presence;

وَمَهَّدتُّ لَهُ تَمْهِيدًا ۝

14. and I have smoothed for him by smoothening,

ثُمَّ يَطْمَعُ أَنْ أَزِيدَ ۝

15. and yet who desires that I should give more!

كَلَّا إِنَّهُ كَانَ لِآيَٰتِنَا عَنِيدًا ۝

16. Never! Surely he is hostile to Our Messages.

سَأُرْهِقُهُ صَعُودًا ۝

17. I shall soon inflict him with a heavy load.

إِنَّهُ فَكَّرَ وَقَدَّرَ ۝

18. Surely he reflected, and he weighed,

فَقُتِلَ كَيْفَ قَدَّرَ ۝

19. but may he be destroyed, how he weighed!

ثُمَّ قُتِلَ كَيْفَ قَدَّرَ ۝

20. Again—may he be destroyed, how he weighed!

ثُمَّ نَظَرَ ۝

21. Then he looked about,

ثُمَّ عَبَسَ وَبَسَرَ ۝

22. then he frowned and scowled;

ثُمَّ أَدْبَرَ وَٱسْتَكْبَرَ ۝

23. then he deliberated and swelled with pride,

فَقَالَ إِنْ هَـٰذَآ إِلَّا سِحْرٌ يُؤْثَرُ ﴿٢٤﴾

24. and said: "This is nothing but an enchantment derived!

إِنْ هَـٰذَآ إِلَّا قَوْلُ ٱلْبَشَرِ ﴿٢٥﴾

25. "This is nothing but the sayings of a man."

سَأُصْلِيهِ سَقَرَ ﴿٢٦﴾

26. I shall soon throw him into a scorching Fire.

وَمَآ أَدْرَىٰكَ مَا سَقَرُ ﴿٢٧﴾

27. Ha! What will make you understand what the scorching Fire is!

لَا تُبْقِى وَلَا تَذَرُ ﴿٢٨﴾

28. It leaves nothing, nor does it spare.

لَوَّاحَةٌ لِّلْبَشَرِ ﴿٢٩﴾

29. It is scorching for the mortal.

عَلَيْهَا تِسْعَةَ عَشَرَ ﴿٣٠﴾

30. Over it is Nineteen.

وَمَا جَعَلْنَآ أَصْحَـٰبَ ٱلنَّارِ إِلَّا مَلَـٰئِكَةً وَمَا جَعَلْنَا عِدَّتَهُمْ إِلَّا فِتْنَةً لِّلَّذِينَ كَفَرُواْ لِيَسْتَيْقِنَ ٱلَّذِينَ أُوتُواْ ٱلْكِتَـٰبَ وَيَزْدَادَ ٱلَّذِينَ ءَامَنُواْ إِيمَـٰنًا وَلَا يَرْتَابَ ٱلَّذِينَ أُوتُواْ ٱلْكِتَـٰبَ وَٱلْمُؤْمِنُونَ وَلِيَقُولَ ٱلَّذِينَ فِى قُلُوبِهِم مَّرَضٌ وَٱلْكَـٰفِرُونَ مَاذَآ أَرَادَ ٱللَّهُ بِهَـٰذَا مَثَلًا كَذَٰلِكَ يُضِلُّ ٱللَّهُ مَن يَشَآءُ وَيَهْدِى مَن يَشَآءُ وَمَا يَعْلَمُ جُنُودَ رَبِّكَ إِلَّا هُوَ وَمَا هِىَ إِلَّا ذِكْرَىٰ لِلْبَشَرِ ﴿٣١﴾

31. And We have not appointed guardians of the Fire except the angels, and we have not made their numbering but as a test for those who disbelieve, in order to make convinced those who have been given the Scripture, and to increase the faith of those who believe, and that those who have been given the Scripture and the Believers may not doubt; and that those in whose hearts there is a disease and the non-believers may say: "What does Allāh intend by this parable?" Thus does Allāh leave in straying whom He pleases and guides whom He pleases. And nobody knows the hosts of your Rabb except Himself. And this is nothing but a Reminder to the mortals.

Explanation:

1. The first seven āyāt of this sūrah was the second revelation sent after the first five āyāt of sūrah al-'Alaq. There was a break of several months between the first set of revelations and the second set now revealed. This break is known as *fatrat al-wahi*.

   The sūrah derives its title from the mention of *muddaththir* (one who is wrapped up). This title is identical in meaning to *muzzammil* (one who is covered up, or enwrapped) used in the previous sūrah. Both titles are affectionately used to address Rasūlullāh (S), drawing attention to the incident when he scurried back home, trembling from to shock and fear, and asked his wife to wrap him up in blankets to stop his shivering. The message of sūrah Muzzammil was to prepare Rasūlullāh (S) to carry on the huge responsibility of delivering the divine message. The message of sūrah Muddaththir explains the actual responsibility. This responsibility is to openly invite people to accept Islam.

2. The command "arise and warn" was the first divine instruction to Rasūlullāh (S), asking him to begin the public call to convey the divine message. Until this point in time, Rasūlullāh (S) did not engage in any active propagation of the divine message first received on Mount Hira. During the initial stage, lasting for about six months, Rasūlullāh (S) mostly confined his preaching to close family members and friends. After the instruction came to make the public call, Rasūlullāh (S) began gradually, starting with his wider circle of family members and Hāshim clan, and then expanding to all of the Quraish.

3. In sūrah al-'Alaq, the word Rabb was used twice—first as the Rabb who created and then as Rabb, the most Honorable. This āyah asks Rasūlullāh (S) and all of us to "magnify" or "applaud" Him. By using the word *Rabb*, Allāh (swt) establishes His relationship with us. He is "Rabb," that is, He is the Lord and Master who is also the maintainer, the provider, the regulator, the rewarder, the ruler, and the sustainer. The best way to applaud the Almighty is to exalt His attributes through the performance of salāt and meditation. This command is similar to the previous sūrah where Rasūlullāh (S) was asked to devote time to similar activity (73:2–4).

4. The word *thiyāb* (garments) can be interpreted in its literal sense, implying the need for a clean garment before performing salāt. However, many classical commentators think that rather than outward purification, the āyah is urging purification of one's heart and intentions. In classical usage, the word *thiyāb* also means the object that the garment encloses—a person's body and in wider sense, his or her soul or heart, or even one's inclinations.

5. Most classical commentators interpreted *rujz* as idols. Literally, the term means pollution, impurity or uncleanliness, referring to one's moral and physical conditions, particularly those originating from loyalty to idols and false gods. People are asked to abandon the idols and shun the evils so that they can recognize their Rabb and worship Him alone.

6. Rasūlullāh (S) is primarily addressed in this āyah, therefore, he is advised not to expect any earthly gain for the time and effort he would be exerting to preach the divine message. The moral for us is this: receiving benefits should not be the motive when we confer benefits upon others.

7. With this āyah, the second set of revelations ended. After this, the theme of the sūrah changes in the next āyah. Now that Rasūlullāh (S) was asked to make the public call, evidently opposition toward his message would increase. Therefore, Allāh (swt) asks him to persevere in his mission. The word *sabr* means endurance, perseverance, patience and fortitude. He is required to be constant in his belief and not to waver or weaken during the difficulties that he will face. He has to continue doing his job.

8–10. Āyāt in this section were revealed several years after the previous passage. Rasūlullāh (S) and his companions were openly inviting people to accept Islam. However, many people and the leaders in Makkah were reluctant. The leaders began to oppose the religion and prevented others from listening to Muhammad's (S) message. In response to their opposition, Allāh (swt) now clarified the warning (nadhir) mentioned in āyah 2. A distressing day will come when the non-believers will find it difficult to cope. That day would be the Day of Awakening. A trumpet (nāqur) would be blown to announce the beginning of the Day of Judgment. The day is referred to as a "distressing day" because the calamity of the day will cause tremendous agony in the minds of sinners.

11. The āyah seems to indicate that someone who opposes the message of Islam should be left alone. No specific name is mentioned, so the underlying message applies to everyone who opposes the message during every time period.

The meaning of the āyah can be understood in two different ways based on which meaning is applied to the phrase "created singly" (wahīdan). On one hand, wahid (one, alone or single) can refer to Allāh's (swt) oneness, stressing His almightiness in creating everything in the universe without seeking assistance from anyone. Thus, He is, the sole creator of human beings. Allāh's (swt) right to deal with human beings stems from His exclusive position of being our creator. Alternately, wahid can also refer to man's final destiny when he will be individually held accountable for his deeds, with no help allowed from any friends or relatives.

12–14. The unnamed person mentioned in the previous āyah symbolizes all those who oppose the truth and deny Allāh's (swt) message. These people actually enjoy many of Allāh's (swt) blessings. For example, Allāh (swt) gave this person wealth and children. In many examples in the Qur'ān, the number of children is mentioned as an indication of one's power and wealth because people in Arabia considered a larger family to be a sign of one's valor. In addition, with the progression of time, the affairs of life were made easier and more comfortable, and at the same time, various challenges in the path of man's progression were made conquerable.

15. In spite of receiving all the blessings mentioned in the previous āyāt, human greed is insatiable. Human beings solicit from their Rabb fulfillment of all their desires, but they fail to acknowledge the Provider and forget to offer gratitude to Him.

16. Generally, the use of the word kalla in the beginning of an āyah cancels the ideas in the previous āyah and reinforces the ideas in the subsequent āyāt. In the previous āyah, non-religious people wanted more affluence from Allāh (swt). The word kalla emphasizes that affluence will never be given to them; instead, they will be afflicted with heavy loads, as stated in the next āyah. In the classical commentaries of the Qur'ān, the person referred to here was identified as Walīd ibn Mughīrah, who was vehemently opposed to Rasūlullāh (S). In a broad sense, the person mentioned here represents all people who are opposed to the truth. This is further implied by the word 'anīd derived from the verb 'anada (rebellious, stubborn and disobedient).

17. Despite what the non-religious people wished for in āyah 15, the opposite will happen to them, as the word kalla in the previous āyah implied. The word arhaqa (to impose a difficult task on someone, to afflict with troubles and difficulties) is further qualified by the word sa'ūd (ascent, mount), which also means "a calamity," "a torment" and "mountain of fire in Hell." People who oppose the truth and neglect Allāh's (swt) teachings will soon be afflicted with insurmountable troubles and difficulties, both physical and emotional. These afflictions will be suffered in this world, implied by the prefix

"*sa*" in the beginning of the āyah—the usage of which signifies the near future. However, painful consequences will continue to affect them in the Hereafter.

18. The non-religious people sometimes do reflect (*fakhr*) on the divine message, however, with the sole intention of contradicting the message and the messenger. The word *qaddara* (to understand, to know) is further evidence of their deceitful way of reflecting on the message.

19–20. The attitude of the non-religious people, mentioned in the previous āyah, will cause their moral and spiritual destruction. The word *qutila* literally means "he has been killed," or "he may be killed." However, the use of *fa* as an auxiliary function to express the wish or desire of *qutila* indicates that it was a curse or an ill will of destruction. Double emphasis of the tragic wish in both āyāt indicates that it will certainly be fulfilled.

21–23. Within a few months of the public call to Islam, it was the Hajj season. The Makkan leaders were very concerned that such a large gathering might become the right platform for Muhammad (S) to spread his message. In order to prevent this from happening, several Quraish leaders came up with different suggestions. Ultimately they accepted the strategy of a Quraish leader named Walid ibn al-Mughira. His strategy is mentioned in the next āyah. The expressions "he looked about" (*nazara*), "he frowned" (*'abasa*), "he scowled" (*basara*) and "he deliberated" (*dabara*) indicate that the Quraish leaders carefully considered the divine message, however, with the intention of finding faults with it.

In a broad sense, non-believers sometimes look carefully look at the divine message—to find fault with the teaching. Even though they reflect on the message, their false pride overpowers them and prevents them from appreciating the truth.

24. Walid ibn al-Mughira suggested that during the time of Hajj, they would spread the rumor that Muhammad (S) was an enchanter. Through the practice of enchantment, he would cause separation between husband and wives, and brothers and sisters. They wanted the pilgrims to stay away from Muhammad (S) and not listen to his message. They were successful; because very few people listened to Muhammad (S). However, this propaganda helped spread his name all over Arabia, and even more people became aware that Muhammad (S) had something to convey.

Non-believers often accused Muhammad (S) of being an enchanter. The term *sihr* means sorcery or magic. In magic act, the magician creates an illusion of changing something into something else by using subtle maneuvers that escape ordinary observation. No lasting impact is desired from such act of illusion except to temporarily enthrall the audience. Rasūlullāh's (S) mission and preaching appeared to challenge the contemporary belief system and societal ideologies to such an extent that the skeptics thought it was unachievable, therefore, illusory in nature (10:2; 21:3; and 38:4).

25. The phrase "the saying of a man" is a wicked remark meant to undermine the divine message. Nobody ever saw who brought the revelations to Rasūlullāh (S). The skeptics were particularly doubtful about whether Rasūlullāh (S) was truly receiving divine revelations or if he was just making them up. In order to defeat the idea of a divine origin of the message, skeptics began to claim that these "messages" were nothing more than the utterances of a man.

26–29. The active opponents of Islam would be thrown into scorching fire (*saqar*). The true nature of the scorching fire cannot be understood other than it does not spare anything and it scorches the sinning mortals. The Qur'ān attempts to describe *saqar*, and then leaves it undefined for two reasons. First, it creates suspense in the minds of readers, and, second, it is something that human beings cannot fully understand because we do not have the appropriate faculties to realize aspects of the unseen.

30. In āyah 69:17, the mention of "eight" is left without a qualifying statement. Here, too, the significance of the number "nineteen" is left undefined. In this passage, the mention of "nineteen" is a continuation of an unknowable reality hinted at in āyah 27. As mentioned previously in the note for āyah 27, it is probably those parts of reality that man will never be able to fully comprehend because they do not have the adequate faculties to understand. For this reason it is mentioned as a parable (*mathal*) in āyah 31. Most of the early commentators indicated "nineteen" refers to angels who stand guard to hell. One of the classical commentators, Rāzī, hypothesized that this number refers to the misuse of man's "nineteen" faculties, including physical, emotional and intellectual abilities. In the twentieth century, some scholars offered a plausible mathematical explanation of the number nineteen that should not be overlooked as a coincidence. Regardless, no single explanation can adequately describe the underlying reality.

31. The word numbering (*'iddat*) refers to the angels mentioned in this āyah, which, in turn, refers to the number mentioned in the previous āyah. It is probably a valid thesis to argue that the number nineteen in the previous āyah refers to angels or angelic powers. Further, the āyah says that the number nineteen is a test (*fitnah*) for all people—Muslims and those who have been given the scriptures. Further research to relate the number nineteen to the Qur'ān could unearth certain flawless facts, which could convincingly usher people's faith toward the Qur'ān. However, the number is also treated as a parable (*mathal*); the purpose is to illustrate a moral attitude or a religious principle for the followers of the Qur'ān (2:26).

Therefore, those who do not believe in the Qur'ān will not find any guidance from it regardless of whether they confine themselves to the literal meaning of the parable or delve into its subtleties. For this reason, the person mentioned in āyāt 21 to 23 pondered, reflected, weighed, and deliberated on the Qur'ān, but could not find any meaning in its message.

Regarding the expression "Allāh (swt) guides whom He pleases," it is important to note that providing guidance is not an arbitrary action of Allāh (swt). Only when a person comes forward to receive guidance, will Allāh guide, and it will be commensurate to one's level of effort.

Words to know:

قُم: you stand. قَامَ: to stand. اِقَامَة: to perform, to establish. قِيَام: normal state. مَقَام: abode, place, residence.

كَبَر: to be great, to become hard. اِستكبَر: to become proud. كَبِير: leader, chief. كِبرِيَاء: greatness, supremacy.

ثِيَابٌ: garments, heart. ثَابَ: to return, to gather. ثَوَّبَ: to reward, to give recompense.

رِجزٌ: pollution, filth, abomination. رِجزٌ: punishment, plague, epidemic.

عَسَر: to be difficult, to be hard. عُسرٌ: hardship. عَسِير: difficult.

مَدَّ: to stretch forth, to cause to increase. مَمدُودٌ: spread out, extend. اَمَدَّ: to be bestowed, assisted, caused to abound.

بَقِيَ: to remain, to leave. لَا تُبقِي: they leave not. بَاقِيَات: the lasting one.

مَرَضَ: to become sick. مَرِيضٌ: sick person.

Sūrah Al-Muddaththir
Word-by-word meaning

بِسْمِ	ٱللَّهِ	ٱلرَّحْمَٰنِ	ٱلرَّحِيمِ
With the name of	Allāh	the most Kind	the most Rewarding
يَٰٓأَيُّهَا	ٱلْمُدَّثِّرُ ۝	قُمْ	فَأَنذِرْ ۝
O you	wrapped up	arise	and warn
وَرَبَّكَ	فَكَبِّرْ ۝	وَثِيَابَكَ	فَطَهِّرْ ۝
and you Rabb	magnify	and your garments	purify
وَٱلرُّجْزَ	فَٱهْجُرْ ۝	وَلَا	تَمْنُن
and filth	keep away from	and not	give a thing
تَسْتَكْثِرُ ۝	وَلِرَبِّكَ	فَٱصْبِرْ ۝	فَإِذَا
in order to increase	and for your Rabb	be patient	then when
نُقِرَ	فِى	ٱلنَّاقُورِ ۝	فَذَٰلِكَ
is sounded	into	trumpet	so that
يَوْمَئِذٍ	يَوْمٌ	عَسِيرٌ ۝	عَلَى
that Day will be	a Day	hard	for
ٱلْكَٰفِرِينَ	غَيْرُ	يَسِيرٍ ۝	ذَرْنِى
the non-believers	not	easy	leave Me alone
وَمَنْ	خَلَقْتُ	وَحِيدًا ۝	وَجَعَلْتُ
with whom	I created	singly, alone	and then granted
لَهُۥ	مَالًا	مَّمْدُودًا ۝	وَبَنِينَ
to him	resources	in abundance	and children
شُهُودًا ۝	وَمَهَّدتُّ	لَهُۥ	تَمْهِيدًا ۝
by his side	and made smooth	for him	settled

أَزِيدَ ۱٥	أَن	يَطْمَعُ	ثُمَّ
I should give more	that	he desires	yet, then
لِأَيَٰتِنَا	كَانَ	إِنَّهُۥ	كَلَّآ
to Our messages	has been	surely he	nay
إِنَّهُۥ	صَعُودًا ۱۷	سَأُرْهِقُهُۥ	عَنِيدًا ۱٦
surely he	a severe torment	I shall oblige him to face	stubborn and opposing
كَيْفَ	فَقُتِلَ	وَقَدَّرَ ۱۸	فَكَّرَ
how	so let him be cursed	and plotted	thought
كَيْفَ	قُتِلَ	ثُمَّ	قَدَّرَ ۱۹
how	let him be cursed	then	he plotted
ثُمَّ	نَظَرَ ۲۱	ثُمَّ	قَدَّرَ ۲۰
then	he looked about	then	he plotted
أَدْبَرَ	ثُمَّ	وَسَرَ ۲۲	عَبَسَ
he turned back	then	and he scowled	he frowned
هَٰذَآ	إِنْ	فَقَالَ	وَٱسْتَكْبَرَ ۲۳
this is	nothing	then he said	and was proud
إِنْ	يُؤْثَرُ ۲٤	سِحْرُ	إِلَّا
only	bought from old	magic	but
ٱلْبَشَرِ ۲٥	قَوْلُ	إِلَّا	هَٰذَآ
of the human being	the word	but	this is
أَدْرَىٰكَ	وَمَآ	سَقَرَ ۲٦	سَأُصْلِيهِ
will make you know	and what	hell fire	I will burn him in
تُبْقِى	لَا	سَقَرُ ۲۷	مَا
it spares	not	Hell fire	what is

لِّلۡبَشَرِ ﴿٢٩﴾	لَوَّاحَةٌ	تَذَرُ ﴿٢٨﴾	وَلَا
the skins	burning	does it leave	nor
جَعَلۡنَآ	وَمَا	تِسۡعَةَ عَشَرَ ﴿٣٠﴾	عَلَيۡهَا
We have set	and not	are nineteen	over it
مَلَٰٓئِكَةً	إِلَّا	ٱلنَّارِ	أَصۡحَٰبَ
angels	but	the Fire	as guardians of
إِلَّا	عِدَّتَهُمۡ	جَعَلۡنَا	وَمَا
except	their numbers	We have fixed	and not
لِيَسۡتَيۡقِنَ	كَفَرُواْ	لِّلَّذِينَ	فِتۡنَةً
in order to convince	who disbelieve	for those	as a trial
وَيَزۡدَادَ ،	ٱلۡكِتَٰبَ	أُوتُواْ	ٱلَّذِينَ
and may increase	the Scripture	were given	those who
وَلَا	إِيمَٰنًا	ءَامَنُواْ	ٱلَّذِينَ
and not	in Faith	who believe	those
ٱلۡكِتَٰبَ	أُوتُواْ	ٱلَّذِينَ	يَرۡتَابَ
the Scripture	were given	those who	may doubt
فِى	ٱلَّذِينَ	وَلِيَقُولَ	وَٱلۡمُؤۡمِنُونَ
in	those	and may say	and the believers
مَاذَآ	وَٱلۡكَٰفِرُونَ	مَّرَضٌ	قُلُوبِهِم
what	and the non-believers	is a disease	whose hearts
مَثَلًا	بِهَٰذَا	ٱللَّهُ	أَرَادَ
example	by this	Allāh	intends

كَذَٰلِكَ	يُضِلُّ	ٱللَّهُ	مَن
thus	leads astray	Allāh	whom

يَشَآءُ	وَيَهْدِى	مَن	يَشَآءُ
He wills	and guides	whom	He wills

وَمَا	يَعْلَمُ	جُنُودَ	رَبِّكَ
and none	knows	the hosts of	your Rabb

إِلَّا	هُوَ	وَمَا	هِىَ
but	He	and not	this is

إِلَّا	ذِكْرَىٰ	لِلْبَشَرِ ۩
but	a reminder	to mankind

A few applications of the message:

The message of this sūrah involves the actions that are needed to enter Paradise and the actions that are needed to avert punishment.

Although the first few āyāt of the sūrah were addressed to Rasūlullāh (S), the message applies to us equally. Among several messages in this section, the one predominantly noticeable is: "for the sake of your Rabb, you persevere." Perseverance means to show forbearance or endurance during times of difficulty. It is a positive approach to the challenges in life. In Islam the importance of perseverance is recognized as one of the most valuable virtues of life.

Every single person faces difficulties and obstacles in life. It is one of Allāh's (swt) divine strategies to test us with difficulties, losses and deaths. All people who lived in the past, including the messengers, were tried and tested. Those who persevered emerged as successful. It is easy to give up and accept defeat. But Allāh (swt) teaches us not to give up. He wants us to overcome our difficulties and achieve success. With the help of Allāh (swt), it is entirely possible to overcome challenges. In the Qur'ān, Allāh (swt) says: "Seek help with patient perseverance and prayer, for Allāh is with those who patiently persevere."[2:153]

We should keep in mind that everyone faces trials and testing in life. We should never feel disheartened or give up hope. We should practice perseverance not only to overcome the difficulties in our lives, but also to become better Muslims.

Questions:

1. In āyah 7 of sūrah al-Muddaththir, why was Rasūlullāh (S) asked to persevere?

2. What did Allāh (swt) give the non-believers, yet they were not satisfied and remained hostile to His message?

3. In āyah 24, why did the Quraish claim Rasūlullāh (S) was an enchanter? What was the motive behind spreading this manner?

4. What is the significance of the number "nineteen" mentioned in āyah 30 of sūrah al-Muddaththir?

5. In āyah 31 of sūrah al-Muddaththir, what is mentioned as a "test" for both Muslims and non-Muslims?

Sūrah 74
Part B

Al-Muddaththir
The One Wrapped Up

Introduction:

In the second part of sūrah Muddaththir, Rasūlullāh (S) was asked to warn the Quraish, and the rest of humanity, about the Day of Judgment. It will certainly be the day of the biggest calamity. On that day, everyone will be paid back in accordance to their deeds. The righteous will be in the blissful Garden of Delight and the sinners will be in the hot fire. This sūrah mentions four evil deeds that will cause sinners to suffer. It also reminds us that no form of intercession will benefit the sinners. Finally, the sūrah points out that Rasūlullāh (S) can only warn people, but he cannot force them to accept Islam. Whoever wished to guard themselves from punishment may pay attention to the divine message.

بِسْمِ ٱللَّهِ ٱلرَّحْمَـٰنِ ٱلرَّحِيمِ

In the name of Allāh, the most Kind, the most Rewarding.

كَلَّا وَٱلْقَمَرِ ۝ 32. Never! Consider the Moon;

وَٱلَّيْلِ إِذْ أَدْبَرَ ۝ 33. and the night as it departs,

وَٱلصُّبْحِ إِذَآ أَسْفَرَ ۝ 34. and the morning as it shines.

إِنَّهَا لَإِحْدَى ٱلْكُبَرِ ۝ 35. Surely it is one of the greatest,

نَذِيرًا لِّلْبَشَرِ ۝ 36. as a warning to mortals—

لِمَن شَآءَ مِنكُمْ أَن يَتَقَدَّمَ أَوْ يَتَأَخَّرَ ۝ 37. for the one among you who wishes to advance, or to fall back.

كُلُّ نَفْسٍ بِمَا كَسَبَتْ رَهِينَةٌ ۝ 38. Every soul is pledged for what it earns;

إِلَّا أَصْحَٰبَ ٱلْيَمِينِ ۝

39. except the Companions of the Right hand.

فِى جَنَّٰتٍ يَتَسَآءَلُونَ ۝

40. In the Garden they will be asking one another

عَنِ ٱلْمُجْرِمِينَ ۝

41. about the guilty—

مَا سَلَكَكُمْ فِى سَقَرَ ۝

42. "What has brought you into the scorching Fire?"

قَالُوا۟ لَمْ نَكُ مِنَ ٱلْمُصَلِّينَ ۝

43. They will say: "We were not among the performers of Salāt,

وَلَمْ نَكُ نُطْعِمُ ٱلْمِسْكِينَ ۝

44. "nor were we who feed the poor;

وَكُنَّا نَخُوضُ مَعَ ٱلْخَآئِضِينَ ۝

45. "but we used to indulge with the indulgers,

وَكُنَّا نُكَذِّبُ بِيَوْمِ ٱلدِّينِ ۝

46. "and we used to belie the Judgment Day

حَتَّىٰٓ أَتَىٰنَا ٱلْيَقِينُ ۝

47. "till the inevitable overtook us."

فَمَا تَنفَعُهُمْ شَفَٰعَةُ ٱلشَّٰفِعِينَ ۝

48. Therefore the intercession of the intercessors will not benefit them.

فَمَا لَهُمْ عَنِ ٱلتَّذْكِرَةِ مُعْرِضِينَ ۝

49. What is then the matter with them that they turn away from the Reminder,

كَأَنَّهُمْ حُمُرٌ مُّسْتَنفِرَةٌ ۝

50. as if they were scared donkeys

فَرَّتْ مِن قَسْوَرَةٍ ۝

51. running away from a lion?

بَلْ يُرِيدُ كُلُّ ٱمْرِئٍ مِّنْهُمْ أَن يُؤْتَىٰ صُحُفًا مُّنَشَّرَةً ۝

52. In fact, every person among them wished that he would be given expanded scrolls.

كَلَّا ۖ بَل لَّا يَخَافُونَ ٱلْأَخِرَةَ ۝ 53. Never! But they do not fear the Hereafter.

كَلَّا إِنَّهُ تَذْكِرَةٌ ۝ 54. Never! Certainly this is a Reminder

فَمَن شَاءَ ذَكَرَهُ ۝ 55. so that whoever wishes may mind it.

وَمَا يَذْكُرُونَ إِلَّا أَن يَشَاءَ ٱللَّهُ ۚ هُوَ أَهْلُ ٱلتَّقْوَىٰ وَأَهْلُ ٱلْمَغْفِرَةِ ۝ 56. And they will not mind except as Allah pleases. He is the most Worthy of reverence, and He is the most Worthy of forgiveness.

Explanation:

32–34. The particle "*wa*" is used as a divine oath to attract the attention of the audience and emphasize the truth that follows in the subsequent passage. The changing phases of the moon and the alternation of day and night are some of the natural phenomena, but the natural explanation for all natural events does not exclude the possibility of the existence of a supreme power. The Qur'ān repeatedly draws human attention toward nature to point out that orderliness in nature is the strongest evidence of one Creator.

35–36. Based on the sequence of the passage that begins with the scorching fire (*saqar*) and its clarification, the pronoun "*ha*" refers to the fire mentioned in āyāt 26 and 27. It is the greatest warning for mankind.

37. The warning of fire applies to everyone regardless of whether a person believes in the divine message or chooses to disregard the teaching.

38. Everyone will be held accountable for what they do and do not do. The word pledge (*ksasabat*) is used in the sense of loads of bad deeds. Instead of accumulating many good deeds, human beings pledge loads of bad deeds—moral and spiritual shortfalls—not realizing that these bad deeds will pull them down in the Hereafter.

39–42. The "right side" or "right hand" is always used symbolically in the Qur'ān in connection with righteous deeds or righteous people. The use of right hand or left hand has nothing to do with a person's biological disposition (56:8, 27–40). The level of righteousness would outweigh any burden of sin; therefore a person will not be pulled down by his or her sins. The person will be in Paradise asking others about the sinners.

Earlier, āyāt 19 and 20 of this sūrah promised that the sinners will be destroyed. Āyāt 26 and 27 warned the sinners that they would be thrown into scorching fire. Now after the judgment, people in Paradise will ask what made the sinners go to the scorching fire.

43. As stated in āyah 38, every soul is pledged for what it earns. The souls of sinners will realize the reality of the pledges that brought them to the scorching fire. One reason was non-performance of

salāt. Formal salāt was yet to be prescribed, but believers were performing it individually. Within a few years formal salāt would become compulsory. Therefore, the message of this verse should be understood from the standpoint of total Qur'ānic message.

44. Additionally, the sinners did not take the initiative to provide food to the poor and hungry. The importance of feeding the poor is repeatedly emphasized in the Qur'ān as a necessary social obligation of well-to-do people. Not fulfilling this obligation adds up to sin, which will eventually cause suffering in the scorching fire.

45–47. During their earthly lives, the sinners indulged in useless pursuits and remained busy with selfish, earthly motives. They believed that they would never be held accountable; therefore, the concept of the Day of Judgment was never a factor in their actions or thoughts. Only after death did their soul realize that it was a mistake to ignore their spiritual duties.

48. The Qur'ān indicates that some forms of intercession (*shafā'at*) will be allowed, only from Muhammad (S), but it would not be able to override the divine judgment (2:48; 6:51; 40:18). No other forms of intercession from any person will be accepted. Everyone will come to Allāh (swt) alone with one's own account (19:95).

49–51. Even after learning about one's worldly and spiritual duties, and learning about the serious consequences of not fulfilling these duties, it is strange that people are turning away from the reminder. In the parable, the lion represents "duties," which people are required to meet. Instead they run away from it, afraid of fulfilling their duties.

52–54. People were reluctant to accept the divine message, assuming that it was only the sayings of a man (āyah 25). They thought that if there was anything divine in the message, they should experience it first. According to them, the best way to experience it would be for each one of them to receive a divine book directly from Heaven. So the next āyah says, *kalla*, indicating this wish will never be fulfilled. The Qur'ān is sufficient as a reminder for all of mankind and guides everyone in all matters of life (21:10; 25:1; 74:37).

55–56. There is no compulsion to believe in the message of the Qur'ān. People are given the freedom of choice to choose any path they like. Allāh (swt) will be happy to guide people on the right course; however, due to the freedom of choice given to them, Allāh (swt) will not force them. The āyah says that people will not pay attention unless it is Allāh's (swt) wish. His wish is not preferential treatment. In the matter of faith, Allāh's wishes will work only after a person desires to seek guidance and demonstrates the necessary efforts to obtain guidance.

Words to know:

دَبَرَ: to turn back, flee. دَبَّرَ: to dispose, to govern. مُدَبِّر: one who manages affairs. أدبَرَ: declining, setting.

سَفَرَ: to disperse, to sweep, to unveil. سَفَر: journey. أَسفَارٌ: large book, journal. سَفَرَةٌ: scribes.

أَخَرَ: to put behind. آخِر: last one. تَأَخَّرَ: delayed, that comes later. آخِرَةٌ: Hereafter.

رَهَنَ: to give in pledge. رَهِينٌ: pledged. رِهَان: pledge.

جَرَمَ: to cut, to commit a crime. مُجرِم: criminal.

خَاضَ: to engage in a topic, to indulge in vain discussion. خَوضٌ: vain talk. نَخُوض: talk falsehood.

شَفَعَ: protect, mediate. شَافِعِين: interceders. شَفَاعَةٌ: intercession.

نَفَرَ: to run away, to flee. مُسْتَنْفِرَةٌ: one who runs away, fugitive.

نَشَرَ: to spread out. مُنْشَرَةٌ: spread open. نُشُور: the Resurrection.

Sūrah Al-Muddaththir
Word-by-word meaning

بِسْمِ	ٱللَّهِ	ٱلرَّحْمَـٰنِ	ٱلرَّحِيمِ
In the name of	Allāh	the most Kind	the most Rewarding
كَلَّا	وَٱلْقَمَرِ	وَٱلَّيْلِ	إِذْ
never!	and by the moon	and by the night	when
أَدْبَرَ	وَٱلصُّبْحِ	إِذَآ	أَسْفَرَ
it withdraws	and by the dawn	when	it brightens
إِنَّهَا	لَإِحْدَى	ٱلْكُبَرِ	نَذِيرًا
surely	it is but one of	the greatest (signs)	a warning
لِّلْبَشَرِ	لِمَن	شَآءَ	مِنكُمْ
to mortals	to any that	chooses	of you
أَن	يَتَقَدَّمَ	أَوْ	يَتَأَخَّرَ
to	go forward	or	remain behind
كُلُّ	نَفْسٍ	بِمَا	كَسَبَتْ
every	souyl	for what	he has earned
رَهِينَةٌ	إِلَّا	أَصْحَـٰبَ	ٱلْيَمِينِ
is a pledge	except	those	on the Right

عَنِ	يَتَسَآءَلُونَ	جَنَّـٰتٍ	فِى
about	they will ask one another	gardens	in
فِى	سَلَكَكُمْ	مَا	ٱلْمُجْرِمِينَ
into	has caused you to enter	what	the guilty
نَكُ	لَمْ	قَالُوا۟	سَقَرَ
we were	not	they will say	scorching fire
نَكُ	وَلَمْ	ٱلْمُصَلِّينَ	مِنَ
we used to	nor	used to offer their salāt	of those who
نَخُوضُ	وَكُنَّا	ٱلْمِسْكِينَ	نُطْعِمُ
talk falsehood	and we used to	the poor	feed
نُكَذِّبُ	وَكُنَّا	ٱلْخَآئِضِينَ	مَعَ
deny	and we used to	the vain talkers	with
أَتَـٰنَا	حَتَّىٰ	ٱلدِّينِ	بِيَوْمِ
there came to us	until	Recompense	the Day of
شَفَـٰعَةُ	تَنفَعُهُمْ	فَمَا	ٱلْيَقِينُ
intercession of	will be of use to them	so not	the certainty
عَنِ	لَهُمْ	فَمَا	ٱلشَّـٰفِعِينَ
from	with them that	then what is wrong	intercessors
حُمُرٌ	كَأَنَّهُمْ	مُعْرِضِينَ	ٱلتَّذْكِرَةِ
donkeys	as if they were	they turn away	the admonition
قَسْوَرَةٍ	مِن	فَرَّتْ	مُّسْتَنفِرَةٌ
a lion	from	fleeing	frightened

بَل	يُرِيدُ	كُلُّ	ٱمْرِئٍ
in fact	desires	every	person

مِّنْهُم	أَن	يُؤْتَىٰ	صُحُفًا
of them	that	he should be given	pages

مُّنَشَّرَةً ۝	كَلَّا	بَل	لَّا
spread out	never	but	not

تَخَافُونَ	ٱلْأَخِرَةَ ۝	كَلَّا	إِنَّهُ
they fear	the Hereafter	never	certainly this

تَذْكِرَةٌ ۝	فَمَن	شَاءَ	ذَكَرَهُ ۝
is an admonition	so whosoever	will	reflect on it

وَمَا	يَذْكُرُونَ	إِلَّآ	أَن
and not	they will reflect	unless	that

يَشَاءَ	ٱللَّهُ	هُوَ	أَهْلُ
wills	Allāh	He is	the One deserving

ٱلتَّقْوَىٰ	وَأَهْلُ	ٱلْمَغْفِرَةِ ۝	
piety	and He is the One worthy	Who Forgives	

A few applications of the message:

One of the key objectives of the Qur'ān is to caution people about the paths they follow. There are fundamentally two different paths: (1) the right path and (2) the wrong path. There is only one right path, but there are several wrong paths. The right path is the one approved by Allāh (swt). If we choose to adopt the right path, Allāh (swt) will be there to guide us. If we choose to adopt the wrong path, Allāh (swt) will not misguide us, but He will leave us without guidance. Any path that does not guide us to perform the righteous deeds will cause our destruction in this life and in the Hereafter. We want to avoid the wrong path at all costs.

We will ultimately be responsible for our good and bad deeds. The load of our good deeds will determine the quality of our life in the Hereafter. This part of the sūrah provides a few examples of good deeds. These are: (1) performance of salāt and (2) feeding the poor. Both duties are so important, Allāh (swt) mentioned them specifically. The sinners neglect to perform these two duties. This negligence will cause them to suffer in the Hereafter.

In light of this sūrah, we must remember to perform salāt at its appointed time and on a regular basis. At the same time, we should remember poor people and always help them. Salāt is a duty that benefits one's own soul, and feeding the poor is a communal duty that benefits society.

Questions:

1. According to sūrah Muddaththir, what are the four reasons sinners will be in scorching fire?

2. According to the explanation, what is the meaning of the parable about the donkey running from the lion?

3. Āyah 36 of sūrah Muddaththir speaks about a warning. Who are supposed to benefit from the warning?

4. In āyah 52 of sūrah Muddaththir, what is the reason each person wanted to receive a scroll in his or her hands?

5. What is the significance of the phrase "except as Allāh wishes," as mentioned in āyah 56 of sūrah Muddaththir?

Sūrah 75
Part A

Revealed in Makkah

Al-Qiyamah

The Awakening

Introduction:

The central theme of the sūrah is the Awakening, implied from its title. This sūrah was revealed during the early period of Rasūlullāh's (S) career in Makkah. During this period, a steady flow of revelations continued to point out the moral and social evils of the Quraish. They were also told about the Day of Awakening and the importance of the Day of Judgment. It was a novel concept that seemed unbelievable to them. They could not understand how all the dead people from the past and present could become alive again on the Day of Awakening. In response to this doubt, the Qur'ān explains that it is absolutely possible for Allāh (swt) to recreate life forms just as He had created all life forms in the first place. The sūrah describes the time when the Awakening will happen. It also provides a vivid description of the conditions of the righteous and the sinners. The middle of the sūrah advises Rasūlullāh (S) not to rush to remember all the revelations, for it is Allāh's (swt) responsibility to gather all the revelations, make Muhammad (S) remember them and explain their meanings.

بِسْمِ ٱللَّهِ ٱلرَّحْمَـٰنِ ٱلرَّحِيمِ

In the name of Allāh, the most Kind, the most Rewarding.

لَآ أُقْسِمُ بِيَوْمِ ٱلْقِيَـٰمَةِ ۝	1. NAY! I call to witness the day of the Awakening!
وَلَآ أُقْسِمُ بِٱلنَّفْسِ ٱللَّوَّامَةِ ۝	2. And nay! I call to witness the self-accusing soul.
أَيَحْسَبُ ٱلْإِنسَـٰنُ أَلَّن نَّجْمَعَ عِظَامَهُۥ ۝	3. Does man reckon that We shall not gather his bones?
بَلَىٰ قَـٰدِرِينَ عَلَىٰ أَن نُّسَوِّىَ بَنَانَهُۥ ۝	4. Yes! We are Capable of restoring his finger bones.
بَلْ يُرِيدُ ٱلْإِنسَـٰنُ لِيَفْجُرَ أَمَامَهُۥ ۝	5. But man desires to act wickedly in front of him.

6. He asks: "When is the day of the Awakening?"

يَسْـَٔلُ أَيَّانَ يَوْمُ ٱلْقِيَٰمَةِ ۝

7. So that when the sight is confused;

فَإِذَا بَرِقَ ٱلْبَصَرُ ۝

8. and the moon is eclipsed;

وَخَسَفَ ٱلْقَمَرُ ۝

9. and the sun and the moon are brought together;

وَجُمِعَ ٱلشَّمْسُ وَٱلْقَمَرُ ۝

10. on that day, man will say: "Where is the place of refuge?"

يَقُولُ ٱلْإِنسَٰنُ يَوْمَئِذٍ أَيْنَ ٱلْمَفَرُّ ۝

11. Nowhere! There is no refuge!

كَلَّا لَا وَزَرَ ۝

12. Toward your Rabb that day is the resting place.

إِلَىٰ رَبِّكَ يَوْمَئِذٍ ٱلْمُسْتَقَرُّ ۝

13. Man will, on that day, be informed about what he sent forward, and what he left behind.

يُنَبَّؤُا۟ ٱلْإِنسَٰنُ يَوْمَئِذٍ بِمَا قَدَّمَ وَأَخَّرَ ۝

14. In fact, man is enlightened against his own soul,

بَلِ ٱلْإِنسَٰنُ عَلَىٰ نَفْسِهِۦ بَصِيرَةٌ ۝

15. even though he puts forth his excuses.

وَلَوْ أَلْقَىٰ مَعَاذِيرَهُۥ ۝

16. Do not move your tongue with it, so as to make haste with it.

لَا تُحَرِّكْ بِهِۦ لِسَانَكَ لِتَعْجَلَ بِهِۦٓ ۝

17. Surely upon Us rests the collection of it, and the recitation of it.

إِنَّ عَلَيْنَا جَمْعَهُۥ وَقُرْءَانَهُۥ ۝

18. Therefore when We have recited it, then you follow its recital.

فَإِذَا قَرَأْنَٰهُ فَٱتَّبِعْ قُرْءَانَهُۥ ۝

19. Then again, upon Us, indeed, rests the explaining of it.

ثُمَّ إِنَّ عَلَيْنَا بَيَانَهُۥ ۝

20. Never, yet you love the transitory,

كَلَّا بَلْ تُحِبُّونَ ٱلْعَاجِلَةَ ﴿٢٠﴾

21. and forsake the Hereafter.

وَتَذَرُونَ ٱلْأَخِرَةَ ﴿٢١﴾

22. Faces on that day will be shining,

وُجُوهٌ يَوْمَئِذٍ نَّاضِرَةٌ ﴿٢٢﴾

23. looking toward their Rabb,

إِلَىٰ رَبِّهَا نَاظِرَةٌ ﴿٢٣﴾

24. And faces on that day will be gloomy,

وَوُجُوهٌ يَوْمَئِذٍ بَاسِرَةٌ ﴿٢٤﴾

25. thinking that some back-breaking calamity is going to fall upon them.

تَظُنُّ أَن يُفْعَلَ بِهَا فَاقِرَةٌ ﴿٢٥﴾

26. No, when it reaches the throat,

كَلَّا إِذَا بَلَغَتِ ٱلتَّرَاقِيَ ﴿٢٦﴾

27. it will then be said: "Who is the charmer?"

وَقِيلَ مَنْ رَاقٍ ﴿٢٧﴾

28. And he thinks that it is the departing,

وَظَنَّ أَنَّهُ ٱلْفِرَاقُ ﴿٢٨﴾

29. and one shin will rub against the other shin;

وَٱلْتَفَّتِ ٱلسَّاقُ بِٱلسَّاقِ ﴿٢٩﴾

30. toward your Rabb that day is the driving.

إِلَىٰ رَبِّكَ يَوْمَئِذٍ ٱلْمَسَاقُ ﴿٣٠﴾

Explanation:

1. There are two different opinions about the use of the particle *lā* (no, not) in the beginning of the sūrah. The first opinion is the particle *lā* rejects some notion that was already in circulation. The specific notion is not mentioned, but as the sūrah continues, we find that the notion was about the Awakening, which the Quraish denied. By beginning the sūrah with the particle *lā*, the Qur'ān is rejecting the notion that the Awakening would not happen.

   The second opinion is the particle *lā* (no, not) is used as an oath, rather than a particle of negation, in order to provide a more forceful emphasis on the message. By using the first-person singular form, Allāh (swt) calls to witness the certainty of the Day of Awakening (*qiyāmah*). Such rare first-person singular testimony in the Qur'ān draws attention to the eventful Day, which is under the absolute control of Allāh (swt). This testimony further imparts divine confidence in its inevitable happening.

2. The divine oath is also taken in the name of a self-accusing soul (*lawwāmah*). The significance of the self-accusing soul can be understood in relation to the three stages of the human soul, hinted on in the Qur'ān (12:53; 89:27–30). A person whose soul is stagnant in *ammārah* or the animal stage (12:53), will submit to animal passion and behave like an animal. It will be difficult for a person in the *ammārah* stage to achieve spiritual progress. The next highest stage, *lawwāmah*, is the self-accusing stage. When the soul of a person reaches this stage, he or she is able to recognize the failures, shortcomings or negligence in fulfilling his or her duties. This realization will enable the person to correct his or her lapses and progress to the next level of a human soul. The final stage of a human soul is *mutma'innah*, or the Heavenly stage (89:27).

3–4. People seem to doubt whether it is possible for Allāh (swt) to gather the disintegrated bones of millions of dead people on the Day of Awakening to bring forth new lives. The answer to such doubt is given by stating that Allāh (swt) is capable of restoring the smallest finger bone of human beings. Although restoration of finger bones is mentioned, in a broad sense, the entire body is implied. The term *banān* means the fingers or tips of the fingers (phalanges). The emphasis on finger bones is mentioned for two reasons: (1) it is one of the smallest bones in the body, and (2) the ability of expressive manipulation of fingers imparted the superiority of human beings over all other creatures.

5. In spite of receiving divine assurance of resurrection, people remain oblivious to the warning. The main reason people deny the Awakening is not because they consider it impossible, but because their selfish motives do not allow them to affirm it. The use of the word *insān* (man) indicates that both believers and non-believers are covered by its definition. They think that an accounting of their deeds will not happen or if it does happen, they will find a way to subvert it. As a result of such conviction, they continue their wickedness.

6–8. With some degree of derision and doubt in mind, people want to know when the Day of Awakening will happen or if it will happen at all. In reply the Qur'ān states that the Day will commence when the sight of human beings is confused and the moon is eclipsed. The covering up of the moon may imply a total lunar eclipse. It could also mean a huge amount of volcanic ash from a super volcanic eruption might cloud the sky for months, causing a clouding of vision and covering the moon from sight. Needless to say, these developments are precursors to the Awakening; therefore, its true reality cannot be explained by available knowledge.

9. The previous āyah says the moon will be eclipsed. This āyah says the sun and the moon will be brought together. The word *jama'a* means to unite, to assemble or to collect. Bringing these objects together

does not mean that they will collide with one another. Study of astronomy does not indicate that they will collide within a few billion years. The sun symbolizes daytime, and the moon symbolizes night time. When both are brought together, the purpose of separating day and night ceases—it is either perpetual day or night.

10–11. On the Day of Awakening, those who are still alive on the earth will try to flee from the calamity of the day. They will seek refuge wherever they can, but they will realize that there is no refuge (42:47).

12–13. While people will unsuccessfully seek refuge wherever they can, they will find instead that their resting place (*mustaqar*) is toward their Lord. The word *mustaqar* indicates a place to stay for a long period of time—either in hell or in paradise. On the Day of Awakening, human beings will be given an objective view of their earthly lives. From the perspective of a third person, everyone will see each and every deed that they sent forward for evaluation. They will also see all the obligatory deeds and opportunities for good deeds that they did not care to fulfill.

14–15. After distinguishing the good deeds and the bad deeds of one's earthly life, human beings will then become witnesses against themselves. Even then they will continue to present poor excuses for leaving the right path and adopting the wrong one. They will try to justify the reasons they adopted a path that was not divinely approved or strictly condemned.

16. Āyāt 16 to 19 interrupts the message about the Awakening to give Rasūlullāh (S) an important message. This sūrah was revealed during the early Makkan period. During this period, Rasūlullāh (S) sometimes used to feel the urgency to commit the revelation to memory as soon as Jibril (A) finished the revelation. He feared that unless he memorized it promptly, he might miss a word or two. Therefore, he was commanded not to hurry to memorize the words, rather to listen attentively to the revelation until it was transmitted completely.

17. During the process of revelation, the Qur'ān referred to itself as a book, but it was far from being a book in the normal sense of the word. Evidently Allāh (swt) had a plan to compile and collect the revelation in book form over the course of time. Rasūlullāh (S) was informed of this divine plan through another revelation, where Allāh (swt) mentions that He, Himself, was the guardian of the revelation (15:9). Thus, Rasūlullāh (S) was released from any additional duty of compiling it into a formal book. However, during his lifetime, and under divine guidance, he arranged the revelations in their present order rather than in the chronological order of revelation (25:32). When the need arose to compile the revelations in a formal book, the khalīfas simply gathered together the manuscripts in the order arranged by Rasūlullāh (S) and made them into a book.

18. The phrase "when we have recited it" does not mean recitation by Allāh (swt). It means revelation through angel Jibril (A) and making the teachings understandable to man. The word *qarā'* (to read, to recite) does not imply mere recitation, but listening and paying attention, primarily to understand the meaning of the teachings.

19. Not only collection of the revelations was a responsibility of Allāh (swt), and explanation of the messages (*bayān*) also rests with Him (11:1; 55:2-4). The manner in which He explains the Qur'ān is by maintaining a textual and informational constancy, keeping uniformity and congruity throughout its entire message and making one verse amplify and supplement another verse. Thus the meaning of the Qur'ān is Qur'ān-bound, and the Qur'ān is its own best commentary. The Qur'ān is the benchmark not only as the basis for its own explanation, but also for other religious works, including Hadīth. It is important to note that explanations of the Qur'ān will always be limited by the boundaries of

an individual's knowledge base, which is, again, restricted to the extent that human knowledge has advanced during a given period of time. Its meaning is dynamic and not fixed by any scholar, past or present.

20-21. After a short interruption of the original message, this āyah returns to the ideas in āyah 15 and continues with the theme of the Awakening. Generally the word *kallā* (never!) negates any argument contrary to the statement in the previous āyah or sequence. Previously Allāh emphasized that explaining the message of the Qur'ān is His responsibility. Contrary to this statement, most people do not accept the teachings; instead, they show excessive love for the transitory life of this world and forsake the Hereafter. If the word *kallā* is said to connect with the previous theme, then we will have to look at where āyah 15 left off. People will present poor excuses for not accumulating enough good deeds during their lifetimes (āyāt 13 to 15). However, they will be told that they did not perform good deeds due to their love for the transitory world.

22-25. A person's face is an indicator of one's feelings, therefore, brightness or gloominess on the face indicates the hope and despair of the righteous and the sinners. The phrase "back-breaking calamity" (*faqara,* meaning to feel excruciating pain on the vertebrae, or to overwhelm with back-breaking calamity) in āyah 25 indicates realization that many bad deeds will make the sinners utterly disappointed in themselves. Loads can be carried on the head, hands, shoulders or back, but excessively heavy loads can only be carried on a person's back. Therefore, the Qur'ān uses the word *faraqa* in relation to the excess load of bad deeds.

26-28. When the soul of a dying person reaches his or her throat, the person will be asked who is the charmer (*rāqin*). The term *rāqin* (charmer, enchanter, physician) alludes to priests, saints and religious leaders, whose charms and deception caused many naïve people to deviate from the truth. The reason for the question is to remind the person, who remained busy with worldly affairs, that they cared the least about the spiritual duties of life. Now in the last moment of life, why are these "charmers" not able to prolong the life that seemed so enduring?

29-30. The shinbone, or shank, is the larger of the two bones in the lower leg of a person that enables him or her to stand up and walk. Rubbing the *sāq* (shank, shinbone) points to an extreme nervous condition, resulting in buckling of the legs. Even though the person would become immobile, one's destiny will still take him or her toward their Master to account for his or her deeds.

Words to know:

سَوِيَ: to be worth, equivalent to. اِسْتَوَىٰ: to establish, become firmly settled. سَوَّى: to proportion, to fashion, to make perfect. نُسَوِّي: reproduce to a complete form.

فَجَرَ: to dig up, to aside from right path. يَفْجُرَ: continues in evil ways. فَجَّرْنَا: we caused to gush forth. فَاجِر: evildoer, sinner. فُجُور: wickedness, evil.

بَرِقَ: to be confused, to be dazzled. بَرَق: lightning, thunderbolt. أَبَارِيق: water jug. اِسْتَبْرَق: brocade, silk of a thick texture.

خَسَفَ: to bring disgrace, to be eclipsed. يَخْسِفُ: he sinks. نَخْسِفُ: we make low.

وَزَرَ: to carry a burden. وَزْرٌ: burden. وَزِير: one who bears the burden of state, a minister or a counsellor.

لَقِيَ: to meet, to experience. أَلْقَى: offered. أَلْقَت: cast forth. أُلْقِيَ: is thrown.

Sūrah Al-Qiyamah
Word-by-word meaning

ٱلرَّحِيمِ	ٱلرَّحۡمَـٰنِ	ٱللَّهِ	بِسۡمِ
the most Rewarding	the most Kind	Allāh	In the name of
ٱلۡقِيَـٰمَةِ ۝١	بِيَوۡمِ	أُقۡسِمُ	لَآ
Awakening	by the Day of	I swear	nay
ٱللَّوَّامَةِ ۝٢	بِٱلنَّفۡسِ	أُقۡسِمُ	وَلَآ
self-reproaching	by the soul	I swear	and nay
نَّجۡمَعَ	أَلَّن	ٱلۡإِنسَـٰنُ	أَيَحۡسَبُ
We assemble	that shall never	man	does think
عَلَىٰ	قَـٰدِرِينَ	بَلَىٰ	عِظَامَهُۥ ۝٣
to	We are Able	yes	his bones
بَلۡ	بَنَانَهُۥ ۝٤	نُّسَوِّيَ	أَن
but	his finger bones	restoring	that
أَمَامَهُۥ ۝٥	لِيَفۡجُرَ	ٱلۡإِنسَـٰنُ	يُرِيدُ
before him	to commit sins	man	desires
ٱلۡقِيَـٰمَةِ ۝٦	يَوۡمُ	أَيَّانَ	يَسۡـَٔلُ
Awakening	this Day of	when will be	he asks
وَخَسَفَ	ٱلۡبَصَرُ ۝٧	بَرِقَ	فَإِذَا
and will be eclipsed	the sight	shall be dazed	so when
وَٱلۡقَمَرُ ۝٩	ٱلشَّمۡسُ	وَجُمِعَ	ٱلۡقَمَرُ ۝٨
and the moon	the sun	and will be joined together	the moon

يَقُولُ	ٱلْإِنسَـٰنُ	يَوْمَئِذٍ	أَيْنَ
will say	man	on that Day	where

ٱلْمَفَرُّ ۝	كَلَّا	لَا	وَزَرَ ۝
to flee	nay	not	(there is) refuge

إِلَىٰ	رَبِّكَ	يَوْمَئِذٍ	ٱلْمُسْتَقَرُّ ۝
unto	your Rabb	that Day	will be the place of rest

يُنَبَّؤُاْ	ٱلْإِنسَـٰنُ	يَوْمَئِذٍ	بِمَا
will be informed	man	on that Day	of what

قَدَّمَ	وَأَخَّرَ ۝	بَلِ	ٱلْإِنسَـٰنُ
he sent forward	and he left behind	in fact	man

عَلَىٰ	نَفْسِهِ	بَصِيرَةٌ ۝	وَلَوْ
against	himself	will be a witness	though

أَلْقَىٰ	مَعَاذِيرَهُ ۝	لَا	تُحَرِّكْ
he may put forth	his excuses	not	move

بِهِ	لِسَانَكَ	لِتَعْجَلَ	بِهِ ۝
with it	your tongue	to make haste	there with

إِنَّ	عَلَيْنَا	جَمْعَهُ	وَقُرْءَانَهُ ۝
surely	upon Us	the collection of it	and the recitation of it

فَإِذَا	قَرَأْنَـٰهُ	فَٱتَّبِعْ	قُرْءَانَهُ ۝
and when	We have recited it	then follow you	its recital

ثُمَّ	إِنَّ	عَلَيْنَا	بَيَانَهُ ۝
then	surely	upon Us	is the explaining of it

ٱلْعَاجِلَةَ ۞	تُحِبُّونَ	بَلْ	كَلَّا
the present life	you love	but	nay

يَوْمَئِذٍ	وُجُوهٌ	ٱلْأَخِرَةَ ۞	وَتَذَرُونَ
that Day	some faces	the Hereafter	and leave

نَاظِرَةٌ ۞	رَبِّهَا	إِلَى	نَّاضِرَةٌ ۞
looking	their Rabb	at	shall be radiant

تَظُنُّ	بَاسِرَةٌ ۞	يَوْمَئِذٍ	وَوُجُوهٌ
thinking	will be frowning	that Day	and some faces

فَاقِرَةٌ ۞	بِهَا	يُفْعَلَ	أَن
some calamity	on them	was about to be done	that

ٱلتَّرَاقِيَ ۞	بَلَغَتِ	إِذَا	كَلَّا
to the throat	it reaches	when	no!

وَظَنَّ	رَاقٍ ۞	مَّنْ	وَقِيلَ
and he thinks	(the) charmer	who is	and it will be said

ٱلسَّاقُ	وَٱلْتَفَّتِ	ٱلْفِرَاقُ ۞	أَنَّهُ
the shin	and will be joined	the time of departing	that it was

يَوْمَئِذٍ	رَبِّكَ	إِلَىٰ	بِٱلسَّاقِ ۞
on that Day	your Rabb	to	with another shin

ٱلْمَسَاقُ ۞
the drive will be

A few applications of the message:

We know from the title of the surah that its message is about the Awakening. All Muslims believe in the Awakening. It is part of our faith. The question is: why does Allāh (swt) caution us about the Awakening? It is because sometimes we forget about the Awakening and become too busy with worldly life. The glamour of life fascinates us. We tend to behave as if this life is all that matters and as if there is no life in the Hereafter. Āyah 20 cautions us about this tendency. We forget that we will be held accountable for all our deeds.

Āyah 5 says that human beings desire to act wickedly. We do wicked things because we want to have fun, pleasure and gratification in this life. Āyah 14 indicates that human beings are enlightened about their souls and able to distinguish between right and wrong, but they present poor excuses for abandoning the right course and following the wrong course. We, the believers, sometimes indulge in such behavior due to weakness in our faith.

As we read the surah, we must remind ourselves about the reality of the Awakening. We should remember that on this Day, we will be informed of all the deeds that we sent forward for accounting, and we will also be informed of the good deeds that we did not perform. We do not want our bad deeds to neutralize our good deeds. We do not want to jeopardize our afterlife by becoming corrupt, wicked, selfish and neglectful in what we do in this life. Allāh (swt) has given us the conscience and ability to differentiate right from wrong. Whenever our conscience tells us something is wrong, we should listen. Shaitān will tempt us to do the wrong things, but we are ultimately responsible for our deeds. We should always remind ourselves that life in this world is transitory in nature, but life in the Hereafter is eternal. We should have many good deeds in our records, which will help us avert punishment in the Hereafter.

Questions:

1. Explain the meaning of the word اللوامة as mentioned in āyah 2.

2. Explain the significance of Allāh (swt) promising to restore the finger bone.

3. What are the reasons the Quraish did not believe in the promise of the Awakening?

4. According to sūrah al-Qiyamah, what three events would indicate the onset of the Awakening?

5. On the Day of Awakening, people will be informed of what they sent forward and what they left behind. What is the meaning of sending deeds forward and leaving deeds behind?

6. What is mentioned in āyāt 20 and 21 as the reason people tend to ignore the promise of the Awakening?

7. Why would one shin bone (ساق) rub against the other? What is the implied meaning?

Sūrah 75
Part B

Revealed in Makkah

Al-Qiyamah

The Awakening

Introduction:

The second half of the sūrah continues with the theme of the Awakening. The Quraish rejected the concept of the Awakening as an impossible premise. Their argument asked: how could Allāh (swt) recreate life after people have died and their bones and flesh have disintegrated in soil? In response, the Qur'ān asks them, and to all human beings, to think about their own creation. Using simple germ cells, Allāh (swt) creates and perfects human beings and makes their spouses. Is that not amazing? Let there be no doubt about it that if He can create life once, He can recreate again.

بِسۡمِ ٱللَّهِ ٱلرَّحۡمَـٰنِ ٱلرَّحِيمِ

In the name of Allāh, the most Kind, the most Rewarding.

فَلَا صَدَّقَ وَلَا صَلَّىٰ ۝

31. So he did not accept the truth, nor did he perform salāt;

وَلَـٰكِن كَذَّبَ وَتَوَلَّىٰ ۝

32. but he belied and turned back.

ثُمَّ ذَهَبَ إِلَىٰٓ أَهۡلِهِۦ يَتَمَطَّىٰٓ ۝

33. Then he went back to his family walking in pride.

أَوۡلَىٰ لَكَ فَأَوۡلَىٰ ۝

34. "Woe be to you! Then woe be to you!

ثُمَّ أَوۡلَىٰ لَكَ فَأَوۡلَىٰٓ ۝

35. "Again, woe be to you, so woe be to you!"

أَيَحۡسَبُ ٱلۡإِنسَـٰنُ أَن يُتۡرَكَ سُدًى ۝

36. Does man think that he will be left unrestrained?

أَلَمۡ يَكُ نُطۡفَةً مِّن مَّنِيٍّ يُمۡنَىٰ ۝

37. Was he not a sperm ejaculated from an ejaculation?

ثُمَّ كَانَ عَلَقَةً فَخَلَقَ فَسَوَّىٰ ۝

38. And then he was a clot, so He created and perfected;

فَجَعَلَ مِنْهُ ٱلزَّوْجَيْنِ ٱلذَّكَرَ وَٱلْأُنثَىٰ ۝

39. then He made from him a pair—the male and the female.

أَلَيْسَ ذَٰلِكَ بِقَٰدِرٍ عَلَىٰ أَن يُحْيِۦَ ٱلْمَوْتَىٰ ۝

40. Is He not capable like this to give life to the dead?

Explanation:

31-32. The āyah does not mention a particular individual, but refers to sinners in general. The suffering of the sinner, mentioned in āyāt 24 to 30 is described for valid reasons. Some of the reasons are mentioned in the following sequence—he did not accept the truth and did not perform salāt. When he was invited to accept truth, he rejected the offer and turned back.

33. Returning to one's family indicates returning to one's belief system, endorsed by family traditions and values. In all probability, most of these traditions are not divinely approved. Most people reject truth because the practice of their forefathers appears valid and justifiable to them. Blind adherence to family traditions makes people proud about their heritage, which is another reason they cling to ancestral faiths.

34-35. The phrase *awlā laka fa'awlā* means "woe be to you! then woe be to you!" The two āyāt repeat the word "woe" four times. Instead of using a frequently used word *wailun* (woe!), the Qur'ān uses another word, *aulā*, the root of which is *waliya*, which means "to be near," "to befriend" or "to turn back." In āyah 32, the Qur'ān uses the same word, *waliya*, to indicate turning back from truth. Therefore, to condemn the sinners' action of turning back from truth, the word *awlā* is used to express woe for their action. The four expressions of woe emphasize how deeply their actions are being condemned. It could also mean that each mention of woe is intended the four different responses mentioned in āyāt 31 and 32: (1) not accepting truth, (2) not performing salāt, (3) belying the truth, and (4) returning to old practices with pride.

36. The word *sada* (to wander freely without obstruction, to be aimless) when used in regard to an animal, means the animal is walking aimlessly without anybody to look after it. The āyah is asking a question: do human beings think they have been left alone to wander about without guidance, and consequently will they be held accountable for deeds that were performed and those that were not performed? Is there not a clear difference between animals and human beings? Animals do not have freedom of choice, they do not lie, they do not reject their natural instincts, and they never invent gods to worship or become gods to other animals. Animals are not answerable for their actions, therefore, they do not deserve rewards or punishment. However, human beings are answerable for their good deeds and bad deeds. The creation of human beings has a definite purpose, therefore, there is a definite need for Judgment.

37-38. Pride and rebellion against divine commands will appear unjustified if human beings ponder their insignificance. Their insignificance is pointed out by drawing our attention to the substance from which we were created—genetic material contained in the despised fluid known as semen. After undergoing various stages of development in the mother's womb, the zygote (*'alaq*) is perfected (*sawwā*) to become a full-size human baby, and, eventually, a fully formed adult.

39–40. A complete, perfected human being, formed from an insignificant substance, now needs a partner (*zawj*) so that the individual, in turn, can reproduce. The pronoun "him," in āyah 39 refers to all of mankind, implied by mention of both male and female. The fact that Allāh (swt) created human beings, from inanimate dust into the most-perfect animate creation, indicates that He is capable of giving life to the dead during the Awakening.

Words to know:

صَدَقَ: to be truthful, speak the truth. صَدَّقَ: to believe. صَدَّقَت: she declared her faith. تَصَدَّقَ: to give alms. صِدّيقٌ: man of truth and veracity.

زَاجَ: to marry someone. زَوَج: spouse, companion. أَزوَاج: husbands, wives, pairs.

Sūrah Al-Qiyamah
Word-by-word meaning

ٱلرَّحِيمِ	ٱلرَّحْمَٰنِ	ٱللَّهِ	بِسْمِ
the most Rewarding	the most Kind	Allāh	In the name of
صَلَّىٰ ٣١	وَلَا	صَدَّقَ	فَلَا
prayed	nor	he believed	so neither
ثُمَّ	وَتَوَلَّىٰ ٣٢	كَذَّبَ	وَلَٰكِن
then	and turned away	he denied	but (on the contrary)
يَتَمَطَّىٰ ٣٣	أَهْلِهِ	إِلَىٰ	ذَهَبَ
admiring himself	his family	to	he went

ثُمَّ	فَأَوْلَىٰ ۞	لَكَ	أَوْلَىٰ
then	and then woe to you	to you	woe
أَتَحْسَبُ	فَأَوْلَىٰ ۞	لَكَ	أَوْلَىٰ
does think	and then woe to you	to you	woe
سُدًى ۞	يُتْرَكَ	أَن	ٱلْإِنسَـٰنُ
without requital	he will be left	that	man
مَّنِيٍّ	مِّن	نُطْفَةً	أَلَمْ يَكُ
semen	from	a sperm	was he not
عَلَقَةً	كَانَ	ثُمَّ	يُمْنَىٰ ۞
a hanging clot	he became	then	poured forth
مِنْهُ	فَجَعَلَ	فَسَوَّىٰ ۞	فَخَلَقَ
from him	and made	and fashioned in due proportion	then He created
أَلَيْسَ	وَٱلْأُنثَىٰ ۞	ٱلذَّكَرَ	ٱلزَّوْجَيْنِ
is not	and female	male	two pairs
أَن	عَلَىٰ	بِقَـٰدِرٍ	ذَٰلِكَ
that	to	is capable	that
		ٱلْمَوْتَىٰ ۞	يُحْۦِىَ
		the dead	He give life to

A few applications of the message:

In this part of sūrah al-Qiyamah, Allāh (swt) cautions us about some of the bad deeds and actions that will cause us to suffer in the Hereafter. These are: (1) not accepting the truth, (2) not performing salāt, and (3) behaving in a proud manner.

As Muslims, we are required to uphold the divine truth as taught to us by our Rasūlullāh (S). We cannot compromise the truth. We cannot say that we will accept one part of the truth and ignore the other part. We have to accept the entire truth and demonstrate it through our actions. Performing salāt regularly and at the prescribed times is extremely important. Therefore, it is specifically mentioned as one of the desirable, righteous deeds. The Qur'ān says that salāt drives away indecencies (11:114; 29:45) and ensures success (108:1–3).

Pride is a forerunner of all evil. In the matter of faith, people show pride because they think they are self-sufficient, they can manage their own lives, and control their own destinies. Pride causes them to ignore their Creator and reject the truth.

As we read this sūrah and understand the gravity of the Awakening, we should remember not to take this event lightly. We should not let our love for the present world distract us from achieving the important objective in life—which is success in the Hereafter. Three good ways to remain focused on the life in the Hereafter is: (1) do not behave proudly, (2) do not reject the truth, and (3) never ignore salāt.

Questions:

1. Why do you think the Quraish refused to believe in the Awakening? Provide three reasons.

2. Why is it mentioned in āyāt 31 to 33, that people go back to their families with pride?

3. What embryological example did Allāh (swt) provide to prove that He can recreate life?

Sūrah 76

Part A

Revealed in Makkah

Al-Insān or Ad-Dahr

The Man *or* The Long Life

Introduction:

This early Makkan sūrah deals with man's humble creation. Allāh (swt) reminds us that He has guided us, however some of us become believers and others becomes non-believer. The non-believers will suffer punishment in fire. The believers will be in paradise because of their faith and righteous actions. The sūrah mentions feeding the poor as one of the examples of the righteous deeds. The believers who perform these duties will inherit paradise, which is described as a kingdom full of blissfulness. Āyāt 5 through 22 provide a captivating depiction of life in Paradise. Believers will dwell in Paradise as a reward for their hard work during their earthly lives.

بِسْمِ ٱللَّهِ ٱلرَّحْمَٰنِ ٱلرَّحِيمِ

In the name of Allāh, the most Kind, the most Rewarding.

هَلْ أَتَىٰ عَلَى ٱلْإِنسَٰنِ حِينٌ مِّنَ ٱلدَّهْرِ لَمْ يَكُن شَيْـًٔا مَّذْكُورًا ۝	1. Did there not pass over man a long time when he was not anything worth mentioning?
إِنَّا خَلَقْنَا ٱلْإِنسَٰنَ مِن نُّطْفَةٍ أَمْشَاجٍ نَّبْتَلِيهِ فَجَعَلْنَٰهُ سَمِيعًا بَصِيرًا ۝	2. We have indeed created man out of a coupled spermatozoa, We are going to discipline him, so We have made him hearing, seeing.
إِنَّا هَدَيْنَٰهُ ٱلسَّبِيلَ إِمَّا شَاكِرًا وَإِمَّا كَفُورًا ۝	3. Surely We have guided him on the Path; he is either grateful, or he is ungrateful.
إِنَّا أَعْتَدْنَا لِلْكَٰفِرِينَ سَلَٰسِلَا۟ وَأَغْلَٰلًا وَسَعِيرًا ۝	4. We have indeed prepared for the non-believers chains and shackles and a burning Fire.
إِنَّ ٱلْأَبْرَارَ يَشْرَبُونَ مِن كَأْسٍ كَانَ مِزَاجُهَا كَافُورًا ۝	5. The virtuous will certainly drink from a cup—the flavor of which is with camphor,—

6. عَيْنًا يَشْرَبُ بِهَا عِبَادُ ٱللَّهِ يُفَجِّرُونَهَا تَفْجِيرًا ۝

a spring from which the bondsmen of Allāh will drink, they will make it flow into a great flowing.

7. يُوفُونَ بِٱلنَّذْرِ وَيَخَافُونَ يَوْمًا كَانَ شَرُّهُۥ مُسْتَطِيرًا ۝

They fulfill vows and fear the day, the calamity of which will be far-reaching.

8. وَيُطْعِمُونَ ٱلطَّعَامَ عَلَىٰ حُبِّهِۦ مِسْكِينًا وَيَتِيمًا وَأَسِيرًا ۝

And out of love for Him they feed food to the poor, the orphan and the captive,

9. إِنَّمَا نُطْعِمُكُمْ لِوَجْهِ ٱللَّهِ لَا نُرِيدُ مِنكُمْ جَزَآءً وَلَا شُكُورًا ۝

"We feed you for the pleasure of Allāh only; we do not desire from you recompense nor thanks.

10. إِنَّا نَخَافُ مِن رَّبِّنَا يَوْمًا عَبُوسًا قَمْطَرِيرًا ۝

"Surely we fear from our Rabb a frowning, distressful day."

11. فَوَقَىٰهُمُ ٱللَّهُ شَرَّ ذَٰلِكَ ٱلْيَوْمِ وَلَقَّىٰهُمْ نَضْرَةً وَسُرُورًا ۝

So Allāh will save them from the evil of that day, and cause them to meet with cheerfulness and happiness;

12. وَجَزَىٰهُم بِمَا صَبَرُوا۟ جَنَّةً وَحَرِيرًا ۝

and reward them, as they had persevered, with a Garden and silk,

13. مُّتَّكِئِينَ فِيهَا عَلَى ٱلْأَرَآئِكِ لَا يَرَوْنَ فِيهَا شَمْسًا وَلَا زَمْهَرِيرًا ۝

reclining in it upon thrones, they will not see in it the sun, nor the biting cold,

14. وَدَانِيَةً عَلَيْهِمْ ظِلَٰلُهَا وَذُلِّلَتْ قُطُوفُهَا تَذْلِيلًا ۝

and close upon them will be the shades, and its clustered fruits will hang low, within easy reach.

15. وَيُطَافُ عَلَيْهِم بِـَٔانِيَةٍ مِّن فِضَّةٍ وَأَكْوَابٍ كَانَتْ قَوَارِيرَا۟ ۝

And around them will pass cups of silver and bowls of crystal glass,

16. قَوَارِيرَا۟ مِن فِضَّةٍ قَدَّرُوهَا تَقْدِيرًا ۝

crystal-clear silver, which they will measure according to a quantity.

17. وَيُسْقَوْنَ فِيهَا كَأْسًا كَانَ مِزَاجُهَا زَنجَبِيلًا ۝

And they will be given in it to drink a cup—the flavor of which is with Zingiber,

عَيۡنًا فِيهَا تُسَمَّىٰ سَلۡسَبِيلًا ۝ 18. a spring in it called Salsabil.

وَيَطُوفُ عَلَيۡهِمۡ وِلۡدَٰنٌ مُّخَلَّدُونَ إِذَا رَأَيۡتَهُمۡ حَسِبۡتَهُمۡ لُؤۡلُؤًا مَّنثُورًا ۝ 19. And youths of perpetual bloom will go around them; when you see them, you will take them for pearls scattered about.

وَإِذَا رَأَيۡتَ ثَمَّ رَأَيۡتَ نَعِيمًا وَمُلۡكًا كَبِيرًا ۝ 20. And whenever you will look there, you will see blissfulness and a great kingdom.

عَٰلِيَهُمۡ ثِيَابُ سُندُسٍ خُضۡرٌ وَإِسۡتَبۡرَقٌ وَحُلُّوٓاْ أَسَاوِرَ مِن فِضَّةٍ وَسَقَىٰهُمۡ رَبُّهُمۡ شَرَابًا طَهُورًا ۝ 21. Over them will be robes of green silk and thick brocade, and they will wear bracelets of silver, and their Rabb will give them to drink a pure drink.

إِنَّ هَٰذَا كَانَ لَكُمۡ جَزَآءً وَكَانَ سَعۡيُكُم مَّشۡكُورًا ۝ 22. "This is indeed a reward for you, and your striving has been appreciated."

Explanation:

1. The question posed in this āyah is to encourage readers to explore where, when, and how human beings existed during a stage of development not worth mentioning. According to some scholars, the āyah referrs to human embryonic stage. According to others, the use of the phrase "long time" (*hāna*), seems to direct our attention to the primordial life of human beings, whose biological identification is *Homo sapiens*. The origin of *Homo sapiens* prior to about 10,000 years ago is fairly well documented, however the finer details are still under investigation. Therefore, the Qur'ān states that during this early development stage, human beings were not anything worth mentioning.

2. The reference to man (*insān*) in both āyāt indicates that it is the story of mankind and its origin. The creation of every human being follows a definite process, initiated by a spermatozoa coupled (*amsaj*, coupled, mixed, mingled) with an ovum. After human beings are created by this process, Allāh (swt) continues to test us. But we cannot be tested unless we are aware of the standards upon which the test will be conducted. In order to do that, human beings are endowed with various faculties; sight and hearing are two faculties that provide the necessary abilities to distinguish between right and wrong and adopting one course of actions over another.

3. Allāh (swt) not only provided human beings the necessary faculties to distinguish right from wrong, but He also guided us toward the right path by revealing the appropriate standards through a large number of messengers. There is no coercion in the matter of religion, therefore, people are free to accept or reject the guidance. Those who accept the guidance recognize their Creator and express gratitude to Him. Those who do not accept the guidance express their devotion in the wrong place; therefore, they are ungrateful to their Creator.

4. The descriptions of chains and shackles provide an impression of disgrace, condemnation and defeat of the sinners. In addition, the description indicates the sinners cannot escape their destiny. The term *salāsil* (singular, *silsilah*) means a flexible series of jointed links, usually chains of metal. The term *aghlāl* (singular, *ghal*) means a yoke, a shackle, a wooden frame or a bar with loops or bows on either end used to harness a pair of bulls. Therefore, the term shackle, in this case, is a heavy iron ring placed on the neck or hands and fastened with a chain.

5. In contrast to the suffering of sinners, a blissful state for the believers is narrated. The word *kafūr* means something that smells good, a fragrant plant, or a delicate aroma derived from the calyx of a fragrant flower. The word is often translated as camphor, a substance that has a strong aromatic odor that suppresses bad odors. Besides relishing such a heavenly drink, the use of the word seems to indicate the drink will suppress all earthly evils, and the environment will be free of any rottenness of human conduct.

6. The Qur'ān frequently mentions pure springs and flowing rivers in the Garden as a description of the pleasing, blissful condition of Paradise. The wholesome, pure, aromatic drinks are often mentioned to contrast the bitter, putrid drink for the sinners. With reference to the spring in Paradise, the word *fajara* (to break, to cause water to flow) is used to imply the breaking down of something in abundance, usually bearing an enormous blessing when used in a positive sense. For example, *fajr*, or morning, occurs when the abundance of daylight breaks the darkness of night. The heavenly spring from which believers will drink flows with abundance.

7. The heavenly blessings mentioned in the previous āyāt abound only for the believers because they fulfilled their spiritual obligations and took precaution against "the day." Evidently, the word "day" refers to the Day of Awakening, which will bring extensive calamity to human beings.

8–10. In an equitable and just society envisioned by Islam, a person should not be self-centered when people around him or her are in basic need of food for survival. Feeding the poor is a virtuous deed of true believers; not feeding the poor is a punishable offense (69:34; 74:44; 89:18; and 107:3). The term *asir* (captives) can be used in a literal sense to mean prisoners, or in general someone who is a captive of the circumstances that made him vulnerable, and consequently, in dire need of help. Believers who qualify to enter Heaven took care of the needy for the pleasure of Allāh (swt) without expecting any reward for their benevolence.

11–12. Because of these virtuous deeds, Allāh (swt) will save the believers from the calamity of the Day. He will reward them with a dwelling in the Garden and provide them with silk clothing (18:31; 22:23). In the seventh century, Arab society considered silk to be very desirable clothing material for the aristocrat. The purpose of such descriptions is to stress the great satisfaction and high quality of life in Paradise.

13. The word *ara'ik* means highly decorated couches with a canopy on which brides usually recline. The mention of such couches for the dwellers of paradise indicates their dignified status. Reference to the sun originates from the perspective of desert Arabs, to whom not seeing the sun is symbolic for not being exposed to extreme heat. But they would not be exposed to extreme cold, either. We should remember that these narrations of paradise are presented entirely in human idiom. The true reality of Paradise is beyond the limits of our comprehension.

14. The word *zill* means shade or shelter to protect from the scorching sun. To understand the importance of the shade, we have to remember that during the summer months, temperatures in Arabia exceed

110 degrees Fahrenheit (42 degrees Celsius). The early audience of the Qur'ān was the Arabs, who fully understood and appreciated the importance of shade. In addition to protection from the heat of the sun, the word *zill* also indicates peace, comfort, contentment and delight in this world. Clusters of fruit hanging low and within reach implies abundant and easy access to all the pleasures and satisfaction in heaven (69:23).

15–16. Cups of silver and bowls of crystal are certainly valued items not only bt today's standards, but also by the standards of the past. Such imagery, used throughout the sūrah, is used to appeal to the fantasy of a rich mercantile Arab audience. The true realities of heaven are incomprehensible by all human standards. Crystal-clear cups made of silver (*qawarir*)—something unthinkable in human concepts, further attests to the fact that the realities of heaven (or hell) cannot be realized unless they are narrated, as in this instance, in language understood by human beings. By definition, these cups are made of silver, but due to their thin sides, the inside of these cups will be visible from the outside, creating the impression that they are made of glass.

17. After the reference to the drink mentioned in āyah 5, now we are told that there will be another type of drink with a *Zanjabeel* or Zingiber flavor. This is a tropical plant grown for its roots, which add an aromatic flavor to a drink. Most commentators think the plant refers to ginger.

18. Continuing with the allegorical nature of the heavenly bliss, yet another pleasure would be the fountain of *salsabīl*—a sweet, free-flowing source of drink.

19–20. The word *mukhalladūn*, derived from *khallada*, means "made immortal" or "eternal." The word is used to connote that life in Paradise will have no decay or death. The surface luster, shape and delicate color of natural pearls impart a unique and exotic value to pieces of jewelry. A comparison to pearls is an indication of the purity of youths (52:24).

21–22. Silk was briefly mentioned in āyah 12. Now silk is mentioned again to add a higher level of splendor and impart a sense of festivity. The dwellers of paradise will wear robes of green silk with thick brocade. A robe with brocade has an intricate floral motif, raised designs and detailed artwork. It is typically worn on special occasions, such as weddings and social celebrations. To complement the festive mood, dwellers will also wear silver bracelets. Earlier the youths were serving them drinks. Now at the peak of the festivity, the Chief Host of the ceremony—the Lord Himself—will give them pure drinks. All of this festivity and splendor is a token of reward for striving to follow the right path.

Words to know:

ذَكَرَ: to remember, to admonish. مَذكُور: mentionable, worth mentioning. ذَكَّرَ: to admonish, to remind.

مَشَجَ: to mix up, to mingle, to unite. أَمشَج: mingled, united, mixed.

بَلاء: to test, to try, to set to trial. نَبتَلِى: we (might) prove, bestow our favor. نَبلُوَ: We shall prove.

عَتُدَ: to be ready. أعتَدنَا: we have prepared. عَتِيدٌ: ready.

بَرَّ: to be pious, just, virtuous. أَبرَار: pious one who is highly righteous. اَلبَرُّ: Benign (one of Allāh's most-beautiful names).

شَرِبَ: to drink, to swallow. يَشرَبُ: he will drink. مُشرَبٌ: drinking place. شَرَابٌ: drink.

وَفَى: to reach the end, to keep one's promise. وَفَّى: fulfilled. يَوَفَّى: he will be paid in full. يُوفُوا: they shall pay in full. تَوَفَّى: He causes to die.

حَرَّ: to be free. حَرِير: silk. حَرُور: sun's heat.

تَذْليل: hanging down. ذَلُول: humble, submissive. ذُلُّ: humility.

يَسْقُونَ: they shall be given to drink. سَقَى: to water, to give drink. سِقَايَةٌ: the act of giving water.

خَلَدَ: to remain, long lasting. مُخَلَّدُون: never altering age, ever-young. يَخْلُدُ: He will abide.

Sūrah Al-Insān
Word-by-word meaning

ٱلرَّحِيمِ	ٱلرَّحْمَـٰنِ	ٱللَّهِ	بِسْمِ
the most Rewarding	the most Kind	Allāh	In the name of
ٱلْإِنسَـٰنِ	عَلَى	أَتَىٰ	هَلْ
man	over	come	has there
لَمْ	ٱلدَّهْرِ	مِّنَ	حِينٌ
not	time when	of	a period
إِنَّا	مَّذْكُورًا ۝	شَيْئًا	يَكُن
surely	to be mentioned	thing	he was
نُّطْفَةٍ	مِن	ٱلْإِنسَـٰنَ	خَلَقْنَا
a sperm drop	from	man	We have created
سَمِيعًا	فَجَعَلْنَـٰهُ	نَّبْتَلِيهِ	أَمْشَاجٍ
hearing	so We made him	in order to try him	mixed
ٱلسَّبِيلَ	هَدَيْنَـٰهُ	إِنَّا	بَصِيرًا ۝
the way	We showed him	surely	sight.
كَفُورًا ۝	وَإِمَّا	شَاكِرًا	إِمَّا
ungrateful.	or	he be grateful	either

سَلَسِلَا۟	لِّلۡكَفِرِينَ	أَعۡتَدۡنَا	إِنَّآ
iron chains	for the non-believers	We have prepared	surely
ٱلۡأَبۡرَارَ	إِنَّ	وَسَعِيرًا	وَأَغۡلَلًا
the righteous	certainly	and a blazing fire	and iron collars
كَانَ	كَأۡسٍ	مِن	يَشۡرَبُونَ
will be	a cup	from	shall drink
يَشۡرَبُ	عَيۡنًا	كَافُورًا	مِزَاجُهَا
will drink	a spring	is camphor	flavor of which
يُفَجِّرُونَهَا	ٱللَّهِ	عِبَادُ	بِهَا
causing it to gush forth	Allāh	the slaves of	where from
وَيَخَافُونَ	بِٱلنَّذۡرِ	يُوفُونَ	تَفۡجِيرًا
and they fear	(their) vows	they fulfill	abundantly
مُسۡتَطِيرًا	شَرُّهُۥ	كَانَ	يَوۡمًا
wide-spreading	its evil	will be	a Day
حُبِّهِۦ	عَلَىٰ	ٱلطَّعَامَ	وَيُطۡعِمُونَ
their love for Him	out of	the food	and they feed
إِنَّمَا	وَأَسِيرًا	وَيَتِيمًا	مِسۡكِينًا
(saying) only	and the captive	and the orphan	to the poor
لَا	ٱللَّهِ	لِوَجۡهِ	نُطۡعِمُكُمۡ
not	of Allāh	seeking the Face	We feed you
وَلَا	جَزَآءً	مِنكُمۡ	نُرِيدُ
nor	reward	from you	we wish for
مِن	نَخَافُ	إِنَّا	شُكُورًا
from	We fear	surely	thanks

قَمْطَرِيرًا ۝	عَبُوسًا	يَوْمًا	رَّبَّنَا
distressful	hard	a Day	Our Rabb
ذَٰلِكَ	شَرَّ	ٱللَّهُ	فَوَقَىٰهُمُ
that	from the evil of	Allāh	so save them
وَسُرُورًا ۝	نَضْرَةً	وَلَقَّىٰهُمْ	ٱلْيَوْمِ
and joy	a radiant light	and gave them	Day
جَنَّةً	صَبَرُواْ	بِمَا	وَجَزَىٰهُم
Paradise	they were patient	because	and He rewarded them
عَلَىٰ	فِيهَا	مُّتَّكِئِينَ	وَحَرِيرًا ۝
on	therein	reclining	and silken garments
فِيهَا	يَرَوْنَ	لَا	ٱلْأَرَائِكِ
therein	they will see	neither	raised thrones
وَدَانِيَةً	زَمْهَرِيرًا ۝	وَلَا	شَمْسًا
and is close	the bitter cold	nor	the heat of the sun
قُطُوفُهَا	وَذُلِّلَتْ	ظِلَٰلُهَا	عَلَيْهِمْ
the fruits thereof	and will hang low	its shade	upon them
بِـَٔانِيَةٍ	عَلَيْهِم	وَيُطَافُ	تَذْلِيلًا ۝
round vessels	amongst them	and will be passed	lowly
كَانَتْ	وَأَكْوَابٍ	فِضَّةٍ	مِّن
that are	and cups	silver	of
فِضَّةٍ	مِن	قَوَارِيرَاْ	قَوَارِيرَا ۝
silver	of	crystal-clear made	of crystal
فِيهَا	وَيُسْقَوْنَ	تَقْدِيرًا ۝	قَدَّرُوهَا
therein	and they will be given to drink	according to their measure.	they will determine the measure thereof

زَنجَبِيلًا ﴿١٧﴾	مِزَاجُهَا	كَانَ	كَأْسًا
is ginger	flavor of it	that is	a cup
سَلْسَبِيلًا ﴿١٨﴾	تُسَمَّىٰ	فِيهَا	عَيْنًا
Salsabil	called	therein	a spring
مُّخَلَّدُونَ	وِلْدَانٌ	عَلَيْهِمْ	۞ وَيَطُوفُ
of perpetual bloom	youths	about them	and going around
لُؤْلُؤًا	حَسِبْتَهُمْ	رَأَيْتَهُمْ	إِذَا
pearls	you would think them	you see them	if
ثَمَّ	رَأَيْتَ	وَإِذَا	مَّنثُورًا ﴿١٩﴾
there	you look	and when	scattered
كَبِيرًا ﴿٢٠﴾	وَمُلْكًا	نَعِيمًا	رَأَيْتَ
a great	and dominion	a delight	you will see
خُضْرٌ	سُندُسٍ	ثِيَابُ	عَلَيْهِمْ
green	made of silk	garments	their honoring
مِن	أَسَاوِرَ	وَحُلُّوا	وَإِسْتَبْرَقٌ
of	bracelets	they will be adorned with	and thick brocade
شَرَابًا	رَبُّهُمْ	وَسَقَاهُمْ	فِضَّةٍ
a drink	their Rabb	and will give them to drink	silver
كَانَ	هَـٰذَا	إِنَّ	طَهُورًا ﴿٢١﴾
is	this	surely	a pure.
سَعْيُكُم	وَكَانَ	جَزَاءً	لَكُم
your endeavour	and has been	a reward	for you
			مَّشْكُورًا ﴿٢٢﴾
			appreciated

A few applications of the message:

It is a divine principle to guide human beings on the right path. However, it is also a divine principle that nobody should be forced to adopt a particular path. For this reason, we see that in spite of receiving guidance, some of us are guided and some of us are not. Those who do not accept guidance will be chained up in shackles and suffer painful punishment in fire.

As we read the sūrah, we have to consider: what kind of end do we want for ourselves? If we want to avoid the shackles and punishment in fire, we need to pay attention to the divine message. We have certain duties to fulfill and certain behavior to avoid. Whatever we do, we must always keep in mind the Day of Awakening, the calamity of which will be far-reaching. Therefore, whatever we do, we should do it for the pleasure of Allāh (swt). We should develop the habit of questioning our conscience about whether a particular action will invite Allāh's (swt) displeasure. Eventually we will be in a position to identify the wrong path and avoid it. Through such conscious efforts, we will be able to earn the pleasure of Allāh (swt).

We need to ask ourselves: what action did I take today that will save me from the calamity of the Day? We need to ask ourselves: what action did I take today that will make me cheerful and happy on that Day? If I did not do anything worthy today, I need to begin seriously thinking about what actions to take.

This sūrah provides fascinating details about rewards in the Hereafter. All of these rewards are achievable for each one of us. Allāh (swt) prepared these rewards for us, and we should make our best effort to qualify for these rewards.

Questions:

1. One of the righteous deeds is to feed the needy. As an example, three categories of needy people are mentioned in the sūrah. What are these three categories?

2. What two things should we keep in mind when we feed the poor?

3. The heavenly drinks will have a certain flavor. What two flavors are mentioned in sūrah al-Insān?

4. Briefly discuss the nature of food and drink in Paradise.

5. Briefly discuss the people's clothing in Paradise. Why is such clothing considered worthy?

6. Discuss the overall comfort of people in Paradise.

Sūrah 76

Part B

Revealed in Makkah

Al-Insān or Ad-Dahr

The Man or The Long Life

Introduction:

In the second part of this early Makkan sūrah, Rasūlullāh (S) is reminded that the Qur'ān is being revealed to him by Allāh (swt) in a gradual manner. No matter how long it takes to finish the revelation, and no matter what happens to Rasūlullāh (S) during the process, he should persevere and not yield to the tactics of the non-believers. They are absorbed with the transitory world and ignore life in the Hereafter. If Allāh (swt) wishes, He could replace them with a new generation. It is easy for Him. However, Allāh (swt) will never force faith to anyone. It is a divine principle that human beings have the freedom of choice to adopt any path they choose. Those who adopt the right path will receive Allāh's (swt) mercy and those who adopt the wrong path will suffer painful punishment.

بِسْمِ ٱللَّهِ ٱلرَّحْمَٰنِ ٱلرَّحِيمِ

In the name of Allāh, the most Kind, the most Rewarding.

إِنَّا نَحْنُ نَزَّلْنَا عَلَيْكَ ٱلْقُرْءَانَ تَنزِيلًا ۝	23. Surely We, Ourselves, have revealed to you the Qur'ān in a gradual manner.
فَٱصْبِرْ لِحُكْمِ رَبِّكَ وَلَا تُطِعْ مِنْهُمْ ءَاثِمًا أَوْ كَفُورًا ۝	24. Therefore you persevere for the Judgment of your Rabb, and do not obey a sinner or an ungrateful one among them.
وَٱذْكُرِ ٱسْمَ رَبِّكَ بُكْرَةً وَأَصِيلًا ۝	25. And remember the name of your Rabb at dawn and at evening;
وَمِنَ ٱلَّيْلِ فَٱسْجُدْ لَهُ وَسَبِّحْهُ لَيْلًا طَوِيلًا ۝	26. and during part of the night, prostrate before Him, and glorify Him late at night.

إِنَّ هَـٰٓؤُلَآءِ يُحِبُّونَ ٱلْعَاجِلَةَ وَيَذَرُونَ وَرَآءَهُمْ يَوْمًا ثَقِيلًا ۝

27. Surely these love the transitory life, and leave behind them a grievous day.

نَّحْنُ خَلَقْنَـٰهُمْ وَشَدَدْنَآ أَسْرَهُمْ وَإِذَا شِئْنَا بَدَّلْنَآ أَمْثَـٰلَهُمْ تَبْدِيلًا ۝

28. We, Ourselves, have created them, and We have strengthened their formation; and whenever We please, We can replace the like of them in a substitution.

إِنَّ هَـٰذِهِۦ تَذْكِرَةٌ ۖ فَمَن شَآءَ ٱتَّخَذَ إِلَىٰ رَبِّهِۦ سَبِيلًا ۝

29. Certainly this is a Reminder, so let him whoever wishes take up a way to his Rabb.

وَمَا تَشَآءُونَ إِلَّآ أَن يَشَآءَ ٱللَّهُ ۚ إِنَّ ٱللَّهَ كَانَ عَلِيمًا حَكِيمًا ۝

30. And you do not wish except as Allāh wishes. Surely Allāh is ever all-Knowing, most Wise;

يُدْخِلُ مَن يَشَآءُ فِى رَحْمَتِهِۦ ۚ وَٱلظَّـٰلِمِينَ أَعَدَّ لَهُمْ عَذَابًا أَلِيمًا ۝

31. He admits whom He pleases with His mercy. And as for the unjust— He has prepared for them a painful chastisement.

Explanation:

23. The gradual process of revelation is emphasized by the use of word *tanzila*. The word also means "orderly arrangement" and "authentic compilation." If Allāh (swt) had willed, He could have revealed the Qur'ān in one revelation. However, there is a divine wisdom as to why it was revealed in a gradual manner. Gradual revelation eased the revelation process for Rasūlullāh (S); it simplified memorization and understanding for the companions, it helped the promulgation of laws to occur in a gradual manner, and it answered and explained unique questions and circumstances as they arose.

24. Five important instructions are given to Rasūlullāh (S), and through him, to all believers. The first instruction is to exercise perseverance (*sabr*) for the judgment of Allāh (swt). The significance of the term *sabr* is to be patient, to persevere, and to endure. When a person is required to persevere, he or she is not expected to give up blaming "fate" or engage in idle lamenting. Rather, he or she is expected to bear the pain or trials calmly without complaint, while at the same time undergo hardship without giving in, and demonstrate ability to sustain prolonged stressful efforts or activity in spite of counter-influence, opposition or discouragement. The second instruction, to not obey a sinner or an ungrateful one, emphasizes the first instruction while assuring that it would prevent believers from succumbing to moral and spiritual downfall.

25. The third instruction is to remember (*dhikr*) the names or attributes of Allāh (swt) at dawn and in the evening. Such *dhikr* does not mean chanting His name in a rosary or enacting another form of devotion, but performing the obligatory prayers. At dawn, Fajr prayers are performed, and during the

evening hours, 'Asr or Maghrib prayers are performed. However, the congregational salāt was not yet recommended when this sūrah was revealed. Therefore, without naming salāt, the Qur'ān instructed believers to perform salāt on an individual basis.

26. The fourth instruction completes the requirements of performing the five statutory prayers of each day. The requirement to prostrate during part of the night fulfils the Maghrib and 'Ishā prayers. The fifth instruction is the late-night glorification through the performance of Tahajjud prayer, which is done by waking up during the later half of the night. The exact timing of all these prayers was set by Rasūlullāh (S). His teachings made the Tahajjud prayer optional for all.

27. The requirement to perform the obligatory prayers may sound burdensome to those who do not care about it or those who reject the teachings altogether. By neglecting these compulsory duties, people prove that they love the transitory life of this world. They forget that one day they will die and stand before their Creator to answer for all their unfulfilled deeds and bad deeds. They behave as if this life will last forever and they will never have to face judgment. That particular day is mentioned as *yawman thaqilan* (grievous day). It is so named because the day will be difficult for them because they will not have any means to avert their punishment.

28. By strengthening the formation of the human body, Allāh (swt) provided them a completely perfect shape (32:9; 38:72; and 75:38). After attaining perfection in creation, whenever human beings do not follow the guidance, Allāh (swt) decides to replace them with other people who will follow the guidance. This verse provides a hint as to why so many nations and civilizations collapse after attaining their glory days. They conspired against Allāh (swt) and rejected the divine teachings.

29. The message of the Qur'ān serves as a reminder for all of mankind. It creates awareness of the Creator and His absolute almightiness, and urges people to accept the truth for their own benefit. However, the Qur'ān never compels them to choose Islam. People are free to adopt any path they choose, including the path that will lead them to their Creator.

30. There is no contradiction in the message of the previous āyah with the present āyah. Human beings are in full command of their freedom of choice; Allāh (swt) does not control their choices. However, nothing happens unless it is in accordance with the laws of Allāh (swt). This is implied by the phrase "except as Allāh wishes." One of the attributes of Allāh (swt) is to guide, therefore, Allāh (swt) helps those who wish to be guided with guidance. Allāh (swt) leaves alone whoever wishes to be left alone, but He never misguides them.

31. Allāh's (swt) mercy embraces everything; nonetheless, there are times when Allāh's (swt) mercy specifically benefits certain people. This special favor is not an arbitrary action, but given to those who request for it, through prayer and righteous deeds. Painful punishment is reserved for unjust people. The use of the word *zalim* (unjust), rather than *mushrik* (polytheist) or *munafiq* (hypocrite), indicates the message of the āyah covers a broad group of people, including the believers, should they indulge in unjust activities.

Words to know:

تَنزِيل: sending divine revelation, orderly arrangement and authentic compilation. نَزَّلَ: to descend, to come down. مَنزِل: mansion.

أَثِمَ: to commit sin or crime. إِثمٌ: sin. أَثَمٌ: punishment of sin. أَثِيمٌ: sinful person.

بَكَّرَ: to rise up early in the morning. بُكرَةٌ: morning.

طَوِيلًا: long, prolonged. طَالَ: lasted long, too long. طَاوَلَ: he prolonged.

أَعَدَّ: he prepared. عَدَّ: to count, reckon. عِدَّتُ: counting number, to make up the prescribed number.

Sūrah Al-Insān
Word-by-word meaning

بِسمِ	ٱللَّهِ	ٱلرَّحمَٰنِ	ٱلرَّحِيمِ
In the name of	Allāh	the most Kind	the most Rewarding

إِنَّا	نَحنُ	نَزَّلنَا	عَلَيكَ
surely it is	We who	have sent down	to you

ٱلقُرءَانَ	تَنزِيلًا ۝	فَٱصبِر	لِحُكمِ
the Qur'an	a revelation	therefore be patient	for the Command of

رَبِّكَ	وَلَا	تُطِع	مِنهُم
your Rabb	and not	you obey	among them

ءَاثِمًا	أَو	كَفُورًا ۝	وَٱذكُرِ
a sinner	or	a non-believer	and remember

ٱسمَ	رَبِّكَ	بُكرَةً	وَأَصِيلًا ۝
the Name of	your Rabb	every dawn	and evening

وَمِنَ	ٱلَّيلِ	فَٱسجُد	لَهُۥ
and during	night	prostrate yourself	to Him

وَسَبِّحهُ	لَيلًا	طَوِيلًا ۝	إِنَّ
and glorify Him	night	a long	surely

هَٰٓؤُلَآءِ these	يُحِبُّونَ love	ٱلْعَاجِلَةَ the present life	وَيَذَرُونَ and leave
وَرَآءَهُمْ behind them	يَوْمًا Day	ثَقِيلًا ۝ a heavy	نَّحْنُ it is We
خَلَقْنَٰهُمْ We Who created them	وَشَدَدْنَآ and We have made strong	أَسْرَهُمْ their build	وَإِذَا and when
شِئْنَا We will	بَدَّلْنَآ We can replace	أَمْثَٰلَهُمْ like them	تَبْدِيلًا ۝ with a replacement
إِنَّ surely	هَٰذِهِۦ this is	تَذْكِرَةٌ an admonition	فَمَن so whosoever
شَآءَ wills	ٱتَّخَذَ let him take	إِلَىٰ to	رَبِّهِۦ his Rabb
سَبِيلًا ۝ a path	وَمَا and not	تَشَآءُونَ you can will	إِلَّآ unless
أَن that	يَشَآءَ it wills	ٱللَّهُ Allāh	إِنَّ surely
ٱللَّهَ Allāh	كَانَ is ever	عَلِيمًا All-Knowing	حَكِيمًا ۝ All-Wise
يُدْخِلُ He will admit	مَن whom	يَشَآءُ He wills	فِى to
رَحْمَتِهِۦ His Mercy	وَٱلظَّٰلِمِينَ and as for the wrong doers	أَعَدَّ He has prepared	لَهُمْ for them
عَذَابًا a torment	أَلِيمًا ۝ painful		

A few applications of the message:

We must pay attention to one important message in this part of the sūrah—the love of transitory life mentioned in āyah 27. Due to an excessive love for life in this world, people ignore their duties toward Allāh (swt). Everywhere we look, people are too busy with their worldly affairs. They seem to act as if life on this world will last forever. Little do they know that this life is only transitory in nature. They forget that actual life is in the Hereafter. People forget that they will be held accountable for their deeds on the Day of Judgment. They forget that painful punishment awaits those who neglect their duties and forget to remember Allāh (swt).

As we read this sūrah, we have to ask ourselves: do we want the blissful Paradise to be our final home or do we want to give up? Giving up is very easy to do—just have fun in life and ignore the divine teachings. It is easy because Allāh (swt) does not force anyone to accept faith. However, the consequences of adopting the wrong path are severe. Consider this: the slightest cuts, bruises and burns hurt us very much. Then why would we want to defy Allāh (swt) and suffer punishment in fire? We cannot afford to face this severe punishment. We better not. Let us learn a lesson from this sūrah and remain loyal to the divine message and follow it carefully.

Questions:

1. Discuss the significance of the word تنزيلا used in āyah 23 of sūrah al-Insān.

2. What three things was Rasūlullāh (S) asked to do in āyāt 24–26 of sūrah al-Insān?

3. Why do you think people pay no attention to the Day of Awakening? Explain why in light of sūrah al-Insān.

4. Why does Allāh (swt) destroy a nation and create a new one in its place?

5. After providing divine guidance, what principle did Allāh (swt) establish regarding how human beings follow the guidance?

Sūrah 77
Al-Mursalāt
Revealed in Makkah
Part A
Those Sent Ones

Introduction:

As with many other sūrah, this sūrah also confirms the Awakening, cautions the wrongdoers and provides glad tidings for the righteous. The sūrah warns the non-believers not to mockingly ask for the Awakening to happen. Then it provides a terrifying description of the day when the Awakening will happen. Allāh (swt) reminds them that many past communities denied the Awakening and became corrupt. They were destroyed because of their conduct attitude and rebellion against the Creator. As a testimony to the Awakening becoming possible, Allāh (swt) provides evidence of creation as a sign of His power. Then the sūrah depicts the fate of the sinners as they suffer punishment.

بِسْمِ ٱللَّهِ ٱلرَّحْمَٰنِ ٱلرَّحِيمِ

In the name of Allāh, the most Kind, the most Rewarding.

وَٱلْمُرْسَلَٰتِ عُرْفًا ۝	1. Consider those sent forth in a continual series,
فَٱلْعَٰصِفَٰتِ عَصْفًا ۝	2. then consider the violent wind in violent gusts,
وَٱلنَّٰشِرَٰتِ نَشْرًا ۝	3. and consider those spreading a great spreading,
فَٱلْفَٰرِقَٰتِ فَرْقًا ۝	4. then consider those separating with a complete separation,
فَٱلْمُلْقِيَٰتِ ذِكْرًا ۝	5. then consider those instilling a Reminder,
عُذْرًا أَوْ نُذْرًا ۝	6. as an excuse, and as a warning.
إِنَّمَا تُوعَدُونَ لَوَٰقِعٌ ۝	7. Surely what you are promised must happen.

فَإِذَا ٱلنُّجُومُ طُمِسَتْ ۝

8. So when the stars are dimmed,

وَإِذَا ٱلسَّمَآءُ فُرِجَتْ ۝

9. and when the sky is rent asunder,

وَإِذَا ٱلْجِبَالُ نُسِفَتْ ۝

10. and when the mountains are blown away,

وَإِذَا ٱلرُّسُلُ أُقِّتَتْ ۝

11. and when the rasuls are made to reach the appointed time—

لِأَيِّ يَوْمٍ أُجِّلَتْ ۝

12. for what day is it fixed?

لِيَوْمِ ٱلْفَصْلِ ۝

13. For the Day of Decision.

وَمَآ أَدْرَىٰكَ مَا يَوْمُ ٱلْفَصْلِ ۝

14. And what will make you understand what the Day of Decision is?

وَيْلٌ يَوْمَئِذٍ لِّلْمُكَذِّبِينَ ۝

15. Woe on that Day to the deniers!

أَلَمْ نُهْلِكِ ٱلْأَوَّلِينَ ۝

16. Have We not destroyed the ancients?

ثُمَّ نُتْبِعُهُمُ ٱلْأَخِرِينَ ۝

17. And then We followed them up with later ones.

كَذَٰلِكَ نَفْعَلُ بِٱلْمُجْرِمِينَ ۝

18. Thus We do deal with the guilty.

وَيْلٌ يَوْمَئِذٍ لِّلْمُكَذِّبِينَ ۝

19. Woe on that Day to the deniers!

أَلَمْ نَخْلُقكُّم مِّن مَّآءٍ مَّهِينٍ ۝

20. Did We not create you from an ordinary fluid?

فَجَعَلْنَٰهُ فِى قَرَارٍ مَّكِينٍ ۝

21. Then We placed it in a secure place,

إِلَىٰ قَدَرٍ مَّعْلُومٍ ۝

22. up to a known measure;

فَقَدَرْنَا فَنِعْمَ ٱلْقَٰدِرُونَ ۝

23. thus did We measure; so how excellent Measurers We are!

وَيْلٌ يَوْمَئِذٍ لِّلْمُكَذِّبِينَ ۝

24. Woe on that Day to the deniers!

25. Have We not made the earth to attract—

أَلَمْ نَجْعَلِ ٱلْأَرْضَ كِفَاتًا ٢٥

26. the living and the dead,

أَحْيَآءً وَأَمْوَٰتًا ٢٦

27. and made lofty mountains in it, and given you sweet water to drink?

وَجَعَلْنَا فِيهَا رَوَٰسِيَ شَٰمِخَٰتٍ وَأَسْقَيْنَٰكُم مَّآءً فُرَاتًا ٢٧

28. Woe on that Day to the denies!

وَيْلٌ يَوْمَئِذٍ لِّلْمُكَذِّبِينَ ٢٨

29. "Set out toward that which you used to belie.

ٱنطَلِقُوٓا۟ إِلَىٰ مَا كُنتُم بِهِۦ تُكَذِّبُونَ ٢٩

30. "Set out toward a shade having three columns—

ٱنطَلِقُوٓا۟ إِلَىٰ ظِلٍّ ذِى ثَلَٰثِ شُعَبٍ ٣٠

31. "neither giving shade, and which does not avail against the flaming Fire.

لَّا ظَلِيلٍ وَلَا يُغْنِى مِنَ ٱللَّهَبِ ٣١

32. "Surely it sends up sparks like palaces,

إِنَّهَا تَرْمِى بِشَرَرٍ كَٱلْقَصْرِ ٣٢

33. "as if they were yellow camels."

كَأَنَّهُۥ جِمَٰلَتٌ صُفْرٌ ٣٣

34. Woe on that Day to the deniers!

وَيْلٌ يَوْمَئِذٍ لِّلْمُكَذِّبِينَ ٣٤

35. This is the Day whereon they will not speak,

هَٰذَا يَوْمُ لَا يَنطِقُونَ ٣٥

36. and no permission will be given to them so that they may make an apology.

وَلَا يُؤْذَنُ لَهُمْ فَيَعْتَذِرُونَ ٣٦

37. Woe on that Day to the deniers!

وَيْلٌ يَوْمَئِذٍ لِّلْمُكَذِّبِينَ ٣٧

38. This is the day of the Decision; We have gathered you and the ancients.

هَٰذَا يَوْمُ ٱلْفَصْلِ جَمَعْنَٰكُمْ وَٱلْأَوَّلِينَ ٣٨

فَإِن كَانَ لَكُمْ كَيْدٌ فَكِيدُونِ ﴿٣٩﴾ 39. So if there is for you any plot, then apply the plot against Me.

وَيْلٌ يَوْمَئِذٍ لِّلْمُكَذِّبِينَ ﴿٤٠﴾ 40. Woe on that Day to the deniers!

Explanation:

1–5. The divine oath (*wa*) at the beginning of the first five āyāt are based on five different realities, which draw attention to the realities of the Awakening and the Hereafter, narrated in the subsequent āyāt. The sūrah derives its title from the mention of *mursalāt* (those sent forth) in the first āyah. The word hints at something that appears gradually, or something that comes one after another in succession. It could indicate violent winds (āyah 2) that comes in succession, angels (āyah 3) who spread goodness, the Qur'ān (āyah 4) that appeared piecemeal to separate truth from falsehood, or the messengers (āyah 5) who appeared in succession to instill a divine reminder.

6. The oaths mentioned in the five previous āyāt serve two objectives: (1) as a reminder to justify the idea that those who accept the message will be shown mercy; and (2) as a warning to those who reject the message that they will be punished.

7. All of mankind was promised an event that will certainly happen one day. The promise refers to the beginning of the Awakening. The pronoun "you" in the word *tu'addūna* (you were promised) is plural, indicating all of mankind.

8–9. The Qur'ān uses the term *samā* (sky) to mean the visible sky, universe or the protective atmospheric layer that works as a canopy (2:22) for the earth. The sky is not solid slab, but an endless expanse, so its renting asunder indicates disintegration of the protective atmospheric layer. Large-scale damage to or thinning of this layer would be potentially devastating to life forms on earth. Due to a thinning or clouding of the atmosphere, the bright stars would become invisible or look faded to an observer.

10. The mountains would be blown away as dust (73:14). If this message is taken literally, it seems to indicate a massive earthquake or a super-volcanic eruption would render the mountains into dust and debris, scattered thousands of miles into the atmosphere.

11–13. When the inevitable Day of Awakening begins, the messengers of Allāh (swt) will be summoned to testify for and against the people to whom they conveyed the divine message (4:41–42; 5:109; 7:6; 16:84, 89; 28:75; and 39:69). The phrase *yawm al-fasl*, meaning the Day of Decision, refers to the Day of Awakening (37:21; 44:40; 77:38; and 78:17), when right and wrong, good and evil, righteous and sinners will be separated.

14. The Qur'ān provides various metaphors for the Day of Decision, but its true realities are beyond human comprehension. This is because human beings do not have the necessary faculties to understand the parts of the unseen that are beyond their knowledge.

15. To provide an example of the future human experience is one way to explain the incomprehensible nature of the Day of Decision. Therefore in this āyah, the anguish, sadness and wretchedness of the sinners is pointed out in a simple sentence—woe on that Day to the deniers. This sentence occurs ten times in this sūrah to emphasize the dismal experience of the sinners.

16–19. In addition to providing an example of the human experience in the future, the deniers are also reminded of past human history. Past communities, nations and civilizations were destroyed after their inhabitants invented spiritual corruption and violated moral and ethical standards. The divine principle of dealing with such corruption is the same from generation to generation, —implied by āyah 18—thus We deal with the guilty. Therefore, the passage ends with the warning—woe on that Day to the deniers.

20–24. In the previous passage, the deniers of truth were reminded of past human history. Now their attention is drawn toward their own creation—starting with insignificant sperm, followed by embryonic development, and finally the period of gestation. At the end of the sequence, a baby is born with all the due components that make a perfect human being. It appears that this beautiful sequence of creation does not inspire people to recognize their Creator. Therefore, the passage ends with the warning—woe on that Day to the deniers.

25–26. The attention of the deniers of truth is now drawn toward planet earth. The term *kifat* signifies a place where things are drawn together, thereby implying the gravitational force of the earth. In addition, the earth acts as a repository of sustenance for human beings and animals and assimilates them into the ground upon their death. Thus, an allusion is made to the life cycle of all organic beings from their birth, development, aging and death.

27–28. Continuing with the theme of drawing attention of the deniers, they are now asked to ponder how Earth was made livable to sustain life forms. The contribution of mountains in sustaining life forms is tremendous. Not only do they protect land from becoming desert, they also act act as a barrier for clouds, thereby ensuring monsoon rain to fall in the catchment areas. They help many streams and rivulets to form and merge into larger rivers. They help the growth of vegetation in the lower reaches and help diverse flora and fauna to thrive in their slopes and other areas. Life forms could not have survived unless they had ready access to sweet water, even though two-thirds of the earth contains saline water. If these illustrations do not inspire people to recognize their Creator, they ought to be reminded of the warning—woe on that Day to the deniers.

29. The word *intaliqū* is based on *intilaq*, which means "to depart," "to go one's way without stopping" or "to be free or loose." The allusion is for human beings to move toward the Awakening, which people used to belie.

30. The final fate of the rejecters of truth is stated in this passage. The phrase "shade having three columns" refers to three characteristics rather than three physical columns. If we consider shade to be the coefficient and the three columns as an exponential notation, the equation provides a relatively large value. The characteristics of and purposes for the three (or several) columns can be many, as seen in the following few āyāt.

31. The columns will not provide any shade or protection from the flaming fire. The word *zill* (shade) when used in reference to Paradise, adds a sense of comfort. However, the shade gives neither any comfort nor any coolness for the sinners.

32. The columns will emit sparks (*shararun*), but the sparks are compared to palaces (*qasr*, meaning castle, palace) to emphasize their vastness or magnitude. This comparison seems to provide sarcasm for the sinners. The castle example provides the impression of houses of wealthy oppressors, built with pride as a symbol of comfort, security and majesty. In the Hereafter, the castle of the wealthy sinners turns into a painful metaphor of their discomfort, anxiety and severity. Interestingly, the āyah does not compare the vastness of the sparks with mountains, because in āyah 27 mountains are mentioned as the source of many blessings.

33–34. Fire intensity is the amount of energy released per unit of time/per unit area of the primary flame front. It is used to evaluate the effectiveness of the fuel. Two factors are important to measure the fire intensity—the column height of smoke and flame heights. Earlier, the column height was compared to a castle; flame height is now being compared with yellow camels. The word *sufr* is plural of *asfar*, meaning something yellow or tawny in color, thus a fitting metaphor for a flame. The mention of camels also provides an impression of swiftness because if the flame is not swift enough, it cannot engulf everything within its reach. The word *jimalah* is the plural form of *jamal* (camel), although in some writings it is mentioned as ropes, but that seems to miss the fascinating metaphor presented in the āyah. If people do not pay attention to these illustrations, and do not adopt the right path, they ought to be reminded of the warning—woe on that Day to the deniers.

35–37. Sinners will not be given an opportunity to plead their cases because every action of every human being will be made public. Nobody will be able to hide or deny his or her past deeds; thus, speaking for or against the evidence will not help. Under such circumstances, there will truly be woe on that Day to the deniers.

38. The Day of Decision, first mentioned in āyah 13, and then in āyah 14, is repeated again here. The pronoun "you" refers to everybody who is alive and who will be gathered together on that Day, as well as all their ancestors who passed away.

39–40. The word *kayda* (to contrive a plot) refers to applying or thinking of a remedy, usually in a negative sense (see usage in āyāt 12:76; 21:57; 52:42; and 86:15). If the deniers of truth have any plot to frustrate the divine plans, they will realize their mistake. Therefore, considering all of these circumstances, truly there will be woe on that Day to the deniers.

Words to know:

عَصِف: violent. عَصَفَ: to blow violently, wind gale. عَاصِفَة: storm, whirlwind.

نَشَرَ: to spread out, to expand. نَاشِرَات: spreading ones. أَنشَرَ: brought to life. نُشُور: the resurrection.

عَذَرًا: to beg pardon, to excuse. عُذْرًا: excuse. مُعَاذِّير: excuses.

طَمَسَ: to be effected, to disappear. أُطْمِس: destroy.

نَسَفَ: to uproot, to reduce to powder. نُسِفَت: shall be blown down to pieces.

فَصَلَ: to separate, to distinguish. تَفْصِيلًا: detailing, explaining. فَصِيلَة: kinsfolk, family.

نَطَقَ: to speak, to utter, articulate sound. مَنطِقٌ: language, technique of speech.

Sūrah Al-Mursalāt
Word-by-word meaning

بِسْمِ	ٱللَّهِ	ٱلرَّحْمَـٰنِ	ٱلرَّحِيمِ
In the name of	Allāh	the most Kind	the most Rewarding

وَٱلْمُرْسَلَـٰتِ	عُرْفًا ١	فَٱلْعَـٰصِفَـٰتِ	عَصْفًا ٢
by the winds	one after another	and by the winds that blow	violently

وَٱلنَّـٰشِرَٰتِ	نَشْرًا ٣	فَٱلْفَـٰرِقَـٰتِ	فَرْقًا ٤
and by the winds that scatter	clouds and rain	and consider those separating with a	complete separation

فَٱلْمُلْقِيَـٰتِ	ذِكْرًا ٥	عُذْرًا	أَوْ
and by those offering	reminders	as an excuses	or

نُذْرًا ٦	إِنَّمَا	تُوعَدُونَ	لَوَٰقِعٌ ٧
as a warning	surely what	you are promised	must come to pass.

فَإِذَا	ٱلنُّجُومُ	طُمِسَتْ ٨	وَإِذَا
then when	the stars	are dimmed	and when

ٱلسَّمَآءُ	فُرِجَتْ ٩	وَإِذَا	ٱلْجِبَالُ
the heaven	is cleft asunder	and when	the mountains

نُسِفَتْ ١٠	ٱلرُّسُلُ	أُقِّتَتْ ١١	
are blown away	the Messengers	are gathered to their appointed time	

لِأَيِّ	يَوْمٍ	أُجِّلَتْ ١٢	لِيَوْمِ
for what	Day	is it fixed	for the Day of

ٱلْفَصْلِ ١٣	وَمَآ	أَدْرَىٰكَ	مَا
decision	and what	will make you know	what is

يَوْمُ — that Day	وَيْلٌ — woe	ٱلْفَصْلِ ۝ — sorting out	يَوْمَئِذٍ — that Day
لِّلْمُكَذِّبِينَ ۝ — to the deniers	أَلَمْ — did not	نُهْلِكِ — We destroy	ٱلْأَوَّلِينَ ۝ — the ancients
ثُمَّ — then	نُتْبِعُهُمُ — We make them follow	ٱلْأَخِرِينَ ۝ — later generation	كَذَٰلِكَ — thus do
نَفْعَلُ — We deal	بِٱلْمُجْرِمِينَ ۝ — with the guilty	وَيْلٌ — woe	يَوْمَئِذٍ — that Day
لِّلْمُكَذِّبِينَ ۝ — to the deniers.	أَلَمْ — did not	نَخْلُقكُّم — We create you	مِّن — from
مَّآءٍ — water	مَّهِينٍ ۝ — worthless	فَجَعَلْنَٰهُ — then We placed it	فِى — in
قَرَارٍ — a place of	مَّكِينٍ ۝ — safety	إِلَىٰ — for	قَدَرٍ — a period
مَّعْلُومٍ ۝ — a known	فَقَدَرْنَا — so We did measure	فَنِعْمَ — and We are the best	ٱلْقَٰدِرُونَ ۝ — to measure
وَيْلٌ — woe	يَوْمَئِذٍ — that Day	لِّلْمُكَذِّبِينَ ۝ — to the deniers.	أَلَمْ — have not
نَجْعَلِ — We made	ٱلْأَرْضَ — the earth	كِفَاتًا ۝ — a receptacle	أَحْيَآءً — for the living
وَأَمْوَٰتًا ۝ — and the dead	وَجَعَلْنَا — and have placed	فِيهَا — therein	رَوَٰسِىَ — firm mountains
شَٰمِخَٰتٍ — tall and high	وَأَسْقَيْنَٰكُم — and have given you to drink	مَّآءً — water	فُرَاتًا ۝ — sweet.

ٱنطَلِقُوٓاْ	لِّلْمُكَذِّبِينَ ۝	يَوْمَئِذٍ	وَيْلٌ
depart you	to the deniers	that Day	woe
بِهِۦ	كُنتُم	مَا	إِلَىٰ
in it	you used to	that which	to
ظِلٍّ	إِلَىٰ	ٱنطَلِقُوٓاْ	تُكَذِّبُونَ ۝
a shadow	to	depart you	deny
لَّا	شُعَبٍ ۝	ثَلَٰثِ	ذِى
neither	columns	three	in
مِن	يُغْنِى	وَلَا	ظَلِيلٍ
against	of any use	nor	shading
بِشَرَرٍ	تَرْمِى	إِنَّهَا	ٱللَّهَبِ ۝
sparks	throws	surely it	the fierce flame of the Fire.
صُفْرٌ ۝	جِمَٰلَتٌ	كَأَنَّهُۥ	كَٱلْقَصْرِ ۝
yellow	camels	as if they were	like a castle
هَٰذَا	لِّلْمُكَذِّبِينَ ۝	يَوْمَئِذٍ	وَيْلٌ
this will be	to the deniers	that Day	woe
وَلَا	يَنطِقُونَ ۝	لَا	يَوْمُ
and not	they shall speak	not	a Day when
وَيْلٌ	فَيَعْتَذِرُونَ ۝	هُمْ	يُؤْذَنُ
woe	to put forth any excuse	for them	they will be permitted
يَوْمُ	هَٰذَا	لِّلْمُكَذِّبِينَ ۝	يَوْمَئِذٍ
a Day of	that will be	to the deniers	that Day
فَإِن	وَٱلْأَوَّلِينَ ۝	جَمَعْنَٰكُمْ	ٱلْفَصْلِ
so if	and the men of old	We have brought you together	decision

كَانَ	لَكُمْ	كَيْدٌ	فَكِيدُونِ ﴿٣٩﴾
did	you have	a plot	then plot against Me

وَيْلٌ	يَوْمَئِذٍ	لِّلْمُكَذِّبِينَ ﴿٤٠﴾	
woe	that Day	to the deniers	

A few applications of the message:

The dominant message of the sūrah is "woe on that Day to the deniers." Woe is an interjection used to express grief, regret or distress. This part of the sūrah mentions "woe" seven times to emphasize the central theme and create suspense in the minds of those who reject the message. The sūrah explains why the sinners will experience woe on the Day of Judgment. They will suffer because they not only denied the truth one time, but they continuously and habitually denied the truth, implied by the word *kadhdhāb*. They believed the Day of Judgment would never happen and they would never be held accountable for their deeds. They are wrong. They will realize their fate on the Day of Decision.

We do not want our deeds to become the cause of our woe on the Day of Judgment. The only way we can make sure that we will not cause woe for ourselves is by remaining loyal to the divine message. We should not reject the divine teachings and we should not rebel against Allāh (swt). We should learn lessons from the history of past civilizations that rejected truth, and as a result, suffered severe punishment on earth. Their punishment on earth was not the end of the story. They will continue to suffer in the Hereafter as described in the sūrah.

Questions:

1. In āyāt 8–10, three events that would happen on the Day of Decision (يوم الفصل) are mentioned. What are these three events?

2. What were the reasons past communities wanted to make the Awakening happen sooner?

3. What were the reasons past nations and communities were destroyed?

4. How has Allāh (swt) made the earth habitable for life forms? Explain in light of āyāt 25–27.

5. What is the basic purpose for the setting on the Day of Decision?

6. How many times is the phrase "woe on that Day to the deniers" used in the entire sūrah?

7. Āyah 30 mentions three columns (ثلث شعب). What are a few of the characteristics of the "columns" as explained in the sūrah?

Sūrah 77 · Al-Mursalāt

Revealed in Makkah

Part B

Those Sent Ones

Introduction:

Throughout the sūrah, the fate of those who deny the Hereafter is mentioned. In this section, their fate is contrasted with the fate of the righteous people. Those who affirm their faith during their earthly lives, those who perform righteous deeds and those who abstain from evil will ultimately be rewarded in the Hereafter. The sinners seem to enjoy their earthly lives with wealth, food and fun. However, compared to blissful eternal life in the Hereafter, all these earthly comforts are of short duration.

بِسۡمِ ٱللَّهِ ٱلرَّحۡمَٰنِ ٱلرَّحِيمِ

In the name of Allāh, the most Kind, the most Rewarding.

إِنَّ ٱلۡمُتَّقِينَ فِى ظِلَٰلٍ وَعُيُونٍ ۝

41. The reverent will indeed be in shades and springs,

وَفَوَٰكِهَ مِمَّا يَشۡتَهُونَ ۝

42. and have fruits such as they desire.

كُلُواْ وَٱشۡرَبُواْ هَنِيٓئًۢا بِمَا كُنتُمۡ تَعۡمَلُونَ ۝

43. "You eat and drink in pleasure on account of what you used to do."

إِنَّا كَذَٰلِكَ نَجۡزِى ٱلۡمُحۡسِنِينَ ۝

44. Truly We thus do reward the doers of good deeds.

وَيۡلٌ يَوۡمَئِذٍ لِّلۡمُكَذِّبِينَ ۝

45. Woe on that Day to the deniers!

كُلُواْ وَتَمَتَّعُواْ قَلِيلًا إِنَّكُم مُّجۡرِمُونَ ۝

46. "Eat and enjoy yourselves for a while; you are certainly guilty."

وَيۡلٌ يَوۡمَئِذٍ لِّلۡمُكَذِّبِينَ ۝

47. Woe on that Day to the deniers!

وَإِذَا قِيلَ لَهُمُ ٱرْكَعُواْ لَا يَرْكَعُونَ ۝ 48. And when it is said to them: "Bow down," they do not bow down!

وَيْلٌ يَوْمَئِذٍ لِّلْمُكَذِّبِينَ ۝ 49. Woe on that Day to the deniers!

فَبِأَيِّ حَدِيثٍ بَعْدَهُ يُؤْمِنُونَ ۝ 50. Therefore in what discourse after this will they believe?

Explanation:

41. In contrast to the shade upon the sinners mentioned in āyah 30, the shade upon the believers would bring comfort and serenity. The description of Heaven often refers to presence of shade (4:57; 13:35; 36:56; 56:30; and 76:13–14). We have to remember that during the summer months, temperatures in Arabia exceed 110 degrees Fahrenheit (42 degrees Celsius). The early audience of the Qur'ān was the Arabs, who fully understood and appreciated the importance of shade. In addition to protection from the heat of the sun, the word *zill* also indicates peace, comfort, contentment and delight in this world.

42–45. The Qur'ān uses food as a function of reward or punishment in the Hereafter. In many instances, the Qur'ān states food for the sinners will be such that they cannot eat or digest. In this āyah, food is used as a function of reward. The word *hani* denotes wholesome food without any harmful or side-effects. Eating the wholesome, good food will bring pleasure and satisfaction. The phrase "on account of what you used to do" indicates these foods would be given only to deserving people, and no unworthy person would receive a share. In contrast to the rewards of the dwellers of Heaven, the sinners will experience the total opposite; therefore, there will truly be woe on that Day to the deniers.

46–47. Āyah 43 mentions eating and drinking would be a function of reward for the people in Heaven. In the earthly live, eating and drinking are sometimes made a function of sin. Let us see how. If we eat and drink prohibited and unlawful food, we earn sin. If we eat good food, but do not share with poor and needy people, that is also a sin. In earthly life, the tendency for a large number of people is to eat and enjoy life because they are unduly attached to the comforts and pleasures of life (15:3; 47:12). This tendency causes them to disregard human accountability, and, consequently, the Awakening. The word *qalīla* (a little) refers to two things—(1) the short duration of life in this world, and (2) the few blessings in this world in comparison to the immense blessings in the Hereafter. For those who indulge in earthly motives, the warning is this: woe on that Day to the deniers.

48–49. Bowing down (*raka'a*, meaning to bow down, to bend down on ground—as in prayer) is the highest form of showing submission to Allāh (swt). Angels bow down to Allāh (swt) and so does all the creations in the universe. Messengers of Allāh (swt) and other righteous people bowed down to Allāh (swt). Only the sinners refuse to bow down or submit to Allāh (swt). A sense of pride and self-importance overtakes the minds of those who deny truth. They not only refuse to bow down to Allāh in the literal sense, but they also refuse to submit to His directives sent through the messengers. Therefore, it is said to them, woe on that Day to the deniers.

50. If the deniers of truth do not believe the dire warnings and glad tidings in the Qur'ān, which contains the best of the teachings (29:49; 39:27; and 98:3), no other discourse could make them believe the truth.

Words to know:

مَعِين: spring, water. عَيْنٌ: eye, look.

شَرِبَ: to drink, to swallow. شَرَابٌ: drink, beverage. مَشْرَب: Drinking place.

هَنَاء: be wholesome, make the food wholesome. هَنِيا: may it be be wholesome or profitable.

نَجْزِي: we reward. جَزَى: to reward, to recompense. جَازٍ: given of a reward. جِزْيَة: exemption tax.

تَمَتَّعَ: enjoy. مَتَّعَ: to let anyone enjoy, make life comfortable. تَمَتُّع: to combine. (a type of Hajj where after performing 'Umrah, the pilgrims come out of the state of Ihram, thus "enjoy."

يَرْكَعُونَ: they bow down. رَكَعَ: to bow down. رَاكِعًا: one who bows down.

Sūrah Al-Mursalāt
Word-by-word meaning

بِسْمِ	ٱللَّهِ	ٱلرَّحْمَٰنِ	ٱلرَّحِيمِ
In the name of	Allāh	the most Kind	the most Rewarding
إِنَّ	ٱلْمُتَّقِينَ	فِى	ظِلَٰلٍ
indeed	the pious	shall be in	shades
وَعُيُونٍ ﴿٤١﴾	وَفَوَٰكِهَ	مِمَّا	يَشْتَهُونَ
and springs.	and fruits	such as	they desire
كُلُواْ	وَٱشْرَبُواْ	هَنِيٓـًٔا	بِمَا
eat	and drink	comfortably	for that which
كُنتُمْ	تَعْمَلُونَ ﴿٤٣﴾	إِنَّا	كَذَٰلِكَ
you used to	do	surely We	thus

نَجْزِى	ٱلْمُحْسِنِينَ ۝	وَيْلٌ	يَوْمَئِذٍ
We reward	the good-doers	woe	that Day

لِّلْمُكَذِّبِينَ ۝	كُلُواْ	وَتَمَتَّعُواْ	قَلِيلاً
to the deniers.	eat	and enjoy yourselves	for a little while

إِنَّكُم	مُّجْرِمُونَ ۝	وَيْلٌ	يَوْمَئِذٍ
surely you are	guilty	woe	that Day

لِّلْمُكَذِّبِينَ ۝	وَإِذَا	قِيلَ	هُمُ
to the deniers	and when	it is said	to them

ٱرْكَعُواْ	لَا	يَرْكَعُونَ ۝	وَيْلٌ
bow down yourself	not	they bow down	woe

يَوْمَئِذٍ	لِّلْمُكَذِّبِينَ ۝	فَبِأَيِّ	حَدِيثٍ
that day	to the deniers	then in which	statement

بَعْدَهُۥ	يُؤْمِنُونَ ۝
after it	will they believe

A few applications of the message:

The word "woe" is repeated three more times in this part of the sūrah, indicating the warning continues. The "woe" is directed at the sinners, who will suffer the consequences for their denial of truth. In light of what we learn about their sufferings, we have to ask ourselves: "What can we do so as not to suffer the same fate as that of the sinners?" The answer is provided in the same sūrah. We have to do the opposite of what the deniers do. We have to accept the truth. We have to remain loyal to the divine message and follow the teachings of our Rasūl (S). We have to bow down to our Creator. This is not just the physical bowing down that we do during our salāt, but we must also bow down with our hearts and souls.

In contrast to the suffering of the sinners, the delightful conditions for the righteous is mentioned. The righteous will be in the shade and in the gardens of springs. They will have plenty of fruit to enjoy and experience a state of pleasure because of their deeds. After reading this sūrah, we should remind ourselves to avoid the bad deeds and perform the righteous deeds that will ensure our eternal life in the Hereafter will be blissful.

Questions:

1. Compare and contrast the shade that will be available to the believers and non-believers on the Day of Decision.

2. On the Day of Decision, what type of food will be given to the righteous people?

3. During their earthly lives, the wrongdoers enjoy their life for a short while (قليلا). What is the significance of the word قليلا?

4. Why do people refuse to bow down to their Creator?

Bibliography

Ali, Abdullah Yusuf, *The Meaning of the Holy Qur'an*, Beltsville, Amana Publications, 1999

Asad, Muhammad, *The Message of the Qur'an*, Gibraltar, Dar Al-Andalus, 1980

Hoque, Zohurul, *Translation of the Holy Qur'an*, Dayton, Holy Qur'an Publishing Project, 2000

Hughes, Thomas Patrick, *Dictionary of Islam*, Chicago, Kazi Publications, Inc. 1994

Ibn Hisham, 'Abd al Malik, *The Life of Muhammad: A Translation of Ibn Ishaq's Sirat Rasul Allah*, London and New York, Oxford University Press, 1955

Kathir, Hafiz Ibn, *Tafsir Ibn Kathir (Abridged)*, Houston, Darussalam, 2000

Khalil, Shawqi Abu, *Atlas on the Prophet's Biography: Places, Nations, Landmarks*, New York, Darussalam, 2003

Khan, Aftab Alam, *The Meaning of the Noble Qur'ān*, New Delhi, Islamic Book Service, 2008

Khan, Muhammad Muhsin, *Summarized Sahih Al-Bukhari*, Riyadh, Maktaba Darussalam, 1994

Lings, Martin, *Muhammad: His Life Based on the Earliest Sources*, Kuala Lumpur, Foundation For Traditional Studies, 1983

Mahmoud, Mostafa, *Understanding the Qur'an: A Contemporary Approach*, Maryland, Amana Publications, 2004

Al-Mubarakpuri, Safiur-Rahman, *The Sealed Nectar*, New York, Darussalam, 2002

Murata, Sachiko and William C. Chittick, *The Vision of Islam*, Minnesota, Paragon House, 1994

Nuri, Husain A. and Mansur Ahmad, *Islamic Studies: Level 10*, Columbus, Weekend Learning Publishers, 2010

Omar, Abdul Mannan, *Dictionary of the Holy Qur'an*, Hockessin, Noor Foundation, 2005

Penrice, John, *A Dictionary and Glossary of the Koran*,

Pickthall, Muhammad M., *The Glorious Qur'an*, New York, Tahrike Tarsile Qur'an, 1999

Qutb, Sayyid, *In the Shade of the Qur'an*, Leicestershire, The Islamic Foundation, 1999–2008

Salahi, Adil, *Muhammad Man and Prophet*, Leicestershire, The Islamic Foundation, 2008

Index

Ear

listening ear that listens 69:12.
putting fingers into ears 71:7.

Earth

extensive nature of earth 67:15.
gravitation by which everything is drawn to earth 77:25–26.
man—abode of on earth 71:19–20.
man lives and dies on earth 71:17–18.
motion of the earth 67:15; 77:25.

East and West

Allāh is the Master of East and West 70:40; 73:9.

Evidence

honesty and justice to maintain in 70:33.

Face

brightness of face 75:22.
humiliation of face 67:22.
shame and gloom cover the face of the guilty 67:27; 75:24.

Face of Allāh 76:9.

Fir'awn

punishment of Fir'awn was severe 73:16.
sin and disobedience of Fir'awn 69:9–10; 73:16.

Free will

man's exercise of free will to attain anything is subject to Allāh's will 74:56; 76:29–31.

Fruits

tasting of, fruits in this life also 69:23.

Garden

age does not change in the Garden 76:19.
blessings of the Garden proportionate to the deeds 76:16.
blessings of the Garden to be tasted even in this life 69:23.
bowls and cups presented in the Garden 76:15.
bracelets of silver are offered in the Garden 76:16,21.
camphorated drinks given in the Garden 76:5.
fountains in the Garden 76:6,18;
fruits to relish in the Garden 69:23; 76:14; 77:42–43.
ginger-tempered drinks offered in the Garden 76:17.
inmates of the Garden talk with the inmates of hell 74:40–47.
Lofty Garden 69:22.
picture of the Garden 76:5-22.
pure drink given in the Garden 76:21.
Right-handed people will enter the Garden 74:39–40.
Salsabil—fountain in the Garden 76:18.
shade in the Garden 76:13–14; 77:41.
silk robes presented in the Garden 76:12,21.
sun and cold absent in the Garden 76:13.
thrones provided in the Garden 76:13;

Garden of Bliss 68:34; 70:38; 76:20.

Hell

boiling in Hell 67:7–8.
chains with which one is tied in Hell 69:30–32; 73:12; 76:4.
evil is manifested in Hell 69:25–26.
fire of Hell scorching the entire body 74:29.
inmates of Hell talk with one another 67:8–10.
nature of hell is grief and regrets 69:25–29.
noises of terrifying nature in Hell 67:7.
parable of nineteen relating to Hell 74:30–31.
picture of Hell 67:6-11; 77:29-37.
skin peeled off while being cast into Hell 70:16.
smoke of fire enveloping Hell 77:30–31.

tasting of Hell in this life as well   79:25, 36.

watery grave of the guilty is called fire of Hell   71:25.

Good Deed

causing good to humanity is an ideal good deed   73:20.

Grave

inmates of graves will be raised to life on the Day of Awakening   70:43.

Non-believer's home is like a grave   70:43.

Heaven (meaning sky)

bursting asunder of heaven to change the old order   77:9.

diviners have no access into heaven   67:5; 72:8.

seven numbers of heaven are created alike   67:3; 71:15.

stars that are visible to the human eye exist only in nearer heaven   67:5.

sun and moon in heaven give light   71:16.

Human Soul

believing souls draw the love of Allāh 76:8.

spiritual progress of the human soul has three phases   75:2.

spiritual progress of the human soul has vast realm as compared to material progress   70:4.

Intellectual Development

reasoning and senses should be exercised 67:10.

Islam

compulsion in religion is condemned by Islam   73:19; 76:3, 29.

transformation of mankind through Islam 68:32.

Jinn

Christians are also called jinn   72:1–3.

leaders of evil meaning of jinn   72:6.

Qur'ān is listened to by jinn   72:1.

Judgment Day see also **Awakening**

Allāh possesses the knowledge of Judgement Day   67:26.

assembly on Judgement Day   67:24.

coming of Judgement Day is inevitable   70:42; 72:24; 74:46–47; 77:7.

denial of Judgement Day by Non-believers   74:46.

exposure of secrets on Judgement Day   69:18.

friends will avail nothing on Judgement Day   70:10–11.

relationships will not help anyone on Judgement Day   70:11–14.

Knowledge

pen and ink wherewith to acquire knowledge 68:1; 96:4.

Law

uniformity in the laws of nature   67:3–4.

Life

seriousness of life for utilizing all opportunities 75:36.

Life after Death

denial of life after death by Non-believers 75:21.

higher life is manifested in life after death   69:18.

Man

creation of man from conjugal relations   76:2; 77:20–22.

creation of man from embryo   75:38.

creation of man from finest make 75:38; 76:28.

creation of man from semen   75:37; 77:20; .

creation of man from sperm   75:37–38; 77:20–22.

creation of man from spermatozoon   75:37; 76:2.

creation of man and his impatient nature   70:19.

creation of man so that he can manifest good qualities 75:36.

materialistic attitude of man 76:27.

miserliness is the attitude of most men 70:21.

ungratefulness of man to the bounties of Allāh 74:11–25.

Masjids

deities other than Allāh must not be worshipped in a masjid 72:18.

Moon

darkening of the moon 75:8.
sun and moon are brought together 75:9.

Morals

patience and perseverance bring success 70:5; 73:10; 74:7.
unselfishness 76:8–9.

Mountains

crushing of mountains into pieces 69:14.
passing away of mountains 69:14; 73:14; 77:10.

Muhammad

allegations against Muhammad as enchanter 74:18–25.
allegations against Muhammad as forger 69:44–47.
allegations against Muhammad as madman 68:2, 6, 51.
allegations against Muhammad as magician 74:24.
allegations against Muhammad as poet and soothsayer 69:40–43.
angels guard the revelations to Muhammad 72:26–28.
companions of Muhammad prayed long hours in the night 73:20.
disobedience to Allāh will never be tolerated from Muhammad 69:44–47.
help of Allāh granted to Muhammad 72:24.
Message of Allāh entrusted to be delivered by Muhammad 72:23.
Message of Muhammad universal for mankind 68:52.
morals of Muhammad is sublime 68:4.
obedience to, a duty upon all nations 72:23.
opponents of Muhammad abased 73:10–14.
opponents of Muhammad will face doom 77:12–40.
opposition to Muhammad will be brought to naught 68:17–33; 75:10–13.
patience of Muhammad to bear the task 70:5; 73:10; 74:7.
plots against Muhammad were frustrated 77:39–40.
prayer performed by Muhammad at night time 73:1–9, 20.
Qur'ān cannot be fabricated by Muhammad 69:44–47.
reward not demanded by Muhammad from people for his preaching 74:6.
slandering Muhammad by opponents 68:11.
triumph of Muhammad prophesied 68:3.
warner—plain and simple 67:26.
warning for which Muhammad was commanded 74:2.
witness for humanity 73:15.
witness over his people 73:15.

Muslims

nights spent by Muslims in prayer and devotion 73:20.
promises made by Muslims must be fulfilled 70:32.
victory of Muslims is promised 70:40–44.

Nabis

Divine help given to all Nabis 72:26–27.
doom of the opponents of Nabis 77:12.
rejection of Nabis in every age 67:9.
revelation is correctly delivered to Nabis 72:27–28.

Night

prayer offered at night yields better fruit 73:2–8.

Nūh

history of Nūh 71:1–28.
rasul of Allāh 71:1.

Oaths

oath-mongers should not be trusted 68:10.

Parable

gardener boasting of harvest finds everything barren 68:17–33.
nineteen used as a parable reflecting a mathematical miracle 74:30.
water drying up 67:30.

Pen

prophecies in the Qur'ān are put down with a pen 68:1.

Pledge in which everybody is bound for his deeds 74:38.

Prayer
    benefits derived from prayer 71:10–12.
    ideal prayer against oppressors 71:28.
    ideal prayer by Nūh for deliverance from enemies 71:28.
    ideal prayer for parents, brethren and others 71:28.

Purity
    Salāt to be performed in garments having purity 74:4.

Qur'ān
    compilation of āyāt and chapters of the Qur'ān was done under divine guidance 75:17–18.
    non-Arabs believe in the Qur'ān 72:1–14.
    poets cannot compose a book like the Qur'ān 69:41.
    procedure of recitation of the Qur'ān 75:16–18.
    prophecies of the Qur'ān gradually made clearer 75:16.
    reminder of the Right Path for the Believers 69:48; 73:19; 74:31; 76:29; 77:5.
    revelation of the Qur'ān directly from Allāh 76:23.
    revelation of the Qur'ān to Muhammad 76:23.
    salāt wherein recitation of the Qur'ān should be done 73:4, 20.
    truth abounds in the Qur'ān 69:51.
    universal nature of the message of the Qur'ān 68:52.
    writing of the Qur'ān testimony thereto 68:1–2, 47.

Respite
    guilty ones are impatient of the prolonged respite 67:25.

Revelation
    higher life is manifested by revelation 69:18; 75:36.
    moral development achieved through revelation 70:23–35.
    Non-believers wanted revelation directly to them 74:52.

Reverence
    Allāh deserves due reverence 74:56.

Right Path
    Straight Path for which everyone should strive 67:22.

Righteous
    description of the righteous 76:5–10.

Salāt
    Tahajjud salāt has great value 73:20; 76:26.
    timings of salāt are five in a day 76:25–26.

Scientific Truths
    man—early life was primitive in nature 76:1.
    superiority of man lies in delicate movements of his fingers 75:4.

Scripture
    the Qur'ān is meant by scripture 74:31.

Shaitān
    lying of Shaitān in ambush to trap man 7:16.

Shin
    terror-stricken condition of doomsday will make, exposed 68:42; 75:29.

Slander
    condemned is he who spreads slander 68:10–13.

Solar System 71:15–16.

Soul
    individual responsibility of deeds is vested upon every soul 74:38.
    three spiritual stages of the soul 75:2.

Spirit
    Jibril is meant by the Spirit 70:4.

Suwa' a female deity of the ancient Arabs 71:23

Ta'if
    Muhammad was persecuted even in Ta'if 72:24.

Thamūd
    punishment of Thamūd 69:5.
    Sālih was rejected by Thamūd 69:4.

Time

mankind lived a primitive life for a long time 76:1.

Truth

Certain Truth 69:51.

Unbelievers

disaster upon non-believers, which they arrogantly ask for 68:5–7.

respite given to non-believers increases their wickedness 68:44–45.

Wadd an idol of Arabs 71:23.

Water

man is created out of water 77:20.

sinking of water 67:30.

Wealth

earning of wealth by traveling 73:20.

earning of wealth recommended 67:15.

withholding of wealth disallowed 70:18.

Worldly Life

love of worldly life should not make people deviate from the right path 75:20–21; 76:27.

Yaghuth the lion-god of Arabs 71:23.

Ya'uq the horse-god of Arabs 71:23.

Yūnus

Companion of the Fish 68:48.

fish carried Yūnus and cast him on the shore 68:49.

nabi of Allāh 68:50.

Zakāt

obligatory nature of zakāt 73:20.